VETERAN & VINTAGE CARS

15

VETERAN & VINTAGE CARS

Text & Photography by
PEDR DAVIS

DAVID & CHARLES
Newton Abbot. London

APOLOGIES

At my request well over one hundred owners went to appreciable trouble to make their vehicles available for photography. Undoubtedly some will be disappointed to find their cars do not appear in this book. The omission does not reflect on the quality of their restoration in any way, simply the expediency of selecting and publishing a comprehensive and representative range of cars.

If anyone feels the author's choice could be improved, or that some deserving cases have been left out, please accept my apologies.

Pedr Davis.
November, 1980.

Published by Lansdowne Press, London
for David and Charles 1981

Produced in Australia by the Publisher
Typeset in Australia by S.A. Typecentre Pty. Ltd., Adelaide
Printed by Toppan Printing Co. (Singapore) (Pte.) Limited
38 Liu Fang Road, Jurong, Singapore 22

ISBN 0 7153 8134 2

List of Veteran & Vintage Cars

Sic Transit Gloria

Gleaming brass, Klaxton horns and wisps of blue exhaust have long held an irresistible appeal. The 1978 International Veteran and Vintage Rally, held between Sydney and Brisbane, attracted more than one million people who lined the routes or inspected the old cars at the various stopover points.

The interest was not confined to the spectators. Though this was only the second International Rally held in Australia, the number of entries received was so great that the organisers were forced to place a limit of 400 cars and 50 motorcycles. In early 1980 a quick count showed there were some 180 clubs across the country devoted to the affairs of historic cars and vintage motor sport.

The trend to restoring and driving old cars has been gathering pace for some years and is now in top gear, with nostalgia at its peak throughout the world.

Australia is remarkably fortunate in having some of the world's finest veteran and vintage cars, not just in museums but regularly used on the highways and byways.

A proper count has never been done but it is almost certain that there are more fully restored veteran and vintage cars in Australia per head of population than in any other country. This includes Britain, the home of the veteran car movement. Another interesting observation is that South Australia boasts the nation's best selection of enthusiasts' cars, possibly because Adelaide motorists formed the world's second oldest club devoting itself to veteran car affairs.

The diversity of makes and models located throughout Australia drew unconcealed admiration from the overseas visitors attending the two International rallies held here. It is possible that the non-corrosive climate of the inland helped to preserve some cars which would otherwise have dissolved in a heap of rust. An even more important factor has been the enthusiasm and hard work of owners who, in some cases, have spent thousands of hours building up a complete car from bits and pieces which others had rejected as unrestorable.

Some reconstructions have added immeasurably to the nation's motoring heritage, for many cars in Australia are unique to the world.

One would expect this from locally built cars such as the Australian Six (built in Sydney between 1919 and 1930), the Melbourne-made Tarrant (built between 1901 to 1907) or the Ohlmeyer (a one-of-a-kind car constructed by a watchmaker in the Barossa Valley, South Australia). Yet, Australian collectors also own fully restored French, British, German, Swiss, American and Italian cars which have no surviving counterparts anywhere in the world.

This book alone depicts the Alfa Romeo Tipo G1, four-cylinder Aquila Italiana, 1924 Berliet prototype, Carlton, Clement Bayard Phaeton, Crossley sports car, Delage Type S, Essex coupé, 1900 Gardner-Serpollet steam carriage, Girling tri-car, 8HP Phanomobile, 15 HP S.C.A.T. and a Sizaire-Naudin with a Victoria coupé bodywork. All are the only surviving models of their type to be seen anywhere.

Equally interesting, if less rare, are machines such as a front-wheel-drive supercharged Alvis, an Austin 7 'Chummy' with Holden body, a Type 39 racing Bugatti, a Chalmers Raceabout, a glorious 1900 De Dion, a luxury Fiat 519A, an air cooled, six-cylinder Franklin and an extremely rare Little, the mini-car that led to the launching of Chevrolet. There is also a superlative Mercedes Targa, built for the Targa Florio races, a friction-drive Metz, a genuine Riley Redwing, a tiny Toledo steam buggy and a most unusual Willys Knight.

To the rare and the unusual we add such old favourites as Bentley, Buick, Cadillac, Chevrolet, Citroen, Daimler, Ford, Hispano-Suiza, Isotta-Fraschini, Lancia, M.G., Morgan, Packard, Rolls-Royce, Oldsmobile, Talbot and Vauxhall.

A few of them have been kept in prime condition almost since new, but the majority have been painstakingly restored by their owners, often with help from fellow club members. A typical machine is discovered as a heap of rust, eating its heart out in a country paddock, with trees growing through the chassis. The owner spends between 2000 and 4000 man-hours seeking missing parts, attending swap-meetings, rebuilding worn components, fabricating a new body and restoring the chassis. The aim is always to produce a vehicle which is indistinguishable from the original.

Modernising an old car is blasphemy to a true believer, though superior brake linings, tyres, fuels and oils make the machine far more pleasant to drive now than when it was new.

Modern 'improvements' are not only frowned upon but greatly detract from the vehicle's value. This is becoming an increasingly important consideration as owners have seen their cars appreciate at an astonishing rate in recent years.

A Sydney solicitor bought a 1909 Rolls-Royce Silver Ghost for $A200 in 1952. Two years later, after some restoration work, he found it necessary to sell and was happy to accept $A300. Recently, the same car – this time without a body – was sold again. It fetched $A22,000.

Similar price rises have been reported around the world. In 1960, a 1927 Mercedes SS sports car sold at a London auction for $A1000. In November 1973 the same car went under the hammer again and changed hands for $A40,000.

Some astronomic prices have been paid during the past few years. In 1979 at Christies Auction in Los Angeles, a Mercedes 500K special roadster sold for $US400,000 and a Mercedes 540K Cabriolet sold for $US320,000.

No car has appreciated more than the Royale — the supreme accomplishment of Ettore Bugatti, an Alsace car maker. Only seven Bugatti Royales are known to exist. Yet in 1953, Charles Chayne, then chief engineer for General Motors, sighted one in a New York junk yard. He bought it for $A350. In the early 1970s, Fritz Schlumf, a noted French collector, paid $A150,000 for a different Royale. Both cars are now worth around $A400,000 each.

No one can put a figure on the value of a veteran or vintage car. So much depends on the supply and demand at the time of sale, as well as the thoroughness of the restoration and the degree of magic associated with the car itself. A marque such as Bugatti commands unbelievable prices and few come up for sale. Rolls-Royce Silver Ghosts are also in high demand, as are Bentleys, Vauxhall's Prince Henry and 30/98 and some Mercedes models. All have that special aura which epitomises the design, construction and appeal of veteran and vintage cars.

Owners are finding it difficult to handle the older cars in traffic, especially those with two wheel brakes. In very recent times the strongest demand has been for cars made during the 1920s, with four wheel brakes and sufficient performance to keep up with modern traffic. Many of these oldtimers have a surprising

performance. The 1921 four-cylinder Stutz, the Prince Henry Vauxhall, most Bugattis and the big Bentleys are only some of the models which can hold their own with modern machinery in all but the braking department.

Veteran or Vintage?

Once lumped into a single category, old cars are now clearly defined as being 'veteran', 'vintage' or 'post-vintage'. The definitions are confused a little because Australian clubs do not quite conform with their British counterparts.

When British auto historians set out to define the 'veteran' motoring period, they concluded that all worthwhile inventions which made the motor vehicle reliable and practical had been tested by 1904. They decided that, in Britain at least a veteran car should be one built prior to 1 January 1905.

The next recognisable period of motoring history is between 1905 and the end of World War One. During this time cars ceased to be just practical and became fast, reliable and often exciting. The British enthusiasts designated these cars as 'Edwardian', a tribute to King Edward whose patronage of motoring enhanced the prestige of motor vehicles during these formative years.

Australian clubs, however, decided against using the term Edwardian, and, in this country, any vehicle built before 31 December 1918, is called a Veteran.

The local definition of Vintage is the same as that used in Britain and the United States. That is to say, any car built between 1 January 1919 and 31 December 1930 is Vintage.

The rate of restoration of both veteran and vintage cars has slowed down in recent years. Most of the relatively easy-to-restore vehicles have been found and are back on the roads. Search parties have scoured much of the land, including such out-of-the-way places as the Birdsville track, bringing to light many valuable cars abandoned by previous owners. Because so much ground has been covered, such 'finds' are becoming increasingly rare. Fortunately, from time to time news still ripples through the veteran and vintage clubs telling of members who have discovered worthwhile cars in old sheds, suburban garages or under houses.

Another reason why restoration has slowed down is that the cost of having work done professionally has soared. It can cost up to $20,000 to have a craftsman build a new body in the old tradition, or $3000 to have new gears cut for a transmission. Most of the bodywork seen on these pages has been done by the vehicle's owner, with or without some professional help. Many enthusiasts have joined panel forming and vehicle painting classes at technical colleges through the country, learning the skills to fabricate a replica body or cut corroded panels out of existing structures. Mechanical restoration can be extremely expensive, even when the owner does much of the work himself, because complicated machining costs, such as cutting a new crown wheel and pinion, can be prohibitive. This is why a gulf exists between the price of a restored and an unrestored car.

With many mass produced models, especially the Model T Ford, it is possible to buy some components over the counter, provided you know where to look. With a rare car, the owner must seek a similar vehicle to use as a 'spare', or have the missing parts specially made. Many borrow a component from a fellow club member owning a similar vehicle and use it as a pattern for the casting and machining of an identical part.

The magic figure of 60 miles an hour, or a mile-a-minute, was first broken in 1899 when an electric car driven by Jenatzy streaked over a flying kilometre at 65.8 mph (105.88 km/h). At the time, medical experts said motorists would not be able to breathe at such a speed. Three years later medical opinion was dumbfounded again as a petrol driven Mors recorded 77.13 mph (123.4 km/h). In 1903 Henry Ford, in his racing special, lifted the figure to 91.37 mph (146.2 km/h), and in 1910 Barney Oldfield fired up his huge Blitzen Benz and roared along at 131.72 mph (210.7 km/h). By the end of the vintage era, Henry Segrave had set a world land speed record of 231.3 mph (370 km/h), but record-breaking attempts had long ceased to bear much resemblance to normal motoring.

Even so, standard production cars were anything but slow. In 1919 the Vauxhall

30/98 was sold with a guaranteed maximum speed of 100 mph (160 km/h) when fitted with a competition body, or 85 mph (136 km/h) fully equipped for touring.

Just as speed was no stranger to early motorists, many of the gadgets and engineering refinements we associate with modern motor cars were available. Flip through these pages and you will be impressed by just how advanced some of the cars were. The 1925 Fiat 519A, for example, was sold with power-assisted four wheel hydraulic brakes as standard equipment and power steering as optional. The Italian company was also building overhead valve engines in 1905

and a twin overhead camshaft engine in 1911.

On the subject of engines, the Delage Type S specifications are quite remarkable. It not only had a twin overhead camshaft engine, but also desmondronic valves, four wheel brakes and a five-speed gearbox — in 1912!

The 1927 Lancia Lambda was another prophetic design, with the chassis and body structure built as an integrated unit. It also featured independent front suspension, remarkably effective four-wheel brakes, a hide-away all-weather hood and one of the first proper luggage boots fitted to a volume produced car.

Another interesting Lambda feature is the V-4 engine, but it was hardly a pioneer in the 'vee' field. In 1910 Dion-Bouton put its V-8 into volume production, the first firm to do so, though Rolls-Royce earlier built a handful of V-8s and other firms were using V-8 engines in racing cars. Another interesting development was Peugeot's use of a full hemispherical combustion chamber in 1913. You may recall that Chrysler launched its 'hemi' with great fanfare only a few years ago. Five bearing crankshafts have also been widely publicised during the last decade, yet the 1904 four-cylinder Cadillac had this very feature.

Modern motorists impressed by

Citroen's single spoke steering wheel should take a close look at the photographs of the 1903 Humberette. This delightful little car not only has this feature but its steering column is adjustable and the car boasts pendant-type foot pedals.

The time, money and effort expended can be considerable, but most count it well worthwhile. Not only is the finished machine a great joy to drive and own, it is also a near-irreplaceable slice of motoring history.

Probably no mechanical invention has transformed the lives of ordinary people more than the motor car. Ever since Gottlieb Daimler and Karl Benz independently constructed the first practical light weight motor vehicles in the 1880s, the car has revolutionised the world's economic structure and the social lives of its people.

Before the turn of the present century, Germany and especially France had established themselves as great car-marking nations, which is why many of the very early cars to come here were French. England's progress during the dawn of motoring was more leisurely, mainly because of two repressive laws which actively discouraged car ownership. One, repealed in 1896, required motorists to slow down to a walking pace in built-up areas and proceed with a footman ahead carrying a red flag. Outside built-up areas, the motorist was required to 'pull to the side of the road and, with engine stopped, wait for oncoming horse-drawn carriages to pass'.

Australia was not entirely free from prejudice. When David Shearer of Mannum, South Australia, completed his steam carriage in 1896, he required a special permit to take it into the city to show it to the Adelaide Chamber of Manufacturers. Even then he was told to travel only on the main roads!

The obvious advantages of the motor car and its ability to link isolated communities with main centres were apparent before the turn of the century. More than fifty attempts were made during the veteran and vintage periods to launch Australian-made cars. None prospered, mainly because the local companies could not compete with the

volume-produced vehicles built overseas. Once Ford Model Ts started to flood into the country from 1910 onwards, no one could hope to produce a local car to sell at the same price. At one time Ford was building Model Ts at the rate of one million a year, with 40,000 a year coming to Australia. A local car making industry could not possibly take on such a formidable competitor without a massive government subsidy and none was offered.

Henry Ford is often credited with being the 'father of mass production' but this over-states the case. Louis Renault in France and Ransome E. Olds in America were both using assembly line techniques before the Ford Motor Company was founded. In 1909, the year that the Model T Ford production really got under way, American firms produced 121,000 new vehicles, compared with 12,000 in Britain. Ford's new car was such a success, and he exploited its sales potential so cleverly, that by 1914 United States production had rocketed to 543,000 vehicles with Ford accounting for 42 per cent of them. Some 99 other firms shared the remaining production.

Another popular fallacy concerns speed. Not all old cars are slow by any means. Even today there are veteran and vintage cars capable of exceeding the legal speed limit on expressways.

Several early cars had steering column gear shifts, including the earliest De Dions, and it is interesting to see that earlier attempts were made to introduce rudimentary forms of automatic transmission. These include the De Dion epicyclic system and the later friction transmission featured in the 1913 Metz.

Technical refinements in other cars depicted in this book include the four-speed gearbox built into the rear axle of the 1913 Aquila-Italiana. This idea is now used in such high performance cars as Alfa Romeo's Alfetta. The 1910 Hupmobile, a racy looking sportster, has rack and pinion steering still employed on most high performance cars. The Sizaire et Naudin has independent front suspension, so has the 1911 Girling. Even before that date, the S.C.A.T. was offering a self-starter working on compressed air; Calthorpe was building engines with positive crankcase ventilation.

Reo was quick to recognise the need for convertible passenger/luggage space and the 1905 model shown on page 29 has a detachable rumble seat which, when removed, gives a flat luggage tray. Only two years later, Swift was building what today would be called a genuine mini car. The tiny but practical machine had the same length as a modern Mini Minor. Similarly, the 1913 Hillman anticipated the Austin 7 by nearly ten years.

The Spyker shown on page 126 is a 1921 model with conventional engineering but it is worth noting that as early as 1903 the Dutch company built the world's first four-wheel-drive car. It also had the first six-cylinder engine.

Even today's conveniences were not overlooked. The 1911 Armstrong Whitworth has the manoeuvrability of a London cab with a turning circle of only 30 ft. (9.1 m). The 1929 Gardner coupé has wind-up windows and twin mirrors, the latter shielding the driver from night-time dazzle. One year later Nash was offering central chassis lubrication.

Durability was perfected during the vintage era, with many cars capable of covering very long distances with complete reliability. Studebaker gave a graphic display in 1929 when four President 8s each covered 30,000 miles (48,000 km) in 30,000 minutes or less, thus averaging 60 mph, or 100km/h for the distance. The feat earned the American company eleven world records.

As Australia enters the 1980s it is increasingly evident that motoring and the motor car will greatly change. New forms of personal transportation will evolve as pressures build up for greater fuel economy, more convenience in city congestion, cleaner exhaust emissions and improved safety. No one can confidently predict the shape, size and motive power of the coming generations of cars. But we can say with certainty that the type of

car which reached its peak during the vintage years can never be produced again.

Readers progressing through this book will possibly share the author's opinion that motoring experienced its greatest challenge during the veteran period but reached its most exciting times in the vintage years.

SIC TRANSIT GLORIA.

VETERAN CAR
GARDNER-SERPOLLET
4 CYLINDERS.
STEAM CAR
FRANCE

1899/1900 Gardner-Serpollet Steamer

THE MARQUE

Leon Serpollet, a former employee of Peugeot, started his own business in 1897. Between then and his death in 1907 he built around 1000 steam vehicles, several of which came to Australia. His partner, Frank Gardner, was an American who provided working capital for the company.

Serpollet had invented the multi-tube flash boiler in 1888, making it possible for steam to be raised quickly by the instantaneous boiling of water in heated tubes. The steam was further heated in the tubes to a state known as super-heat, a technique still used today.

Like all steam cars, the Gardner-Serpollet had certain important advantages: quietness and no gear changing. It also had the ability to run on low grade fuel, which was more easily obtained during the veteran and vintage years than the fuel we now call petrol.

There were drawbacks too. Steamers were less convenient to start than petrol cars, requiring at least five minutes to raise steam pressure when cold, and they were heavy on fuel. According to the owner's handbook, this 18HP Gardner-Serpollet achieves 9 miles per gallon (40 litres/100 km), which means that it uses twice as much fuel as a petrol car of similar size and performance.

Routine servicing included cleaning out all sixteen burners.

The Gardner-Serpollet has 122 metres of condenser tubes under the floor, plus a large water tank with separate boiler and burners. However, it could cruise all day at 70 km/h, brisk motoring in 1900, and could reach 77 km/h. Leon Serpollet once clocked 120 km/h with a similar car specially geared for speed. In normal road conditions, the standard model can travel up to 320 km on a tankful of water — thanks to the elaborate condensing system.

1900 GARDNER-SERPOLLET

Believed to be the only car of its type surviving in the world, this steamer has its chassis stamped 1899, making it one of the oldest road-going cars in Australia. At least three other Gardner-Serpollet's, all with smaller engines, are known to survive in Australia, but this is probably the only fully restored example.

Now owned by Jim Eisenhauer, of Sydney, this unique car was completed either in 1899 or 1900 and shipped from Paris to York, England. It came to Australia in 1902 with the French Consul, possibly because Madamoiselle Serpollet, the designer's energetic sister, had previously visited Sydney, Melbourne and Adelaide to sell petrol driven Dion-Bouton tricycles. She also spread the word concerning Leon Serpollet's steamers.

Costing 600 golden guineas when new, the 18 HP Serpollet was known as the King model, because a similar car had been supplied to His Majesty King Edward VII. As it still carries the Royal Coat of Arms, this may have been the original Royal car.

After four years of use, the French consul sold the Serpollet at auction. The purchaser, a Mr Chargeois, was a travelling photographer who rumbled throughout Queensland in it, plying for trade. Eventually he sold it to a Mr Green, a grazier near Cape York Peninsula, who used it mainly as a tractor. In 1918 the car was abandoned near a large mango tree. It lay there, sinking further and further into the ground, until 1961. That was the year that Lucien Chabaud, a Frenchman living in Atherton, Queensland, and fossicking in the old gold-mining areas, heard about it. He visited the station, then owned by the daughter of the original Mr Green, who gave him the car provided that it was restored to its former glory.

Lucien Chabaud did much of the early restoration work, including a complete rebuild of the body. In 1975 he sold it to Sydney collector Jim Eisenhauer who completed the restoration and turned what was a static showpiece into a fully functioning steam car. The car had the honour of being No. 1 entry in the 1978 International Veteran and Vintage Rally.

MECHANICAL FEATURES

Engine: Four-cylinder, horizontally opposed, 18 HP, poppet valves. Coil-type flash boiler with 16 paraffin burner jets. 82 x 90 mm bore and stroke.
Transmission: Chain drive to rear wheels. Engine can be reversed for travelling backwards.
Chassis: Channel sections, riveted, with hand forged axles stamped Lemois Paris, 1899.
Brakes: Reversing the engine when travelling forward slows down the car. There is also a handbrake operating on the rear tyres and a foot brake operating on externally contracting drums bolted to the rear wheels.
Dimensions: Overall length 12 ft 0 ins (3658 mm). Overall width 5 ft 3 ins (2230 mm). Overall height 5 ft 6 ins (1676 mm). Kerb weight 32 cwt (1630 kg).
Performance: Maximum speed when new — 48 mph (77 km/h). Normal cruising speed — 43 mph (70 km/h). Fuel consumption at highway speeds — 9 mpg (40 litres/100 km).

1900 De Dion-Bouton Vis-A-Vis

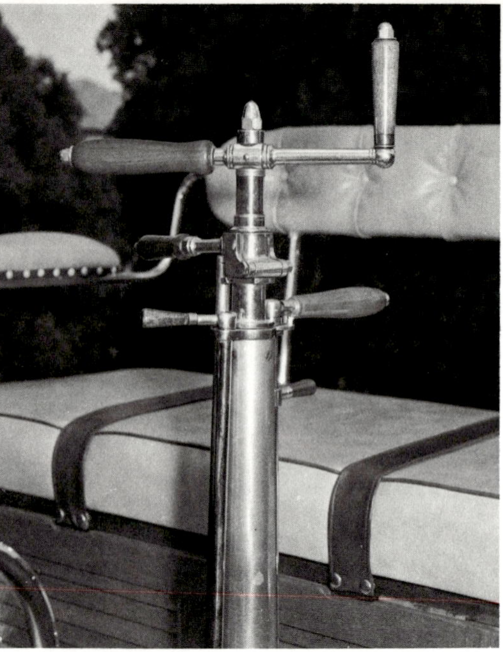

THE MARQUE

De Dion-Bouton, the Paris based manufacturer, was one of the few car manufacturers with a swinging business in 1900. It is not known how many cars the Marquis De Dion built that year, but three 1900 models survive in Australia and at least eight in Britain. A vehicle count in South Australia as early as 1909 shows that there were 990 De Dion-Boutons on register in that State alone.

A description of the founding of the De Dion-Bouton is given with the 1904 De Dion on page 22.

1900 DE DION-BOUTON 4½ HP

One of the finest fully restored 1900 De Dion's in the world, this superlative little car is owned by Miss Diana Hecker of Maryborough, Queensland. Her father, Sam Hecker, a noted veteran car collector, fully restored the car for her and built the vis-a-vis body as an authentic replica of the original De Dion style.

The body type is called a 'Vis-a-Vis' (face-to-face), as the driver sits on the rear bench, facing his passengers. The beautifully built body has timber guards. One seat is hinged to expose the engine, the other lifts, giving access to a tool box and cooling system water tank. The replica body was trimmed by C. E. and M. P. Popp, of Maryborough.

The 1900 De Dion was reputedly owned by Sydney department store owner, Mr Mark Foy, and was one of the first De Dion cars in the country. It was possibly this car which inspired Mark Foy to start his own car importing business.

The parts to rebuild it were collected by De Dion enthusiast, Len Masser, though Sam Hecker found the engine driving a water pump in his home town. After acquiring Len Masser's collection of parts, Sam Hecker wrote to the Veteran Car Club of Great Britain and obtained the names of eight British owners of 1900 De Dion-Boutons. He wrote to them, and later visited each in turn, acquiring a wealth of information about the model, as well as some much needed parts.

After restoration commenced, he discovered that the two-speed gearbox was in very good order, apart from worn bushes. A reverse gear had been originally fitted. In 1900 De Dion featured reverse as a £10 ($20) optional extra. A later owner apparently removed the reverse gear, apart from the winding handle fitted on the driver's side of the front seat. Once engaged it was a major operation to get it out of gear again.

Another peculiarity is that the rear wheel brake system is operated by placing the gear handle in neutral and pressing down on the gear lever. The brake remained on until released by pressing a floor pedal. The brakes themselves are mounted inboard, close to the differential.

Unlike later De Dion-Boutons, this 1900 model has its single-cylinder engine located at the rear, coupled directly to a gearbox with a large spur gear and pinion. The differential is very small.

The car has a tubular steel chassis frame and rack-and-pinion steering, with steering handles on the column. The steering column also houses the controls for advancing the ignition and changing the fuel mixture. There is no accelerator as such, as the engine normally runs at a steady 1500 rpm, but the speed can be very effectively reduced by lifting the exhaust valve.

Riding comfort is surprisingly good and the steering is excellent but engine vibration is very noticeable.

MECHANICAL FEATURES

Engine: Single-cylinder, 84 x 90 mm bore and stroke giving 492 cc capacity. Rated at 4½ HP. Rear mounted, water-cooled with pump on end of gearbox. Battery ignition with trembler coil.
Gearbox: Two-speed expanding clutch gearbox with no reverse.
Suspension: Semi-elliptic springs at front with a transverse cross spring. Three-quarter elliptics at rear, tubular steel frame.
Brakes: External contracting brakes on rear wheels.
Steering: Rack-and-pinion with steering handles on vertical column.
Wheels: Wire wheels, 3.50 x 19 tyres.
Dimensions: Wheelbase 5 ft 1 in (1550 mm). Width 4 ft 5 ins (1346 mm). Overall length 7 ft 5 ins (2260 mm). Height 4 ft 5 ins (1346 mm). Kerb weight 7 cwt (356 kg).
Performance: Maximum speed when new — 28 mph (45 km/h). Normal cruising speed — 20 mph (32 km/h). Fuel consumption at highway speeds — 30 mpg (9.4 litres/100 km).

OLD
VETERAN
003

1900 Toledo Steamer

THE MARQUE

Though the world's auto industry once built more steamers than petrol or electric cars, a steamer in full flight is a rare sight today.

This enchanting Toledo demonstrates why the steamer ceased to remain competitive. It travels quietly and briskly enough on level roads but lacks the steam capacity to tackle steep hills. Even on satisfactory terrain, it travels about 10 miles per gallon of kerosene (3.5 km per litre) and between 2 and 3 miles per gallon of water.

Unlike more sophisticated steamers, the Toledo lacks a system to recondense the steam waste, and its total range between fresh charges of water is 50 miles, or 80 kilometres.

Toledo was never in the forefront of steamer design, building only ten cars or so during three years of production. The marque does not rate a mention in Lord Montagu's book, *Steam Cars,* probably because hundreds of small firms were then attempting to compete with the thriving Stanley brothers.

The Toledo was named after the city in Ohio, United States, where it was built. The American Bicycle Company launched the firm but after building a few cars changed the name to the International Motor Car Company. They achieved some export success; though only ten Toledos were made, four exist in the United States, two in Australia and one each in England, South Africa and Mexico.

In 1902 the company abandoned steam car production and switched to Pope-Toledo petrol cars. Production lasted a further six years.

1900 TOLEDO BUGGY

Little is known of the early background of this car. The present owners, Roger and Lesley Young of Rockhampton, Queensland, acquired the car in mid 1977. The previous owner, Tim Osborne of Brisbane, had restored the tiny buggy during the 1950s but its boiler deteriorated to the point where it became necessary to take the car off the road in the late 1960s.

Complete and in original condition, the steamer still has the two seater body made by the American Bicycle Company. It is sprung from a rigid chassis.

The twin-cylinder, double acting steam engine develops 6¼ HP and is suspended from the chassis by a hollow ball joint, providing a steam passage as well as adjustment for the chain drive to the back axle.

After the car was purchased, Roger Young, a machine inspector, removed the boiler and designed a replacement which conforms with today's safety standards, though it is as close to the original specifications as possible. Tested to 300 pounds per square inch (2067 kpa), the semi-flash type boiler is heated by a kerosene burner. Liquid petroleum gas (instead of petrol) is used in the pilot burner. The 35 gallon (160 litre) water tank surrounds the boiler.

When the car is mobile, water is circulated by an engine-driven pump but when stationary, the tiller doubles as a hand pump. The engine also drives an air pump, maintaining 60-80 psi pressure in the fuel tank. No gearbox is fitted but the engine can run backwards to provide reverse.

The main driving control is a single lever which varies engine speed and provides forward or reverse direction. The tiller has a very quick action and the brake pedal can be locked down for parking. There is also a foot-operated, two-tonne clarion bell.

The driver has three gauges to keep an eye on — one showing steam pressure, one fuel pressure and one water level. The latter is read by means of a mirror.

MECHANICAL FEATURES

Engine: Twin-cylinder, double acting steamer with piston valves and inside admission. Rated at 6.25 HP. Burns kerosene, with semi-flash boiler.
Gearbox: No gearbox or clutch, but chain drive provides a 2 to 1 reduction between engine and rear differential.
Suspension: Double semi-elliptic (transverse at front), elliptic at rear.
Steering: Tiller steering with only ¼ movement turning wheels lock-to-lock. Turning circle 25 ft (7.6 m).
Wheels: Pneumatic tyres on wire spoked well base wheels, 4.00 x 18. The original 28 x 3 bolt-on-type tyres not now available.
Dimensions: Wheelbase 4 ft 10 ins (1470 mm). Overall length 7 ft 6 ins (2285 mm). Height 5 ft 7 ins (1700 mm). Kerb weight 10 cwt (510 kg).
Performance: Maximum speed when new — 30 mph (48 km/h). Normal cruising speed — 15 mph (24 km/h). Fuel consumption at highway speeds — 10 mpg (28 litres/100 km) fuel, 3 mpg (94 litres/100 km) water.

OLDSMOBILE
1901 MODEL
VETERAN CAR
017
12

1901 'Merry' Oldsmobile

THE MARQUE

The car which inspired the song, "Come Away with me, Lucille, in my Merry Oldsmobile", was this curved dash runabout. The tiny two seater was a phenomenal success. It not only introduced cheap motoring to the American masses but proved that cars could be reliable, durable and fun to own.

Designed and built by Ransome E. Olds in 1900, the runabout is still one of the most desirable and easily recognised cars of its type available.

Olds built his first vehicle — a steamer — in 1892. After experimenting with several steam designs, he switched to petrol. During 1900 he built several prototype cars but the factory burned down, destroying all except the single-cylinder spinderly runabout with the curved dash.

To recoup his losses, Olds rushed it into production, selling the runabout for $750 in the United States. He promoted it with some interesting stunts, including a drive from the east to west coast of America. Production commenced in 1901. Some 2100 cars were built in 1902, the figure increasing to 5000 in 1904. When production ceased two years later, more than 20,000 runabouts had been built, and the factory was using assembly line techniques.

Gus Edward's song, inviting Lucille to elope in a Merry Oldsmobile, helped make it one of the most famous cars of all time. The little machine was also an astonishingly attractive performer. A single-cylinder water-cooled engine, placed horizontally across the chassis frame, was rated at 5 HP, developing 7 BHP at 790 rpm. This gave a road speed of 30 mph (48 km/h). Most owners cruised with the engine running at about 500 rpm, hence the expression 'one chug per telegraph pole'.

The engine turned the rear wheels via a two-speed epicyclic gearbox and central chain drive. The unusual controls included tiller steering and a foot operated reverse gear. Owners claimed they needed three legs and three arms to drive it properly.

In 1904 Ransome E. Olds sold his company to William Durant, founder of General Motors, for $3 million in stock. Olds then founded REO, initially manufacturing a twin-cylinder buggy.

1901 CURVED DASH RUNABOUT

This completely original Oldsmobile was acquired second hand in 1910 by the Oxford Street Tyre Retreading Company of Paddington, New South Wales. In 1937 Mr W. H. Lober, a major car distributor, purchased it for £50 ($100). The car has been in the Lober family ever since.

For several years it was used to advertise W. H. Lober & Co., which distributed Oldsmobile, Cadillac and La Salle cars throughout New South Wales. It was driven daily to the centre of Sydney to collect the company's mail.

The original instruction book provides some interesting glimpses of early motoring:

"Don't do anything to your motor car without good reason and without knowing what you are doing."

"Don't imagine that your motor runs well on equal parts of water and gasoline."

"Don't make improvements without writing to the factory."

"Never make a quick turn of the steering lever while the vehicle is running at high speeds; it is liable to cause a bad accident."

This particular Oldsmobile has been a faultless performer for most of its life. It has made two trips from Sydney to Melbourne, one in 1938 and again in 1970, competing in the Australian Bi-Centenary International Rally.

At least 40 Curved Dash Oldsmobiles are known to survive around the world, including about ten in Australia. For some unexplained reason, half the Australian survivors have been found in Tasmania.

MECHANICAL FEATURES

Engine: Single-cylinder side valve unit of 1478 ccs. Rated at 5 HP, developing 7 HP at 790 rpm. Water-cooled, Oldsmobile carburettor, jump spark ignition.
Gearbox: Two-speed epicyclic with reverse gear and chain drive to rear axle. Clutch effected by means of bands in gearbox.
Suspension: Semi-elliptic springs running from front to rear.
Brakes: Internal expanding brake in differential housing.
Steering: Tiller with only half turn lock-to-lock.
Wheels: 28 inch timber artillery 750 x 90 tyres.
Dimensions: Wheel base 5 ft 6 ins (1676 mm). Overall length 8 ft 2 ins (2490 mm). Height 4 ft 9½ ins (1460 mm). Kerb weight 7 cwt (356 kg).
Performance: Maximum speed when new — 30 mph (48 km/h). Normal cruising speed — 15 mph (24 km/h). Fuel consumption at highway speeds — 30 mpg (9.4 litres/100 km).

1903 Carlton Rear Entrance Tonneau

THE MARQUE

During the past century more than 4000 different firms have set up in the car making business. Around one hundred survive. The majority have fallen into obscurity because either the product was basically uncompetitive or the maker had insufficient capital to develop the design and commence production.

Some cars are so obscure that they are almost ignored by the most comprehensive reference books available. Georgano's *Complete Encyclopaedia of Motor Cars 1885-1968*, for example, simply notes that the Carlton Motor Company of Coventry, Warwickshire (England) made three models between 1901 and 1902. They are listed as a 6 HP single, a 12 HP twin and a 24 HP four-cylinder model, all using Aster engines.

When Eric Rainsford, one of Australia's premier collectors and restoration experts, uncovered the world's only surviving Carlton, he could find only the sketchiest references to its origin.

On his behalf, George Brooks and the late Dennis Field spent many hours in Britain investigating the history of the Carlton Motor Company. They concluded that although Rainsford's car may have been built prior to 1903, it was not sold until that year. They also considered that the car was probably built up from proprietary components which were commercially available at the time. Even this is speculative, as Carlton was listed at the time as being a manufacturer of engines and other components.

Whether Georgano is right and the surviving Carlton has an Aster-made engine is not known. The engine bears the inscription 'Carlton Motor Company, London', though this does not necessarily mean that Carlton manufactured it. There is no identification on the engine or anywhere else to indicate who made what.

1903 CARLTON

It is not known why or when this extremely rare car came to Australia, but possibly it was imported with a view to establishing an Australian agency for the British firm. The car itself was found in Stawell, Victoria, disassembled in boxes and listed amongst the assets of a deceased estate. Complete in most respects, it lacked only a steering wheel and gear lever.

An inspection showed several unusual features. The front wheels are smaller in diameter than the rear. The engine runs in an anti-clockwise direction; the steering is almost impossibly high in its gearing. This makes the car quite treacherous to drive. Eric Rainsford thinks that possibly the original design had a lever or tiller steering which would provide a greater degree of control, but in the absence of any other information, a steering wheel was manufactured and fitted during restoration. It has only one quarter turn from lock-to-lock!

The single-cylinder engine of 950 cc capacity drives the rear wheels through a two-speed epicyclic gearbox. There is no reverse gear. Unlike many cars of the time, the Carlton has shaft drive, not chains.

This unusual and fairly small car was completely restored by Eric Rainsford. The chassis was given a new rear entrance tonneau type body, similar to that widely used by British firms in 1903. D. Davey trimmed the replica body.

The 1903 Carlton is now on display at the National Motor Museum, Birdwood Mill, South Australia.

MECHANICAL FEATURES

Engine: Single-cylinder engine of 950 cc capacity rated at 8 HP. It has an automatic inlet valve and side exhaust, with water cooling and coil ignition. The engine runs in an anti-clockwise direction with a maximum speed of approximately 1200 rpm.

Gearbox: Epicyclic unit with external band for low gear and cone clutch for top. No reverse.

Suspension: Semi-elliptic leaf springs front and rear.

Brakes: External contracting bands on rear wheels.

Steering: Gear-and-pinion, with 26 ft (7.9 m) turning circle; only one quarter turn lock-to-lock.

Wheels: Artillery wheels, front 26 x 3, rear 710 x 90.

Dimensions: Wheelbase 6 ft 4 ins (1930 mm). Overall length 10 ft 2 ins (3099 mm). Height 4 ft 6 ins (1372 mm).

Performance: Maximum speed when new - about 25 mph (40 km/h). Normal cruising speed - 20 mph (32 km/h). Fuel consumption at highway speeds - 30 mpg (9.4 litres/100 km).

11

1903 Humberette

THE MARQUE

In a humble backyard workshop in Nottingham, England, Thomas Humber built a curious looking cycle, making every part himself, down to the timber wheels. In 1896 he turned his talents to motor vehicles, starting with motorcycles and tricycles. His first four-wheeler, a quadricycle built in 1899, was fitted with a 2¼ HP De Dion-Bouton engine. Front-wheel-drive and rear wheel steering made it an original, if highly unusual, design. Two experimental cars later, Humber settled on a conventionally designed Voiturette, borrowing heavily from De Dion practice.

The new car had several novel ideas, including a tubular frame with the radiator mounted on hinges, allowing it to be easily moved out of the way when working on the engine. Other innovations included a single spoke steering wheel, adjustable steering column, a bonnet lifting from the front and pendant-type pedals. The 4½ HP engine was conventionally located with shaft drive to the rear.

The new car, which came to be known as the Humberette, was a great success. It quickly proved to be Britain's first really popular light car and, by late 1901, was being produced at the rate of 50 a week.

A completely new model with a 5 HP engine was introduced in 1903. The engine was a close copy of De Dion's but turned in an anti-clockwise direction, an idea said to have neatly circumvented the De Dion Patent. With successive improvements, the model continued until 1908 when the company began concentrating on a line of larger models produced some years earlier.

Though pretty and practical, the Humberette was unusually difficult to drive. Gear changing was so slow that when climbing a hill the car lost most of its speed before the driver could change from top to bottom gear. Another drawback was that the mixture and ignition controls (located on the steering column) needed constant adjustment.

Eleven 5 HP Humberettes are known to survive. Ten are in Britain and one is in Australia.

1903 HUMBERETTE VOITURETTE

Owned and completely rebuilt by Len and Joan Clarke of Adelaide, this beautifully finished car has won several Concours awards and is at least equal to new in all respects.

It was originally imported into Western Australia by Cobb & Co. to carry mail between Nanine and Meekatharra in the Murchison area. In 1908 Cobb & Co. ceased their operations in Western Australia and gave the car to a Catholic priest in the township of Cue. He found it rather too difficult to drive and passed it on to a local prospector, Frank Johns, brother of a well known Cobb & Co. driver.

In 1914 Johns also decided that the Humberette was an unsatisfactory car to drive and left it unused in a shed. Over a number of years, the car slowly deteriorated. The front seat was taken for use on a verandah, the body was ripped up for its aluminium and the steering column disappeared, along with the steering wheel and the controls. Someone pulled out the gearbox and radiator and left them beside the wreck.

Little more happened until 1950 when a visitor trucked some of the bits to Mount Magnet. He probably intended to restore the car but soon abandoned the idea.

A man from Kalgoorlie found the remains on the Mount Magnet rubbish dump. He took them to his home town, cut up the chassis for its tubing and converted the engine to an air compressor. Fortunately, Adelaide old car enthusiast, Len Clarke, heard the story, acquired what was left of the car in Kalgoorlie and then back-tracked to Cue where the original radiator (damaged when run over by a truck) and gearbox were recovered.

With the help of an Englishman who

owned a similar Humberette, Len undertook the long job of completely rebuilding the car to its original specifications. The trim restoration was done by Don Davey, the mechanical and body work by Len Clarke. The job took seven years, but yielded the only known 5 HP Humberette outside of Britain.

MECHANICAL FEATURES

Engine: Single-cylinder engine of 655 ccs, with automatic overhead inlet valve and side exhaust. The cooling water is circulated by pump. Longemere carburettor; trembler coil ignition. Maximum engine speed is 1500 rpm.
Transmission: Two-speed, continuous mesh, with gears engaged by locking shafts and dog clutches. Leather-faced cone clutch.
Suspension: Semi-elliptic springs front and rear.
Brakes: External contracting on rear wheels.
Steering: Ackerman type with extremely direct action. Wire wheels 650 x 65; kerb weight 6½ cwt (331 kg).
Performance: Maximum speed when new — 25 mph (40 km/h). Normal cruising speed — 20-22 mph (32-35 km/h). Fuel consumption at highway speeds — 50 mpg (5.6 litres/100 km).

1903 Rambler Runabout

THE MARQUE

The firm we now know as American Motors traces its ancestors back to the Rambler Runabout and still builds a car by the same name. But between then and now have passed such names as Jeffery (1914-17), Nash (1918-57), Ajax (1919-32), La Fayette (1934-39), Hudson (1909-57), Essex (1919-32), Terraplane (1933-38), Metropolitan (1954-62), Nash-Healey (1951-54), Hudson-Railton (1933-38) and Hudson-Italia (1954).

Thomas B. Jeffery helped to build and sell Rambler cycles from 1878 to 1900, when he constructed his first car. His interesting prototype had a front mounted engine and a steering wheel but Jeffery's father talked him out of such radical innovations. When the first Rambler was ready for production, it featured a tiller steering system and the engine under the seat.

Though little more than a motorised buggy with a timber body, large artillery wheels and a single-cylinder 900 cc engine, the Rambler had some ingenious ideas. Jeffery was no doubt mindful of the song "Get Out and Get Under", for he made sure that all mechanical components could be serviced or repaired from above, through trapdoors in the floor and a hinged seat.

Very early in his automotive career, Jeffery hired two men — Harry Stutz and Ned Jordan — both of whom later made a success of their own car companies.

Production of the lightweight Rambler commenced in 1902, soon after the Merry Oldsmobile had taken the country by storm. In 1903, Jeffery sold 1350 cars. He adopted the assembly line technique, no doubt after taking a look at the Oldsmobile operation. Late in 1903, he switched to a steering wheel and a larger single-cylinder engine of 1.9 litres. By 1904 the American public was demanding more power and added sophistication, so production of the single seater runabout was dropped in favour of a larger twin-cylinder model.

Jeffery then moved into a range of designs and body types, including a five

passenger $2500 Rambler powered by a 40 HP four-cylinder engine.

When he died at a comparatively young age in 1910, his son Charles took over. He introduced some innovations, including an adjustable steering column, and changed the car's name to Jeffery, possibly in honour of his father. Charles Jeffery's greatest contribution was a remarkable truck called the Quad which boasted four-wheel-drive and four-wheel-steering. He sold 21,494 Quads to the United States Army and, at one time, claimed to be the largest truck maker in the world.

In 1916 Charles Jeffery was on board the *SS Lusitania* when it was torpedoed. Though he was rescued, he was very badly shaken and immediately looked around for a buyer for his company. Meanwhile Charles Nash, president of General Motors, resigned abruptly and bought the Jeffery Company for $6 million. He introduced the Nash Six and later bought the LaFayette Corporation. For some years he also produced a low cost light six called Ajax and, in 1926, the Nash companies announced total

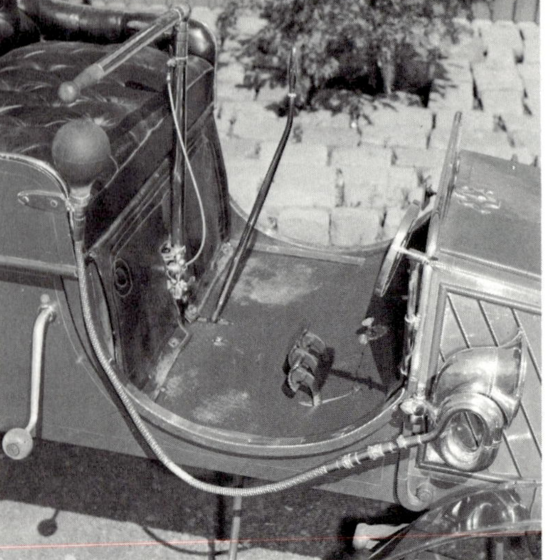

production of 100,000 vehicles for the year. This remarkable effort helped Nash survive the coming depression.

After World War Two, Nash brought out a small car called the Rambler. The Nash-Healey followed and, in 1954, the company merged with Hudson, forming American Motors. The names Hudson and Nash finally disappeared in 1957 but Rambler survived.

1903 RAMBLER RUNABOUT

Typical of the motorised buggies with which America entered the auto business, the 1902-3 Rambler had its single-cylinder engine mounted horizontally under the seat. It has a large flywheel, two-speed epicyclic gearbox and chain drive to the rear wheel. An interesting feature was an ignition advance-and-retard mechanism similar to the centrifugal type used today.

The history of the car in these photographs is not known, but the car was beautifully restored by John Alderson of East Ivanhoe, Victoria. In 1970 it was purchased by the late Jack Jeffery of Sydney and later changed hands again. The present owner, a Sydney collector, displays the car at Green's Motorcade, near Liverpool, New South Wales.

MECHANICAL FEATURES

Engine: Single-cylinder, side valve, 900 cc capacity (approx.), developing 10 HP at 950 rpm. Water cooling, Stromberg carburettor, battery ignition.
Gearbox: Two-speed epicyclic with external bands and chain drive to rear axle.
Suspension: Full elliptic springs at front and rear.
Brakes: External contracting brakes on rear wheels.
Steering: Tiller with 40 ft (12.2 m).
Wheels: Artillery type, timber spokes 710 x 90.
Dimensions: Wheelbase 6 ft 6 ins (2011 mm). Overall length 9 ft 2 ins (2794 mm). Height 5 ft 1 in (1549 mm).
Performance: Maximum speed when new — 28 mph (45 km/h). Normal cruising speed — 20 mph (32 km/h). Fuel consumption at highway speeds — 25 mpg (11.3 litres/100 km).

Rambler
1902
NSW
RV·9371

1904 De Dion-Bouton

THE MARQUE

The cars made by Count Albert De Dion, M. Trepardoux and workshop foreman, Georges Bouton, were the pace setters of France at the turn of the century. The firm had commenced building steam carriages as early as 1883. Count De Dion and Bouton (who did the early designing) built a highly successful single-cylinder petrol engine in 1895. It happily revved to 1500 rpm — a high speed at the time — giving more power than contemporary engines. In 1899, the new engine was fitted to the rear of a tubular steel frame which formed the basis of a successful light weight voiturette.

De Dion introduced a remarkable gearbox designed by Bouton, employing the basic principles of the modern automatic transmission, including epicyclic gears and automatic clutches. Another important invention was a new type of rear axle. Most cars of the time had chain drive, but Trepardoux devised a system of shaft drive, with a differential unit bolted to the chassis frame and two universally jointed shafts turning the rear wheels. The system is still in use in some high performance cars today.

De Dion was building four-cylinder cars by 1904. A year later his cars were so popular that the factory employed 3000 people and was exporting around the world.

For sheer innovation, the Count reached his peak in 1908 when he announced that a new luxury car, with a 35 HP V-8 engine, would be produced the following year. His was not the first V-8 (Ader, Darracq and Rolls-Royce had V-8 cars in 1905) but unlike the others, De Dion's engine stayed in production until 1923. It inspired Cadillac and the rest of Detroit to follow the same route. About ten V-8 De Dion cars are believed to survive, several being in Australia.

After World War One De Dion's innovative spark died. Car sales dwindled accordingly, the last one being built in 1931. At the time, the Marquis De Dion was aged 74 and in robust health. He lived a further ten years.

1904 DE DION-BOUTON TYPE V

One of the few almost completely original 1904 cars anywhere in the world, this remarkably sound De Dion has never been restored. A coat of paint, normal maintenance and a few repairs have kept it in excellent shape during a long and busy life.

The car is believed to have arrived here in 1905. It was fitted with a De Dion made tonneau style body, incorporating bench seats and a rear door. No weather protection was provided.

The first owner, a Dr J. Sangster of Burra, South Australia, sold it to an Adelaide doctor, Dr E. Kinmont. Kinmont was a noted car enthusiast and when living in Port Lincoln, had commissioned a local cycle maker, Puckridge Brothers, to build him a car in 1903. After moving to Adelaide, Dr Kinmont used this De Dion for many years, but finally abandoned it when the engine failed to start one evening.

Veteran car enthusiast Percy Wien-Smith heard about the De Dion in 1933. He instituted a search and in early 1934 located the car, complete and unharmed, in a dry building behind the Royal Adelaide Hospital. Dr Kinmont was dead by then, but Percy Wien-Smith acquired the car from the executors of his estate. He took it in South Australia's first Veteran Car Rally, held in May 1934.

In the hands of the late Percy Wien-Smith and more recently with his son John at the wheel, the 1904 De Dion has won an impressive number of rally and concours successes. It is one of the most original De Dion of its type in the world.

MECHANICAL FEATURES

Engine: Single-cylinder, 940 cc capacity with side exhaust valve and automatic overhead inlet, RAC rating 8 HP. Water-cooled with a De Dion carburettor and make-and-break coil ignition.
Gearbox: Epicyclic gearbox, gears in constant mesh, three forward speeds plus reverse, engaged by expanding clutches. Gear lever mounted below steering wheel.
Suspension: Semi-elliptic at front; De Dion axle at rear with two semi-elliptics and one transverse spring.
Brakes: Contracting type brakes on rear wheels with contracting bands on drums. Transmission brake in front of gearbox.
Steering: Rack-and-pinion, with a 32 ft (9.7 m) diameter and only ¾ turns lock-to-lock.
Wheels: Woodspoke wheels with 760 x 90 beaded edge tyres.
Dimensions: Wheelbase 6 ft 1½ ins (1867 mm). Overall length 9 ft 0 ins (2743 mm). Height 4 ft 9 ins (1448 mm). Kerb weight 12 cwt (611 kg).
Performance: Maximum speed when new — 32 mph (51 km/h). Normal cruising speed — 20 mph (32 km/h). Fuel consumption at highway speeds — 30 mpg (9.4 litres/100 km).

1

1904 Minerva Voiturette

THE MARQUE

Like so many firms, Belgium's most successful car firm started as a cycle manufacturer, moving into the automotive field at the turn of the century. The cycle factory had been open for only three years when Sylvain de Jong and his brother built firstly, a motorcycle, then a car. For the next few years they launched a succession of models, ranging from a 5 HP voiturette to a massive 12 litre racer.

The early Minervas were chain driven and it was not until 1905 that the firm moved into shaft drive.

This delightful voiturette, built in 1904, was one of the very first cars made in Antwerp and is powered by a 5 HP, single-cylinder side valve engine, with water cooling. The two-speed gearbox is mounted in unit with the engine which lies east-west across the chassis. A cone clutch disconnects the primary chain from the secondary chain which drives the rear wheels.

The 5 HP voiturette was designed for the British market where it was sold as the Minervette. Only two are known to survive — one in Queensland, owned by Frank Hack, the other in Britain.

Though Belgium has no motor industry today, it was home to several notable makes, including F.N., Excelsior and Metallurgique. Minerva is probably the best known of all Belgium cars, but the name is associated more with the luxury tourers and the huge limousines the company built before and after World War One. Its big 6 litre sleeve valve engine pulled some of the most luxurious coachwork of the day. Minerva also produced a 6½ litre straight eight engine and its silence was a by-word in the stables of British and European aristocracy.

A more complete story on the development and demise of this interesting marque is given with the 1924 Minerva Tourer (see page 142).

1904 5 HP VOITURETTE

This extremely rare car was probably one of the special models built for the British market before Minerva had found its feet as a car maker. Unfortunately, the car's origin and history are lost in obscurity. All that is conclusively known is that the little car was put in a packing case and stored under a house in Melbourne during World War One. There it stayed for many years, but in 1960 the voiturette turned up in Maryborough, Victoria, and was acquired and restored by John Alderson, of Victoria.

In 1962, it won the Award of Merit from the Veteran Car Club of Australia (Vic). Since being acquired by the present owner, Frank Hack, of Rochedale, Queensland, it has deservedly won several Concours d'Elegance events.

MECHANICAL FEATURES

Engine: Single-cylinder, side valve design, 635 cc rated at 5 HP, water-cooled with induction coil ignition. Engine mounted east-west across the chassis frame. Bore 90 x 100 mm stroke.
Gearbox: Two-speed sliding dog type built in unit with the engine.
Suspension: Semi-elliptic leaf springs front and rear.
Brakes: Contracting drum brakes on rear wheels.
Steering: Direct crank. Turning circle: 23 ft approximately.
Wheels: Wire wheels, originally beaded edge, now 19 x 300 well base.
Dimensions: Wheelbase 6 ft 3 ins (1900 mm). Overall length 8 ft 0 ins (2438 mm). Height 4 ft 2 ins (1270 mm). Kerb weight 8 cwt (407 kg).
Performance: Maximum speed when new — 25 mph (40 km/h). Normal cruising speed — 20 mph (32 km/h). Fuel consumption at highway speeds — 30 mpg (9.4 litres/100 km).

1904 Ohlmeyer Jigger

THE MARQUE

Dubbed the 'Jigger' by the maker's family, this was one of several home-made cars built in the Barossa Valley, South Australia, soon after the turn of the century.

The constructor, Albert Ohlmeyer, was a member of a group of Barossa Valley motoring enthusiasts who assembled each Sunday morning with their motorcycles or home-made cars. His friend, Fred Modistach, also built a four-wheeler based on cycle parts, known as the 'Quad', and the two cars frequently travelled together.

Ohlmeyer was an unusually versatile man, being a watchmaker by profession, an inventor by instinct, and both a violin player and photographer by choice. He owned a Minerva and a Gritzner motorcycle before building his own car.

The Jigger was a true buckboard style, with cycle wheels and seating for two. Its name was appropriate because there were no suspension springs. Road shocks were absorbed by the pneumatic tyres and by two sturdy hickory bearers running from front to rear of each side. The seat, similar to a sulky type, also had a soft cushion and, according to Jule Ohlmeyer, the present owner, the ride was quite comfortable, even on the rough roads of the day.

Jule and Ernst Ohlmeyer were small boys when their father built the Jigger and had previously travelled in a wicker basket towed by their father's motorcycle before the Jigger was ready. After using the home made car for twelve years, Albert Ohlmeyer bought a Model T Ford and passed the Jigger to his sons who used it regularly until 1923 when it was deemed too old-fashioned for further use.

It was dismantled and put in a shed, untouched for forty years. Then Jule reassembled the car. He last drove it in 1969 when he took part in the Barossa Vintage Festival. The car is still complete and in working order in Adelaide, owned by Mr Jule Ohlmeyer, but it is no longer taken on the road.

The design is simple but ingenious. The engine is a British built 4½ HP Automotor, built as a stationary engine to drive a water pump. The single-cylinder unit has an automatic inlet valve, dry battery, coil ignition and a simple surface carburettor. The engine is mounted on its side at the front of the car, driving the rear wheels through a flat belt which turns a pair of pulleys on a counter shaft at the rear. The drive is taken from there by chains and sprockets to the back wheels. The countershaft also carries a pulley for the foot brake which operates externally on the rear tyres. There is also

a clutch to engage top gear. Power is applied to one wheel at a time, the nearside being the low gear and the offside the high gear — a system which eliminated the need for a differential.

Equally simple was the wire-and-bobbin steering, incorporating an articulated steering column. The

universal joint in the steering column helped to reduce road shock and vibration and made it easier for the driver to get in and out of the car. But the main advantage was that the driver could walk beside the moving car, steering from the side when travelling over sand or up a steep hill.

During its first year, the Jigger gave its full share of mechanical trouble, mainly caused by slipping belts and 'missing' ignition. Punctures were frequent. The surface carburettor consisted of a metal box with a float to control the fuel level, the air being drawn over the fuel. It gave fantastic fuel economy, with figures around 70 miles per gallon, but vehicle motion created a surging effect, making the car hard to drive smoothly. Mr Ohlmeyer replaced the surface carburettor with a jet-type motorcycle carburettor and, though fuel consumption rose, the car was easier to handle.

After the bugs were ironed out, the Jigger proved very reliable. It has covered an estimated 50,000 km since being built, the only major breakdown occurring when a bolt came loose in the engine's gudgeon pin, scoring the cylinder.

After Jule and Ernst took over the car in 1916, they modernised the carburettor and ignition and used it as every day transport for seven years.

MECHANICAL FEATURES

Engine: Single-cylinder, water-cooled Automotor of 4½ HP, with coil ignition and, originally, a surface type carburettor.
Gearbox: Two forward ratios (and no reverse) effected by belt and pulley, with chain drive to the rear wheels.
Suspension: None.
Brakes: External metal shoes rubbing against rear tyres; foot pedal operated.
Steering: Wire and bobbin type, with articulated steering column.
Dimensions: Overall Length 9 ft 4 ins (2845 mm). Width 4 ft 4 ins (1321 mm). Height 4 ft 3 ins (1295 mm). Kerb weight 4½ cwt (230 kg).
Performance: Maximum speed when new — 25 mph (40 km/h). Normal cruising speed — 20 mph (32 km/h). Miles per gallon — 40 to 70 mpg, depending on carburettor.

1904
OHLMEYER
SA217

THE MARQUE

Ransome E. Olds was remarkably prophetic when he introduced this 'Gentleman's Runabout' in 1905. The single-cylinder engine was placed across the chassis. The body introduced the rumble seat. This could be quickly unbolted, leaving a load carrying platform — the forerunner of the utility.

Olds retired from his Merry Oldsmobile concern in 1905, a self-made American millionaire. He immediately plunged into the design of this new model, offered with a single or a twin-cylinder engine. The two cars were a great success, 25,000 being built by 1910 when a four-cylinder car was introduced.

Apart from the engine, the single and twin Runabouts were virtually the same, with the engine mounted in the middle of the chassis. An extension of the crankshaft allowed a 'side winder' crank handle.

When new, the single-cylinder model sold in the United States for $US675, including the optional rumble seat. Olds marketed it with the rather ambiguous slogan, 'Built For What Happens'. Some owners considered it well named, for driving the car was anything but easy. To reverse uphill the driver needs one leg for the parking brake, one to keep down the reversing pedal and a third to operate the pendant accelerator. Both hands are fully occupied as well!

Reo cars sold well after conventional four and six-cylinder models were introduced. The company survived the American Depression and celebrated by introducing a straight eight, the Flying Cloud (in 1931) and a four-speed automatic transmission (1933). Sales dropped sharply in 1935 and, a year later, the company discontinued car production to concentrate on its truck operation.

Ed Sims finds the Reo less difficult to drive than folklore remembers. Quiet and astonishingly reliable, it has never let him down.

The Reo was one of a pair brought to Australia by the Steggall family, of Yandina, near Nambour, Queensland. It was extensively used until 1924, then left under a house. In 1950, Ed Sims heard about the car and bought if for £10 ($20). The car was complete but fairly dilapidated, as white ants had declared open season on the timber. Two days later the car was running; within months it competed in its first veteran car rally.

Ed re-restored the Reo to take part in the 1970 International Veteran and Vintage Rally, doing the body and mechanical work himself. Keith Albury, of Brisbane, looked after the trim, Graham Crittenden, of Kingaroy, making the hood. The car won the prestigious trophy for the one, two and three-cylinder classes in the International Rally.

The only other restored 1905 single-cylinder Reo in Australia is at St. Ives, New South Wales, and a 1908 model can be found in Queensland.

1905 REO MODEL B

This 'Gentleman's Runabout', owned by Ed Sims, of Kenilworth, Queensland, is one of the most active veteran cars in the country. Since restoring it in 1950, Ed has covered more than 10,000 miles (16,000 km) in rallies and outings. He has won dozens of events, with 24 trophies to prove it.

1905 Reo Runabout

MECHANICAL FEATURES

Engine: Single-cylinder, horizontal engine of 675 ccs, developing 8 HP at about 1300 rpm. Side valve design. Reo-made carburettor with vibrator coil ignition.
Gearbox: Engine chain drives the rear axle through a two-speed epicyclic gearbox, with reverse. Clutch has two steel and one copper plate immersed in oil.
Suspension: Three-quarter elliptics at front, full elliptics at rear.
Brakes: External contracting brakes on rear wheels. Pedal has a locking device on toe-board, providing a type of parking brake.
Steering: Gear-and-segment with a 42 ft (12.8 m) turning circle and only ⅝ turn lock-to-lock.
Wheels: Wooden artillery type with 23 inch tyres.
Dimensions: Wheelbase 6 ft 6 ins (1981 mm). Overall length 9 ft 3.5 ins (2832 mm). Height 6 ft 8.5 ins (2045 mm). Kerb weight 8.7 cwt (443 kg).
Performance: Maximum speed when new — 35 mph (56 km/h). Normal cruising speed — 25 mph (40 km/h). Fuel consumption at highway speeds — 40 mpg (7.1 litres/100 km).

1906 Rover 6 HP

THE MARQUE

Rover is now noted for powerful and luxurious cars, but the firm's beginnings were founded in pedal cycles and this delightful but diminutive single-cylinder car.

After pioneering the B.S.A. safety cycle (the modern bicycle shape), the company grew to be a large and prosperous cycle maker. In 1902, an experimental motorcycle was built and, in 1904, a four wheeler light car followed. Known as the 8 HP model, it was a quality machine designed by Edmund Lewis, with an aluminium backbone frame, enclosing the clutch, gearbox, and propeller shaft. The single-cylinder, water-cooled engine had a robust crankshaft mounted in ball bearings.

The 8 HP sold for £200 ($400) and was soon supplemented by a slightly smaller car, the 6 HP, with a conventional chassis frame and such modern ideas as

rack-and-pinion steering and a steering column gear change.

When the English price of £105 ($210) was announced, buyers beat a path to the factory. Like the 8 HP, it proved solid and reliable, despite some design eccentricities. The carburettor for example, is mounted on the side of the gearbox and connected to the inlet valve by an 18 inch (457 mm) long tube. The crankcase is cast in magnesium alloy with upper and lower sections, incorporating the clutch and gearbox.

Despite the small power output, the lightweight car was a real vehicle in all respects. One of the 8 HP models was used by Dr Jefferson in 1906 for an interesting journey from London to Constantinople.

ROVER 6 HP 1906

This car has an interesting history. The original owner is not known, but in 1908 Mr Tom Cantrell of Annandale, New South Wales, bought the 6 HP second hand. As an organ and piano maker, Mr Cantrell used the Rover extensively, at one time making weekly trips from Sydney to Wollongong. He developed a great affection for it and when he bought a larger, more powerful Renault, the 6 HP was stored in a shed behind a mounting collection of piano and organ parts.

It remained undisturbed for many years. In 1954 George Williams, a well known Sydney veteran car enthusiast and restorer, heard about the Rover. He approached Mr Cantrell, who showed no interest in selling.

George Williams continued visiting him on a weekly basis. Six months and innumerable cups of tea later, Mr Cantrell agreed to sell provided that George had approval from the family. A conference was called. The family agreed not only to sell the Rover but also three other old cars (a Renault, Bullnose Morris and Terraplane). As the oldest car in the 'collection', the Rover fetched the highest price — £50 ($100).

The years had treated the Rover sadly. The body had been changed and 'modernised', the engine was in poor shape. George Williams made new guards and bonnet to the original specifications and rebuilt the body to the correct shape. A well known competition driver, Teddy Behman, overhauled the engine and soon the car was in sound running order.

By 1961, George Williams had acquired other cars and sold the Rover to Sydney collector Laurie O'Neil. He placed it in the hands of Arthur Garthon, who has been custodian ever since. The most complicated mechanical job he has done during that time was a valve grind, which took twenty minutes. The trim restoration was done by Fred Thompson.

Four similar cars are in Australia. The United Kingdom boasts at least as many again.

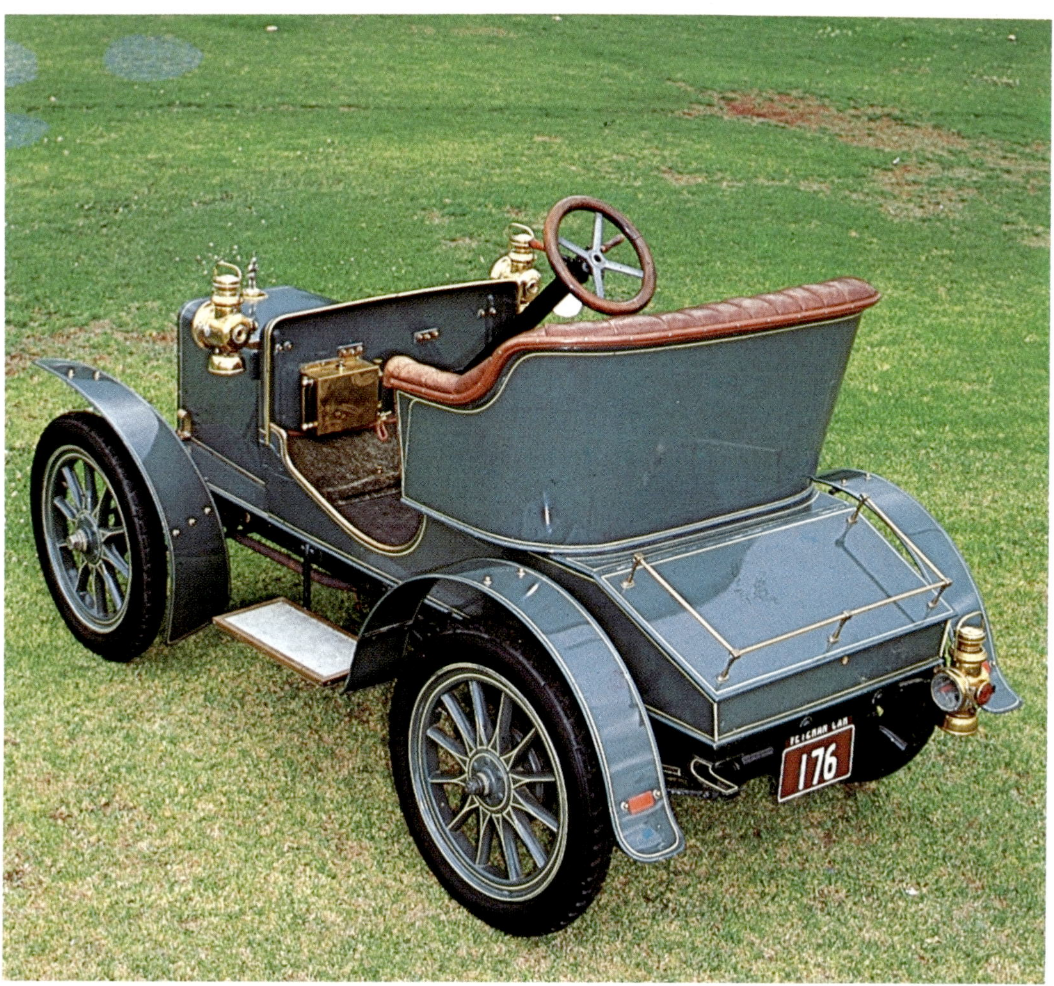

MECHANICAL FEATURES

Engine: Single-cylinder of 780 ccs with 97 x 100 mm bore and stroke and side valves. Rated at 6 HP. Fan and water pump cooling. Zenith carburettor. Magneto is chain driven from the crankshaft. The engine features Rover 'noiseless tappets'.
Gearbox: Sliding pinion type with three forward gears and quadrant change on the steering column. Clutch consists of a metal-to-metal multi disc running in oil and operated by the same pedal as the brake.
Suspension: Semi-elliptic springs front and rear, both sets having sliding trunions instead of shackles.
Brakes: Rear wheel brakes, external contracting with steel bands and an equaliser to both sides of the car.
Steering: Rack-and-pinion steering, with 20 ft (6 m) turning circle and ⅞ turn lock-to-lock.

Wheels: Wooden artillery type size 710 x 90.
Dimensions: Wheelbase 5 ft 8½ ins (1740 mm). Track 4 ft 0 ins (1220 mm). Overall length 9 ft 4 ins (2845 mm). Height 4 ft 5 ins (1346 mm). Kerb weight 7 cwt (356 kg).
Performance: Maximum speed when new — 24 mph (38 km/h). Normal cruising speed — 18 mph (29 km/h). Fuel consumption at highway speeds — 35 mpg (8 litres/100 km).

1906 Star Tourer

general Panhard layout. In 1902, he introduced the 8 HP model with a vertical twin engine, featuring automatic inlet valve. Though the Star catalogue said the engine was 'British built throughout', it was certainly European inspired. According to Lord Montagu in his book *Lost Causes of Motoring*: ". . . it is an indisputable fact that anyone would have found it hard to distinguish it from a contemporary Panhard."

Be that as it may, Star cars earned an enviable record for thoroughness of construction and long life. In particular the marque was noted for the excellent bodywork. In 1904 the company catalogued a light delivery van with side windows and removable seats — an idea which later found favour as the station waggon.

Star boomed and, by 1914, was Britain's sixth largest car maker. Edward Lisle had little interest in mass production. He once said that he would rather 'build one good car a day than commit himself to mass production'.

The company's success continued during the 1920s but as its products grew larger and more powerful, so the world

THE MARQUE

No less than five different cars named 'Star' were lauched during the veteran and vintage period — two in the United States and one each in Britain, Italy and Peru. This Star, representing the light car style of its day, was built by Star Engineering Company of Wolverhampton, England.

Like many early car companies, Star Engineering was derived from a successful cycle maker. Yet, Edward Lisle, the guiding force behind the car division, was ahead of his time in that he strove to make his cars trouble-free, durable and easy to drive.

The story of Star is complex because several companies were interwoven and, at various times, Edward Lisle's three sons came into the picture as heads of various companies. Probably they operated as a family concern with the sons given separate responsibilities for different jobs.

Edward Lisle built his first car in 1898, using an imported single-cylinder Benz engine with belt drive. Called the

Starling, it had the driver and passengers facing each other in vis-a-vis style. At least one Starling came to Australia and was owned by Mr Charles Free, who, in 1906, traded it in on the larger more powerful Star shown on this page.

Lisle's second car, a twin-cylinder model, was also based on Benz components but when he launched the 'A' series in 1900, he switched to the more

depression squeezed a growing number of firms out of business. In 1928 Star was taken over by Guy trucks; four years later the last Star car was built.

1906 STAR MODEL 7

This delightful tourer, believed to be the only Model 7 Star in Australia, was originally purchased in Sydney by Charles Free, who traded in his 1898 Starling for the car. He proudly drove the car to its new home in Tamworth where it created quite a sensation. Towards the end of 1907, Mr and Mrs Free took the Star to their property at Clifton on the Darling Downs, Queensland.

They kept it in meticulous order until 1954 when it was sold to Ed Uebergang who commenced restoration. In 1975 he sold it to the present owners, Kevin and Joyce Bartenstein of Toowoomba, Queensland.

MECHANICAL FEATURES

Engine: Twin-cylinder, water-cooled, rated at 8 HP, with maximum speed of 900 rpm. Star carburettor, magneto ignition and semi-dry sump lubrication.
Gearbox: Three-speed, with gears selected in succession; one reverse gear. Cone clutch and chain drive to rear wheels.
Suspension: Semi-elliptic springs, front and rear.
Brakes: Mechanical brakes on rear wheels.
Steering: Turning circle approximately 35 ft (10.7 m).
Wheels: Wooden spoked, size 30 x 3½ ins.
Dimensions: Wheelbase 7 ft 0 ins (2134 mm). Track 4 ft 0½ ins (1232 mm). Overall length 10 ft 1 in (3073 mm). Height 7 ft 1 in (2159 mm). Kerb weight 12½ cwt (636 kg).
Performance: Maximum speed when new — 20 mph (32 km/h). Normal cruising speed — 15 mph (24 km/h). Fuel consumption at highway speeds — 40 mpg (7.0 litres/100 km).

1906 Tarrant

THE MARQUE

Victorian-born Harley Tarrant was the first man to attempt to launch an Australian motor industry. His car-making ventures failed but he succeeded in building up Melbourne's largest car selling and body-building operation.

During the 1890s Tarrant experimented with his own internal combustion engine and, in 1897, built an unsuccessful twin-cylinder buggy. Undeterred, in 1897 he launched a new business, manufacturing stationary engines. Within months he was again experimenting with cars. In partnership with Howard Lewis, Tarrant designed and built a lightweight car, powered by a 6 HP Benz engine. It was launched in 1901.

This car was sold to a Melbourne merchant firm of Chandler Brothers who used it for several years. It was thus the first Australian car to be sold and successfully operated by the purchaser.

A third man, Bill Ross, joined the partners. They established a new car agency selling Argylls, De Dion-Boutons and, later, a wide range of other marques. Recognising the need for local production facilities, Tarrant also founded the Melbourne Motor Body Works, which survived until after World War Two when it was purchased by the Austin Motor Company.

Despite his hectic business life, Harley Tarrant was determined to launch his own car. In 1903, he built a twin-cylinder 8 HP model, with 90 per cent local content. Only the radiator, magneto and carburettor were imported. This car won Australia's first properly organised car race, held on Sandown Park Racecourse on 12 March, 1904. Tarrant developed an abiding interest in motor sport and in 1905 went on to win Australia's first long distance event, the Dunlop Reliability Trial from Sydney to Melbourne, driving an Argyll. Not surprisingly, he entered his own 8 HP car in the second Dunlop Trial, also held later in 1905, and conducted over nearly 900 km of dreadful roads between Melbourne and Sydney. Only five of the 29 starters completed the trip, including Tarrant. The five were declared joint winners.

Tarrant's next venture was to design a four-cylinder 14/16 HP tourer which he intended building in quantity to compete against similar sized imports. Despite his eagerness, only a handful were made before production ceased in 1907. In all, a total of sixteen Tarrants were built over a span of ten years.

Tarrant himself became wealthy, largely as a result of the Ford Model T distributorship. He retired from his company in 1920, following a bout of ill health but recovered and lived until 1949, aged 89 years.

1906 TARRANT 14/16 HP

The early history of the car is not known but it was purchased at auction in 1932 by the late Mr Maurice Shmith, a prominent Melbourne businessman. Prior to then it had been used as a delivery van for Smiths Furniture Store of Prahran.

After some work on the Tarrant, Shmith gave it to Kenneth and Peter Holmes, the sons of Harley Tarrant's daughter. They completely restored the chassis and engaged local craftsmen to make a replica of the original two seater open tourer body.

The work was done between 1963 and 1968, bringing the Tarrant to virtually new condition. It is the only known survivor of sixteen cars built by the Melbourne manufacturer.

MECHANICAL FEATURES

Engine: Four-cylinder T-head twin camshaft unit of 3.5 litres, rated at 16 HP at 1000 rpm. Water pump cooling, Zenith updraught carburettor, Bosch magneto. Maximum engine speed 1600 rpm.
Gearbox: Selective sliding three-speed unit in aluminium case. Leather-faced cone clutch.
Suspension: Semi-elliptic springs at front, three-quarter elliptics at rear.
Brakes: Handbrake actuates external expanding brakes on rear wheels, foot pedal operates two wheel and transmission brake.
Steering: Worm-and-nut, with 50 ft (15.2 metres); one turn lock-to-lock.
Wheels: Timber spoked steel rim, tyre size 30 x 3½.
Dimensions: Wheelbase 9 ft 7 ins (2921 mm). Overall length 13 ft 1 in (3988 mm). Height 5 ft 6 ins (1676 mm). Kerb weight 16 cwt (815 kg).
Performance: Maximum speed when new — 55 mph (88 km/h). Normal cruising speed — 35 mph (56 km/h). Fuel consumption at highway speeds — 15 mpg (18.8 litres/100 km).

651

1907 Alldays & Onion Rear Entrance Tourer

THE MARQUE

Alldays and Onion were primarily established in pneumatic engineering in Birmingham, England, when the firm decided to launch its own car. The first product, a single-cylinder quadricycle, appeared in 1899, designed for parcel carrying and light delivery work. In 1903 the firm had graduated to a more refined passenger car, with a single-cylinder De Dion engine, shaft drive and a higher level of engineering.

In 1905 the firm launched the all new 10/12 HP tourer which stayed in production for seven years and established the company as the builder of well engineered cars, noted for their prodigious hill climbing ability.

Many 10/12s were built with a rear entrance style of body. This legacy from the horse and carriage era remained fashionable for some years, especially with the well-to-do business clientele that Alldays and Onion sought. To establish the new 10/12 model, the company entered hill climbs, managing to beat Fiat and Delage at the famed Shelsley Walsh hill climb and capturing the first three places.

Around 1908 Alldays acquired the Enfield Autocar Company which was auctioned off to pay its debts. Then came a diverse series of models, ranging from a one litre V-twin cyclecar to a 35 HP six, with many models sold under both Alldays and Enfield brands.

After World War One, the firm merged its two car firms and launched the radically different Enfield-Allday. A brilliant machine in many ways, this newcomer had some splendid features, including a five-cylinder, air-cooled, 1.5 litre radial engine. Unhappily, it proved too expensive and probably too different for its time and almost sent the firm broke. Enfield-Allday managed to keep the pot boiling until 1925, with some hurriedly introduced models of more conventional concept. But then an acute lack of customers forced a closure.

1907 ALLDAYS & ONION 10/12 HP

In view of this design's early successes in hill climbs in Britain, it is fitting that within days of being restored, this most attractive twin-cylinder car managed to romp away with the hill climbing trophy in the 1978 International Veteran and Vintage Rally.

The car was originally sold in Adelaide in 1908 and, two years later, taken by Mr Bob Jones (no relation to the present owner) to Julia Creek, Queensland. It was used in the area for many years, finally abandoned on a property, and raided for bits and pieces.

During the 1960s the small pile of rusting debris was inspected by several members of the Veteran Car Club and pronounced unrestorable. But one man decided to have a try. In May 1970 John Jones, of Brisbane, purchased the heap of parts, consisting of an incomplete engine, the differential housing, a steering box and some other bits and pieces.

He spent the next six years advertising in club journals, following leads and accumulating parts, with generous help from Les Ford of New South Wales, Reg Carrol of South Australia and Allan Pickup of the Australian Capital Territory.

In September 1976, John decided there were enough parts to commence restoration. He set a completion target date — the 1978 International Rally. Working for 18 months, up to 40 hours a week, he eventually had the Alldays and Onion ready for a test run. Next day it made a trip by trailer to Sydney for the start of the Rally.

It performed remarkably well, winning the hill climb and developing only a few minor ailments — testimony to the restoration skill of John Jones and his helpers, Graham Wilkinson and Noel Vinall.

MECHANICAL FEATURES

Engine: Twin-cylinder, side valve, capacity 1.63 litres, developing 10 to 12 HP at 2000 rpm. Water pump cooling, Zenith carburettor; Bosch magneto and coil twin ignition system.
Gearbox: Quadrant type with three forward gears. The unit is unusual in that it is a crash box, but the driver cannot double-declutch as there is no neutral. Leather cone clutch.

Suspension: Full elliptics at front, semi-elliptics at rear.
Brakes: Handbrake operates on rear wheels, the foot pedal controls a drum on the tailshaft.
Steering: Worm type with 42 ft (12.8 m) turning circle and only one turn lock-to-lock.
Wheels: Wooden spokes, 30 x 3½ ins tyres.
Dimensions: Wheelbase 9 ft 9 ins (2972 mm). Track 4 ft 6 ins (1372 mm). Overall length 11 ft 8 ins (3556 mm). Height 5 ft 2 ins (1575 mm). Kerb weight 11½ cwt (585 kg).
Performance: Maximum speed when new — 35 mph (56 km/h). Normal cruising speed — 22 mph (35 km/h). Fuel consumption at highway speeds — 35 mpg (8.0 litres/100 km).

1907 Darracq Twin

THE MARQUE

Darracq was a French company which became involved in so many mergers and acquisitions that its history is hard to follow. The company was originally founded in 1898 by Alexander Darracq, who had acquired the rights to build Leon Bollee's four wheel voiturette. Within two years, Darracq was making cars of its own design, using a single-cylinder 785 cc engine, with shaft drive to the rear axle.

A series of successful models followed, powered by single, twin and four-cylinder engines. The company also produced the world's first V-8 engine, by merging four two-cylinder blocks, two each side. The unit was installed in a racing car which clocked 112 mph (180 km/h) — in 1906.

The best known Darracq was the 1904 'Famous Fifteen', a lightweight 3 litre model featuring a pressed steel chassis frame. The car was highly regarded, especially after one had been driven across Europe for 2390 miles (3824 km) without the engine stopping.

The most famous Darracq of all time is undoubtedly Genevieve, one of the two cars starring in the film of that name. Genevieve was later acquired by Gilltraps Museum near Coolangatta on the Gold Coast.

After producing a successful series of cars prior to World War One, Darracq merged with Talbot and Sunbeam. The joint venture continued to call the cars Talbot in Europe and Darracq in other parts of the world. After World War Two the French end of the company was acquired by Simca. It later passed to Chrysler and ultimately to Peugeot.

1907 TYPE R DARRACQ

Car discounting goes back a long way. This delightful looking Darracq was originally sold by an Adelaide firm in 1908 as a 'last year's model'. The man favoured with the special price was Mr H. W. Rasmus of Ucolta, near Peterborough in South Australia. With the selling agent, he drove in one day the 150 mile (240 km) journey from Adelaide to his home, without the benefit of a windscreen.

Five years later, he sold the car to a near neighbour, Mr Schultz, who in turn sold it a few years later to Mr Ern Shackleford who had started a fruit business. He converted the Darracq to a utility and used it until 1925 delivering fruit around the area.

In 1957 an Adelaide old car enthusiast, Ron Bloyd, heard rumours that parts of a Darracq existed in Peterborough. It took him a year to trace them to a Mr Shackleford. The parts formed only the bones of a car, as the engine, radiator and many body parts were missing. Ron Bloyd swapped some trailer components for the remains and trucked them back to Adelaide.

He procured a Darracq engine from Lloyd Culley but soon found that it was unsuitable, being earlier than 1907 when no cooling pan was fitted. Fortunately he found another Darracq enthusiast with the right engine — and a further exchange took place.

By 1962, Ron Bloyd had enough parts to start building a car. He set his sights

on taking part in the 1963 Barossa Valley Rally, little knowing that he would spend 2000 man hours cleaning, welding, shot blasting, rust proofing and rebuilding worn components. With some help from David Lipsham and other friends, he finally had the car ready with only hours to spare.

The rebuilt car distinguished itself by humming through the Rally without a breakdown. Two years later Ron drove it to Mount Gambier and joined in The National Tour 1965 (Sydney, Melbourne, Adelaide) for Veteran and Vintage Cars.

The Darracq also competed in the National Tour 1967, which was a hub rally in Albury, New South Wales, covering 500 miles (800 km) in one week.

The Darracq won the Adelaide Advertiser Trophy in 1969 and again in 1978, by which time it was owned by D. M. Radford of Adelaide.

Though orthodox throughout, the design is interesting. Excellent visibility, with a tight turning circle and very quick ratio steering makes it ideal for driving tests which involve manoeuvrability. The steering is now very light, but originally

it was so heavy that Ron Bloyd fitted thrust races to the stub axles.

The front axle and steering arms are forged, nicely proportioned and beautifully finished. The engine is robust, with the flywheel bolted to the flange on the crankshaft. It can idle smoothly at low speed, despite being a large capacity twin.

In many ways, this 1907 model is typical of the lightweight cars that France excelled in building during the early years of motoring.

MECHANICAL FEATURES

Engine: Twin-cylinder 1.8 litre side valve, rated at 12.4 HP, developing 10-12 BHP at 1800 rpm. Coil and magneto ignition.
Gearbox: Crash type gearbox with three forward speeds and progressive change, i.e. reverse-neutral-first-second-top, operated by steering column change. Leather-faced cone clutch.
Suspension: Semi-elliptics front and rear.
Brakes: Rear wheel, originally cast iron shoes on steel drums but now fitted with bonded linings on the shoes.
Steering: Worm-and-sector steering with 37 ft (11.2 m) turning circle and only one turn lock-to-lock.
Wheels: Non-detachable artillery type wheels 765 x 105 mm, using 30 in x 3½ in tyres.
Dimensions: Wheelbase 8 ft 3 in (2515 mm). Overall length 11 ft 2 ins (3404 mm). Height 5 ft 6 ins (1676 mm). Kerb weight 18 cwt (916 kg).
Performance: Maximum speed when new — 44 mph (70 km/h). Normal cruising speed — 30 mph (50 km/h). Fuel consumption at highway speeds — 22 mpg (12.8 litres/100 km).

THE MARQUE

Yet another firm which progressed from pedal power to petrol, Swift of Coventry Ltd., built a cycle-based quadricar in 1900. The British firm used an M.M.C. engine and later employed a variety of proprietary engines as well as manufacturing its own twin and four-cylinder units.

Swift's first machine had a two-speed rear axle, in which the driver shifted gear by engaging a second crown wheel-and-pinion ratio. In 1903, the firm adopted the more common and less troublesome conventional shaft drive. A twin-cylinder 10 HP engine of its own manufacture followed, with three and four-cylinder engines next.

During their early days, Swift either made or bought single-cylinder 6 HP Fafnir engines and they appear to have supplied them to other firms in the Coventry area.

In 1907 the company came to an arrangement with Herbert Austin who had left Wolseley to manufacture a range of fairly heavy tourers of his own. Exactly who designed the single-cylinder 7 HP roadster is not known, but both Austin and Swift produced virtually identical cars, apart from the radiator design. The vehicle is sometimes called the prototype Austin 7 as it has similar dimensions and weight to the four-cylinder car that made Austin famous during the 1920s.

Neither Swift nor Austin made many single-cylinder models, though production continued until 1912. Swift found their customers preferred the twin-cylinder 10 HP which was a little more expensive but generally considered more like a proper car. Swift replaced the single-cylinder engine of the smaller model with a 7 HP twin in 1912.

The company also brought out a more modern car with a four-cylinder 1.1 litre engine. After World War One, a 2.0 litre four joined the pre-war four-cylinder model. Swift began supplying components to several local firms which had commenced car production immediately after the War. Many were simply 'assembly' jobs made up from proprietary parts; but one, the small sporting Eric-Campbell, is of note because of its later connections with Invicta and Railton.

1907 Swift Single Cylinder Roadster

In common with Austin, Morris, Fiat and Standard, Swift also provided complete chassis to a young man named William Lyons whose Swallow Coach-building company attracted attention for its handsome open and closed bodies. In due course, the firm became S.S. and later Jaguar.

During the 1920s, Swift concentrated on four-cylinder cars noted for being dull but durable. In 1930 they tried the sporting approach with a new 10 HP model with wire wheels, a four-speed gearbox and a streamlined radiator. A year later they proudly announced the small 8 HP Cadet sedan to rival Austin and Morris in the baby car field. The engine was made locally by Coventry Climax.

The venture failed, hastening Swift's bankruptcy. After the factory had closed, Coventry Climax had no trouble selling the unused Cadet engines and R. H. Collier, of Birmingham, purchased the other components to sell as spare parts.

1907 SWIFT 7 HP

A school teacher brought this delightful little car to Warrnambool, Victoria, in 1907. It was regularly used through the 1920s and, during the 1930s, was 'modernised' with various body alterations and electric lights. Eventually it passed to Wheelhouse Motors, Melbourne, who sold it to John Campbell. The car was unrestored but in sound running order, and was used in processions.

Its features include metal-to-metal rear brakes, a total loss engine lubrication system, a decompressor for easy handle-swinging, kerosene lights and a dual ignition system. The engine starts on a coil, then switches to magneto.

In the late 1950s the Swift was bought by Jean Shield, of Diamond Creek, Victoria. After it had taken part in various veteran car runs, husband Frank dismantled the car, rebuilt the mechanical parts and made a new body, a replica of the original. Harry Palmer made the trim.

The resulting car won the V.C.C.A.'s Gold Medallion and the Award of Merit and was named the Best Single Cylinder Car of 1962.

MECHANICAL FEATURES

Engine: Single-cylinder side valve unit of 1092 ccs, rated at 6.8 HP, developing 12 BHP at 1800 rpm. Water-cooled with Zenith carburettor and dual Bosch coil and magneto ignition. Pressurised dead loss oil system.

Gearbox: Selective sliding three-speed unit with white metal bearings and external shift. Leather-faced cone clutch and open prop shaft.
Suspension: Semi-elliptic springs at front, three-quarter elliptics at rear.
Brakes: Metal-to-metal contracting brakes on rear wheels only.
Steering: Worm-and-sector unit with 1⅛ turns lock-to-lock.
Wheels: Timber spoked beaded edge size 710 x 90.
Dimensions: Wheelbase 6 ft 0 ins (1829 mm). Track 4 ft 0 ins (1219 mm). Overall length 9 ft 5 ins (2896 mm). Height 4 ft 2 ins (1270 mm). Kerb weight 10 cwt (509 kg).
Performance: Maximum speed when new — 35 mph (56 km/h). Normal cruising speed — 30 mph (48 km/h). Fuel consumption at highway speeds — 32 mpg (8.8 litres/100 km).

15

1908 Renault

1908 RENAULT AX

Owned by Mr and Mrs Wal Reeve, of Adelaide, this single seat voiturette was restored by the late Bill Buchanan, of Melbourne, and subsequently completely overhauled by the present owner. Correct in every detail, it even carries the original Renault carburettor, whereas most early Renaults were at one time in their lives fitted with other carburettors to improve their performance.

Like all Renaults of its era, it has a coal scuttle bonnet, with the radiator mounted at the rear of the engine. A fan built into the flywheel draws air through the radiator and exhausts it under the floorboards.

Quite a few similar restored AX models are in Australia but this example has won the Veteran Car Club of Australia (Vic) Award of Merit in 1966 and the V.C.C.A. (SA) Percy Wien-Smith Trophy in 1973-74. Regularly driven in veteran car rallies, it has proved a reliable performer being consistently highly placed.

THE MARQUE

Louis Renault was one of the giants of the motor industry. Eccentric and enormously talented, he could design and build an entire car single-handedly, then develop the complex equipment required to produce it in large numbers.

His genius covered all facets of automobile design, from racing engines to one of the world's first self starters — a compressed air device offered as optional equipment in 1906. Well before that time he had patented the first three-speed gearbox with direct drive on top and the royalties collected from rival car makers were enough to make him a rich man. Renault's ideas spread in other directions. In 1902, for example, he built the first fully enclosed car — an innovation which created immediate mirth. Who, among the band of intrepid motorists, would want to hide from the rain?

Renault was also one of the first to realise the potential of motor sport. His fledgling firm dominated the French racing scene for three hectic years, with Louis and brother Marcel as the factory drivers. Unfortunately, Marcel was killed in the 1903 Paris-Madrid race but the interest in racing whipped up by the Renault victories ultimately led to the first French Grand Prix.

Louis Renault had produced his first prototype in 1898, a small voiturette

powered by a single-cylinder, air-cooled 1¾ HP De Dion-Bouton engine. A year later Renault designed and built his own engine and he laid down his unorthodox chassis arrangement, with the radiator placed between the engine and the dash panel. The basic design remained without major changes until 1928, when the factory followed the more usual radiator arrangement.

The three Renault brothers formally went into business as car makers in 1899. They produced 60 cars during the first six months, each one being virtually hand made. By 1902, Renault cars were so popular that buyers were having to wait up to three years for delivery. In 1905 Renault produced the first twin-cylinder Model AX, a design which proved the company's best seller until World War One. This car, initially with a 1.1 litre engine, sold so well that Louis Renault was forced to develop new production techniques, including assembly lines and transfer machines which later proved the basis for Henry Ford's operation in Detroit.

During 1907 the Renault factory built more than 3000 cars. The figure rose to 5000 in 1908 and 10000 by 1913. Renault was soon Europe's largest car maker.

Louis Renault remained firmly in control until the dying days of World War Two when he was gaoled as an alleged collaborator. He was murdered by unknown assassins while in gaol and his factory passed into the hands of the State. It is still one of Europe's largest.

MECHANICAL FEATURES

Engine: Twin-cylinder, water-cooled, rated at 8 HP with a 1.2 litre capacity. Conventional engine design with side valves. Spark provided by a Bosch HT magneto. Total loss oil system.
Gearbox: Renault's patented progressive action three-speed, with the gearbox located separately from the engine and driven by a short shaft extending from the cone clutch.
Suspension: Semi-elliptics all around.
Brakes: The handbrake operates two internal expanding brakes on the rear wheels, the footbrake operates an internal expanding transmission brake at the rear of the gearbox.
Steering: Worm-and-sector with only ¾ turns from lock-to -lock.
Wheels: Sankey wheels are currently fitted but the original car had 710 x 90 artillery wheels.
Dimensions: Wheelbase 7 ft 0 ins (2134 mm). Overall length 10 ft 2 ins (3099 mm). Height 6 ft 6 ins (1981 mm).
Performance: Maximum speed when new — 30 mph (48 km/h). Normal cruising speed — 25 mph (40 km/h). Fuel consumption at highway speeds — 30 mpg (9.4 litres/100 km).

1909 Cadillac Roadster

THE MARQUE

Cadillac — the Crown Prince of American automobiles — was born because Henry Leland made a fine engine that Oldsmobile did not want.

At the time (1903) Leland owned a machine shop which sub-contracted the manufacture of engines for the thriving Oldsmobile factory. Leland figured out a few improvements which he thought would make a real engine out of the one-lunger which was lifting the Merry Oldsmobile to immortality. Leland's modifications had a remarkable effect on the engine, boosting power from 5 to 10.25 HP. However, Ransome E. Olds wanted no part of it. He was way behind on orders, and if he put in the more powerful engine, several other components would have to be changed.

Disappointed, Leland called on the Detroit Automobile Company which happened to have parted company with its founder, Henry Ford, and was surveying the market. Detroit Autos snapped up the new engine and designed a chassis around it. Then the company merged with Leland's machine shop in 1903 forming a new concern, Cadillac Motor Company.

Sales soared and Leland produced the four-cylinder model 'K'. To help launch it in Britain, the new distributors arranged a unique demonstration in which three Model K's were pulled apart, the bits mixed up and then reassembled. The cars were put through their paces on a 500 mile (800 km) endurance run on Brooklands racing circuit. They ran perfectly. The feat won Cadillac the Dewar Trophy, awarded by the Royal Automobile Club in London, for the greatest advance of any car during the year. It also signalled the end of the hand-built era, from henceforth all cars would be built to fine tolerance, so that spare parts could be interchanged without the need for lapping in.

William Durant, the free spending head of General Motors, cast an envious eye on the thriving Cadillac concern and, in 1909, Leland sold out for a cool $US4.5 million.

Cadillac's first volume seller was the four-cylinder Thirty, a 30 HP car with its cylinders cast in separate blocks, surrounded by copper water jackets. It appeared in 1906 and stayed in production until 1913, by which time 75,000 had been built.

When new, the 30 HP cost $1400 in the United States. Prime examples are rare — only one 1909 model is known to exist in Australia.

1909 CADILLAC THIRTY

The early days of this stylish roadster have been lost in obscurity. As far as Dave Fiechtner, the present owner, can tell, nothing is known about the car's history until 1920 when Fred Rickerts, of Clifton, Queensland, bought it secondhand. He dismantled it, using the engine and gearbox to drive a grain harvester. After about seven years, the engine was 'retired' and the dismantled car left unattended on his farm. Dave was out scouting for parts for a 1912 Cadillac when he heard rumours of the remains, and followed them up.

Dave commenced restoration of the 30 HP in January 1974 and completed it later the same year, with G. Crittenden attending to the trim.

For its year, the Thirty is surprisingly well equipped, with side lights, a tail light and an electric horn. A very pleasant car to drive, it pulls evenly in top gear at any speed from 5 to 50 mph. The side valve engine has a five bearing crankshaft and battery ignition. A magneto was an optional extra in 1909.

The Model Thirty was replaced by a similar car with a larger engine and, in 1915, Cadillac introduced its celebrated V-8.

MECHANICAL FEATURES

Engine: Four-cylinder, side valve 3.7 litres rated at 25.6 HP, developing 30 BHP. The water-cooled engine has its cylinders cast singly and features a Schebler carburettor trembler coil ignition and copper water jackets.
Gearbox: Three-speed, selective sliding with the gear change on the driver's right hand side. Cone clutch.
Suspension: Semi-elliptic springs at front with transverse rear springs.
Brakes: Double system of expanding and contracting brakes on the rear wheels.
Steering: Worm-and-sector.
Wheels: Timber wheels with 32 x 3½ inch tyres.
Dimensions: Wheelbase 8 ft 10 ins (2692.4 mm). Track 4 ft 8 ins (1422.4 mm). Overall length 12 ft 4 ins (3759.2 mm). Height 6 ft 11 ins (2108.2 mm). Kerb weight 24 cwt (1222 kg).
Performance: Maximum speed when new — 50 mph (80 km/h). Normal cruising speed — 25 mph (40 km/h). Fuel consumption at highway speeds — 14 mpg (20.2 litres/100 km).

1909 Sizaire et Naudin Phaeton

THE MARQUE

Hardly a European race meeting was held between 1905 and 1910 without a special class for voiturettes. Figuring prominently at these meetings was the highly unusual Sizaire et Naudin. Voiturettes were vehicles weighing less than 400 kg.

When Sizaire et Naudin was in its heyday, competition in the single-cylinder field was so fierce that Peugeot, Delage, De Dion and Sizaire et Naudin produced some extraordinary one-lungers.

Sizaire had the most freakish design of all. One of its racing single-cylinder engines had a stroke of 250 mm, giving a capacity of almost 2 litres and the remarkable output of 42 HP. Not surprisingly, this car won its class on the tricky Compeigne circuit, with the stunning average of 48.7 mph (78 km/h). It once lapped the Dieppe circuit at 54 mph (86 km/h).

The French firm was founded in 1905, the cars being designed by Maurice Sizaire, constructed by Louis Naudin and raced by Georges Naudin. The chassis of the first car was substantially the same as the 1909 model shown on opposite page. The timber-stiffened chassis frame featured sliding pillar, independent front suspension and a most unusual rear axle in which the driver changed ratios as he went along.

The design won the voiturette class in the Coupé de l'Auto races in 1906, 1907 and 1908. The production cars which were similar to the racing voiturettes differed mainly in engine size. By 1909 the production engine had reached 1.6 litres, the largest it became.

In 1910 Sizaire introduced a four-cylinder unit with a more conventional chassis design. The firm virtually finished production just before World War One, when Maurice Sizaire left to found Sizaire-Berwick. The original firm continued until 1921, using engines built for them by Ballot.

1909 SIZAIRE ET NAUDIN F.09 SERIES 4

Despite their initial popularity, only eight single-cylinder Sizaire et Naudins are known to survive, two of them being in Australia. This example, with a custom built Victoria Phaeton body (made by Angus & Sons, Sydney) is unique. There is no other known car like it.

The car was bought new in Sydney, probably by the Apps family and taken to their property at Goulburn, New South Wales. It came to light during the 1950s when Jack Smith (who owned the other Australian single-cylinder Sizaire et Naudin) needed some parts to complete restoration. Fellow V.C.C. member Len Masser heard about a 1909 model left lying in bits at Goulburn. He visited the farm and collected the required parts on behalf of Jack Smith. Later another Sydney collector, Ben Bronk, scoured the three paddocks over which the body and chassis parts were scattered. Ben then restored the body, assembled the chassis and fitted the body. By advertising in V.C.C. journals he obtained two 1909 engines.

The present owners, Denis and Garry Lovell of Peakhurst, New South Wales, acquired the car in 1976. Denis completely stripped the chassis and rebuilt every mechanical component. An interesting discovery was that the two engines he had acquired from Ben Bronk and the engine fitted to Jack Smith's have concurrent numbers. This suggests that three 1909 models came together to Australia.

The chassis design has some fascinating features. One of the first production models with independent front suspension, it has a transverse leaf spring anchored in the middle. Sliding pillars at each end function as king pins. There is a single foot pedal which, when pressed half way down, operates the clutch, the second half of the travel bringing on the transmission brake.

There are self energising metal-to-metal rear brake shoes on this car, but other Sizaire et Naudins have twin rear brake shoes.

The most unusual feature is the huge differential housing with a massive crown wheel plus four pinions. The pinions slide on the end of the propeller shaft and can be moved both longitudinally and laterally by the gear lever working on a quadrant. This is done because the gears engage axially when changing up but radially when changing down. Gear shifts are not so much an art as a life-time study and considerable practice is required to change quietly and quickly. The standard clutch action is extremely heavy.

The final unusual feature is that the high gearing provides a road speed of 40 km/h per 1000 rpm in top gear.

MECHANICAL FEATURES

Engine: Single-cylinder design with overhead inlet and side exhaust valve. Bore and stroke 120 x 140 mm gives capacity of 1595 ccs. Rated at 10 HP, developing about 22 BHP at 2000 rpm. Thermo-syphon cooling and Bosch HT magneto. Speed control by tapered sliding inlet valve cam.

Gearbox: Four pinions in rear axle provide three forward and reverse gears. Pinions engage axially when changing up and radially when changing down. Crown wheel has 76 teeth, the forward pinions having 20, 14 and 8 teeth, respectively. Single plate clutch, cast iron to steel friction action.
Suspension: Independent front suspension with transverse leaf spring. Live rear axle with three-quarter elliptic springs.
Brakes: Self energising cast iron band in steel drum for rear wheels. (Virtually useless when travelling backwards.) Internal differential transmission brake.
Steering: Worm-and-cam with 1½ turns lock-to-lock.
Wheels: Non-detachable artillery wheels, 30 x 3½ beaded edge tyres.
Dimensions: Wheelbase 8 ft 7 ins (2616 mm). Overall length 11 ft 7 ins (3531 mm). Height 6 ft 5 ins (1956 mm). Kerb weight 14 cwt (713 kg).
Performance: Maximum speed when new — 42 mph (67 km/h). Normal cruising speed — 30 mph (48 km/h). Fuel consumption at highway speeds — 32 mpg (8.8 litres/100 km).

VCCA
1909

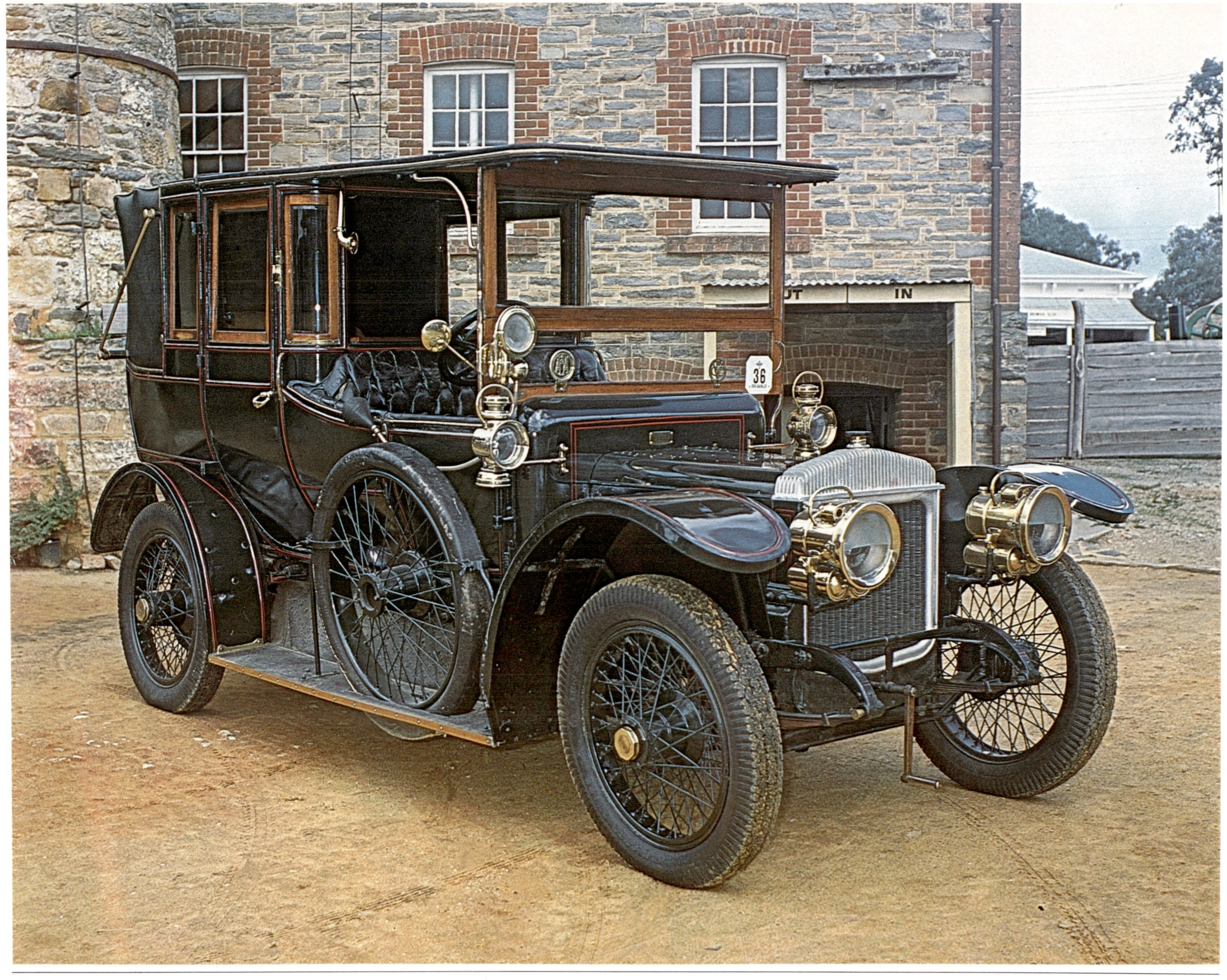
IN
36

1910 Daimler Landaulet

THE MARQUE

Gottlieb Daimler made his first car in 1886. He was soon to meet a remarkably shrewd Englishman, Frederick R. Simms who had seen a Daimler petrol engine on display at an engineering exhibition. Simms called on Daimler and purchased the rights to manufacture Daimler products in Britain. He then formed the Daimler Motor Syndicate in 1893, initially with the view to building cars identical to those made in Germany.

Simms raised £6000 to start the venture. No sooner was the business off the ground when an enterprising company promoter named Harry Lawson (founder of the Great Horseless Carriage Company) offered £35,000 for the Daimler rights. Simms accepted. The new owners went ahead and produced the Daimler waggonette, a crudely designed car with a twin-cylinder 4 HP engine with hot tube ignition, tiller steering and solid tyres. The car made an immediate impact by successfully completing a 929 mile (1486 km) journey from John O'Groats in the extreme north of Britain, to Lands End, in the extreme south west. As the car had a maximum speed of 14 mph (22 km), the journey took 93½ hours running time.

It was a sound beginning. Daimler then collected 16 major awards in the first British long distance sporting event — the 1000 Mile Trial of 1900. Later the company also performed creditably in the second Targa Florio in 1907. Italian-made Daimlers of British design finished 13th, 20th and 26th. The British Daimler company, however, never became seriously involved in motor sport. It was fortunate enough to attract royal patronage as early as 1900 when the Prince of Wales, later King Edward VII, bought a Daimler. The marque quickly became the car for aristocrats as well as the choice of royalty.

Lanchester and Rolls-Royce were both building quieter cars than Daimler, so, in 1908, the company made a bold decision and bought the rights to produce a new kind of engine designed by the American, Charles Yale Knight. This involved a system of double sleeve valves per cylinder, the sleeves being interposed between the cylinder wall and piston. As the sleeves moved up and down the cylinder, they covered and uncovered inlet and exhaust ports at the right moments.

The design had the major advantage of being quiet, as there were no poppet valves. However, there were drawbacks. For instance, relatively large friction areas could make for poor starting in cold weather because of the stickiness of cold oil.

Some Knight engines tended to seize because of poor heat transfer through the sleeves and the resulting cure, over-lubrication, could cause a haze of blue smoke. Daimler, however, made a better job of adapting the design than most and by limiting engine speed to 1500 rpm in the early engines, was able to overcome the major drawback.

The company persevered with the Knight engine until the early 1930s. Long before that, however, they had merged with Birmingham Small Arms (in 1910) and acquired Lanchester (1931). The group was eventually bought by Jaguar and became part of British Motor Corporation and finally British Leyland.

1910 DAIMLER 38 HP

In view of their popularity with royalty, it is not surprising that Daimler manufactured their own landaulet body from the early days. A landaulet is a closed body in which the rear section of the roof can be folded to give open air motoring in suitable weather. The body on this car was not made in England, however, but in Adelaide.

The chassis was imported by Vivian Lewis Ltd. and fitted with the seven seat landaulet built in their own workshop on behalf of Mrs J. Gordon of North Adelaide. Little is known of the vehicle's history, but it was on the roads of Adelaide in 1916 and may have been used as a hire car in its later days.

In 1945 George Brooks of Tranmere, South Australia, found the car in a scrap metal yard. He has owned it since and the car was photographed at the National Motor Museum, Birdwood, South Australia. The car remains amazingly original. The tyre sizes were changed from beaded edge to straight side in 1947 because it was not possible to match the original type. A fresh coat of paint was added in 1954. No other work has been done, apart from routine maintenance and repairs.

Equipment included speaking tube to driver and an odometer with a fitting in the mph section to show maximum speed attained on any journey. An 'electric footman' gives such commands as 'Slow' 'Turn right', 'Home, James' and so on.

MECHANICAL FEATURES

Engine: Four-cylinder 6.3 litre unit with double-sleeve valves, rated at 38 HP, developing 57.25 BHP at 1200 rpm. Daimler carburettor and Bosch magneto. The cast iron cylinders are in two pairs, bolted to an aluminium crankcase. The crankshaft has five main bearings.
Gearbox: Three-speed with constant mesh gears at the propeller shaft end of the gearbox. Leather-lined cone clutch in the massive fly wheel. Open propeller shaft.
Suspension: Semi-elliptic front springs with swivelling shackles at the trailing ends. Rear springs consist of semi-elliptics with auxiliary coil springs in the rear shackles.
Brakes: Internal expanding drum brakes on rear wheels, contracting brake band on propeller shaft behind gearbox.
Steering: Worm-and-sector.
Wheels: Rudge detachable wire, original size 1020 x 120 beaded edge, now 5.00 x 24 straight side.
Dimensions: Wheelbase 10 ft 6 ins (3200 mm). Overall length 14 ft 5 ins (4394 mm). Height 8 ft 0 ins (2438 mm).
Performance: Maximum speed when new — 45 mph (73 km/h). Normal cruising speed — 35 mph (56 km/h). Fuel consumption at highway speeds — 8 mpg (35 litres/100 km).

Kundu Lodge
1910 F.N.
474
018

1910 F.N. Raceabout

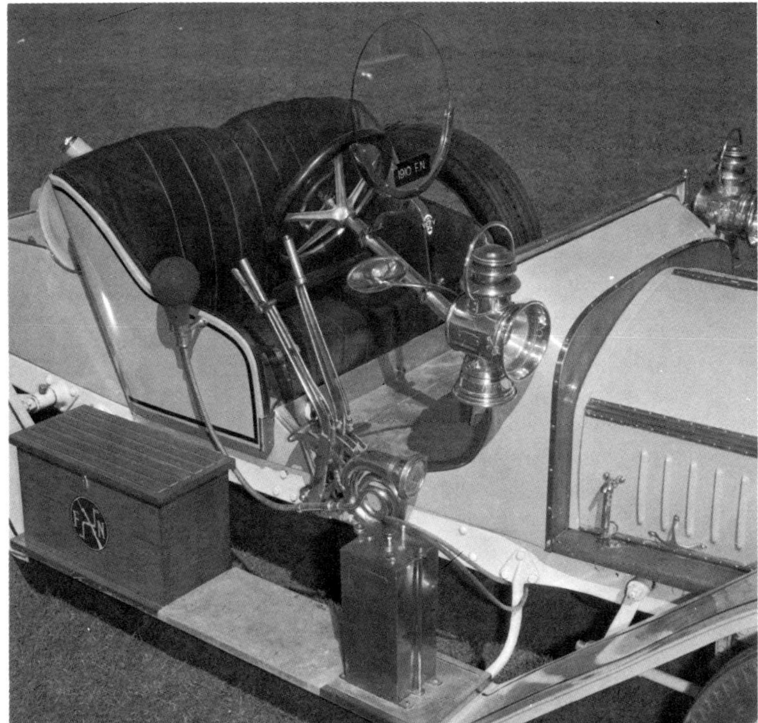

THE MARQUE

The initials 'F.N.' stand for Fabrique Nationale d'Armes de Guerre. This Belgian munitions factory built its first car in 1899 and grew to be Belgium's largest car producer.

Noted for its low cost, conventionally engineered designs, F.N. built passenger cars until World War Two, then continued with truck and motorcycle manufacture.

The first production car, in 1900, came with an air-cooled, twin-cylinder engine and later a water-cooled unit. A two-speed gearbox chain-drove the rear axle. One hundred of these early models were sold and, in 1902, a four-cylinder model followed. Apparently it was not a success as production lapsed and did not resume until 1906 when a big chain-driven tourer was built under licence from Rochet-Schneider.

That model became the springboard for a series of new F.N.'s, starting with the 2 litre Type 2000 in 1908 and continuing with the 2.1 litre Type 2100 in 1910. The firm also produced the smaller Type 1400 and 1500 cars, as well as some interesting motorcycles.

The change from chain-drive to live axle was made in 1906 and by the start of

World War One, F.N. was building five cars a day. The post-war range was based on the earlier models, especially the 1925 and the later 1300, with its 1.3 litre overhead valve engine. It also featured the engine and gearbox built in one unit and front wheel brakes.

F.N.'s motorcycle history was also interesting, especially during the 1920s when a shaft-driven two-wheeler, with a 750 cc four-cylinder engine attracted attention around the world.

In 1925 the firm started a competition program, and one of its 3.2 litre eight-cylinder cars had the distinction of being the only Belgian car to win the celebrated Liege-Rome-Liege rally. (Liege being F.N.'s headquarters.)

The 1300 also did well in motor sport, with a class win in the 1925 Monte Carlo rally and the Spa 24 Hour event. Two years later a 1300 became the first two-wheel-drive car to cross Africa from north to south.

F.N. built a range of more expensive cars, including a straight eight 3.2 litre model from 1930 to 1935. Production of all passenger vehicles ceased in 1939.

1910 TYPE 2100

Owned by Peter Amor, of Ballarat, Victoria, this purposeful looking Raceabout was purchased by Ben Lester, of Geelong, about 1959. After acquiring the F.N., Peter wrote to the Belgian factory and was able to establish that the chassis had been shipped to Australia in 1910, without a body. It is not known when the raceabout body was fitted. Even if it was not of 1910 manufacture, it is certainly typical of the type used at the time.

Peter's father, Eric Amor, rebuilt the raceabout body and completely restored the chassis between 1964 and 1969. Apart from the monocle windscreen, there is no weather protection. When the Amor family competed in the 1978 International Rally, three young children sat in the dickey seat and cheerfully braved the wind and rain.

Around ten early F.N.'s survive in Australia, most of them being in Queensland. One is a 1911 model which had been given as a wedding present to a bride. Following her husband's early death, she stored the car in a loft and, more than forty years later, handed her car to a Veteran Car Club member, without a scratch or blemish. A rare acquisition indeed.

MECHANICAL FEATURES

Engine: Four-cylinder, side valve, 2.1 litres, rated at 16 HP. Water-cooled with Zenith carburettor and magneto ignition.
Gearbox: Conventional selective sliding, three forward speeds and cone clutch.
Suspension: Leaf springs front and rear.
Brakes: Drum brakes on rear wheels.
Steering: Worm-and-gear with one turn lock-to-lock.
Wheels: Sankey type, 30 x 3½ ins.
Dimensions: Wheelbase 9 ft 7 ins (2921 mm). Overall length 13 ft 6 ins (4115 mm). Height 4 ft 0 ins (1220 mm). Kerb weight 21 cwt (1070 kg).
Performance: Maximum speed when new — 60 mph (100 km/h). Normal cruising speed — 35 mph (56 km/h). Fuel consumption at highway speeds — 24 mpg (11.7 litres/100 km).

1910 Hupmobile Runabout

THE MARQUE

Robert and Louis Hupp made their first car in 1908. Though Hupmobile continued in business until 1940, the firm is best known for the stark, sporting and enormously appealing Runabouts manufactured during its earliest years.

Robert Hupp had worked for Ford, which probably explains the similarity between his four-cylinder engine and Ford's Model N. But the rest of the early Hupmobile owed nothing to Ford. Its open body style, bucket seats, bolster tank and rack-and-pinion steering added up to a fine sporting machine. The 2.8 litre engine gave a top speed of 42 mph (67 km/h), matched by good road holding and a double set of brakes in the rear wheels.

The early Raceabout cost $750 in the United States against $US1250 for a car such as the Studebaker roadster. In 1910, one convincingly won an endurance race against some pricey European imports, and the word went out that a Hupmobile was the car for the young bloods of the day.

It offered a high power-to-weight ratio, the relatively large engine pulling an extremely light machine. The conventionally designed unit could rev to 1800 rpm and had a few oddities. The flywheel, with built-in cooling fan, was in front. The camshaft was cast in place in white metal, and had to be melted out to replace the timing gears. The engine was surprisingly modern in at least one respect; the almost 'square' bore-and-stroke configuration — 82.5 mm by 85.7 mm.

It drove through a two-speed sliding gear transmission, with shaft drive to a modern differential, and had no trouble pulling from low speeds in top gear.

Other interesting features include a pressed steel chassis frame, total loss engine lubrication and a very simple cockpit. As the salesman might have said: 'There's nothing to take your mind off the road ahead.'

Hupmobile even put a plaque on the dashboard, saying, 'Guaranteed for Life' and signed by the maker. One wonders how today's Consumer Affairs Bureau would react to such a guarantee!

One excellent feature was the braking system, with two sets of internal expanding shoes and two drums for each wheel. One set is operated by the foot brake, the other by the handbrake. The latter is the more effective by far, thanks to the enormous leverage possible with the long handbrake lever.

Hupmobile continued building the Runabout style for some years but in 1911 they introduced weather protection with touring and roadster bodies. By 1913 they were selling 1000 cars a month. Four-cylinder production models continued until 1925 when the firm produced a Straight Eight, then a Six. Production rose steadily to 1000 cars a week.

Then came the bad news. Sales plummeted with the Depression and Hupmobile was badly hurt. The firm made an interesting but unsuccessful bid to stay in business during the 1930s by buying the discontinued Cord body dies and launching a new model based on Hupmobile running gear. The plant closed with the coming of World War Two.

HUPMOBILE MODEL 20

It took Lionel Jones 18 months to build a virtually brand new car from the wreck he purchased for £5 ($10) in 1959. With the help of Michael Jones and Bert Moore, he had the car completed in time to take part in the 1961 V.C.C.A (NSW) Wollongong Rally — and won the Concours d'Elegance. The car scored a similar triumph in the 1966 Blue Mountains rally.

The Runabout came to Sydney in 1910 with American bodywork and was bought by a Mr Muir, of Ryde, New South Wales. Ten years later he sold it to a Mr Walker, a partner in a plumbing firm, and it was

used for daily calls until the mid 1920s. The partners then dissolved the business and Mr Walker went to live in Gosford, taking the car with him. For some reason it was not used, and was purchased by Lionel Jones in 1959.

'I called on Mr Walker after restoring the car,' recalls Lionel Jones, 'and he was delighted to see the old Hup going again. Over a beer (we left him a dozen) he showed me some old business records in which the Hup appeared to be extremely heavy on oil. He confided that it was not

the car that was thirsty and it wasn't oil that the expense account paid for! And he still enjoyed his beer at 80 odd. Unfortunately, Mr Walker died a year or two later.'

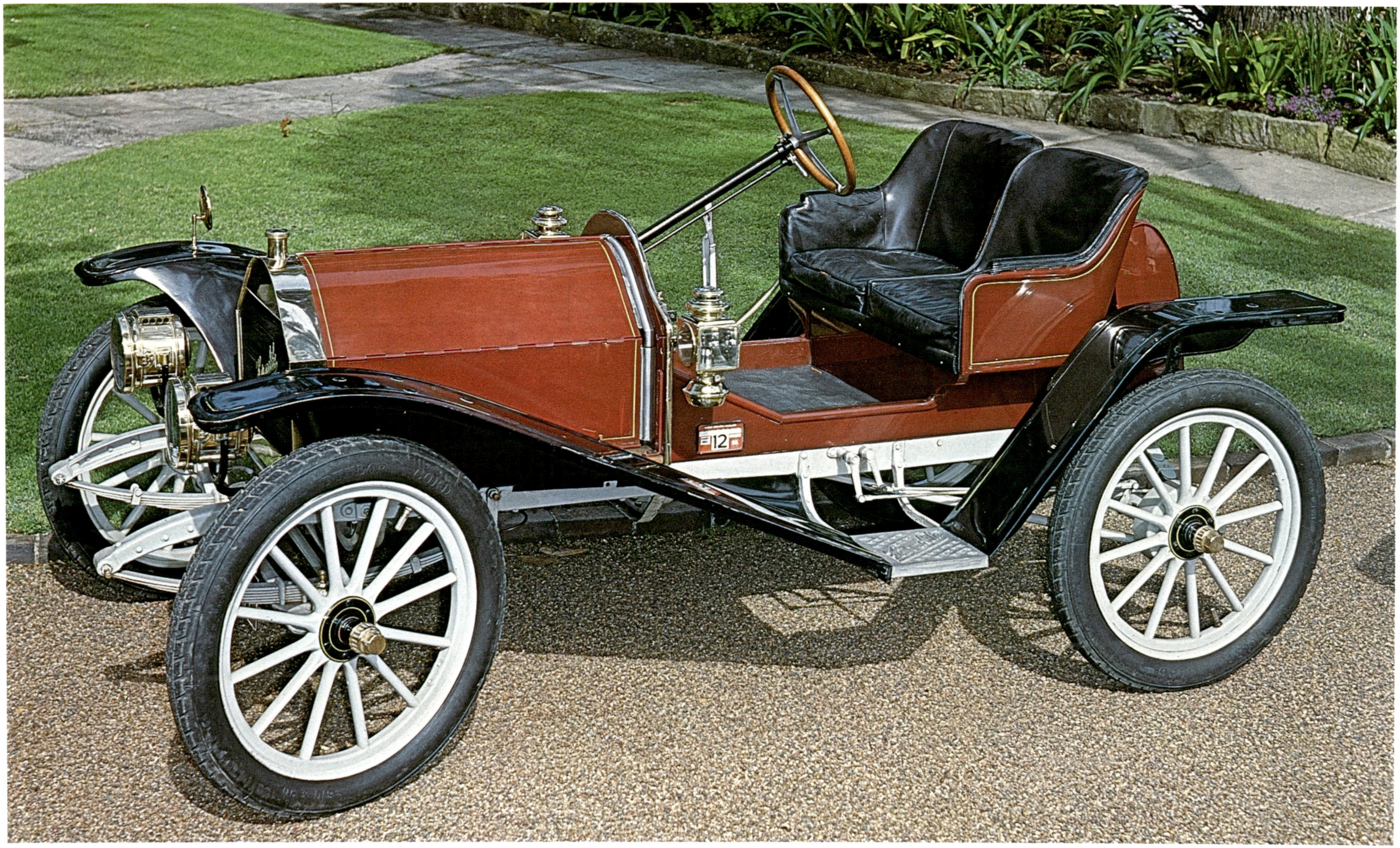

MECHANICAL FEATURES

Engine: Four-cylinder, side valve 1.85 litres, rated at 16.9 HP, developing 20 BHP at 1750 rpm. Thermo-syphon water cooling. Breeze updraught carburettor, Bosch magneto ignition. Flywheel and fan mounted in front of engine.
Gearbox: Two-speed selective sliding with 2.7 to 1 ratio for first gear, direct drive in top. Multi-plate wet clutch, conventional rear axle.
Suspension: Semi-elliptic springs at front, transverse leaf spring at rear.
Brakes: Twin drum shoes in wheels, one set being operated by the foot pedal, the other by the handbrake.
Steering: Rack-and-pinion steering with ⅞ turn lock-to-lock.
Wheels: Beaded edge rims with timber spokes, 30 x 3 ins.
Dimensions: Wheelbase 7 ft 2 ins (2184 mm). Track 4 ft 7 ins (1400 mm). Overall length 9 ft 11½ ins (3035 mm). Height 4 ft 1 in (1245 mm). Kerb weight 9.8 cwt (500 kg).
Performance: Maximum speed when new — 42 mph (67 km/h). Normal cruising speed — 20 mph (32 km/h). Fuel consumption at highway speeds — 27 mpg (10.5 litres/100km).

1910 Phanomobile

and four-cylinder engines, mounted transversely across the forks. The early twins had a capacity of 880 ccs but the Australian vehicle, with a capacity around 990 ccs, may have been a prototype. Two years after it was built the company turned to a 1.5 litre four which boosted the maximum speed.

Phanomen Werke of Saxony also built some four wheeler cars. After World War One the firm developed an advanced overhead cam engine of 3.1 litres developing 50 BHP, which was mainly used in a sports model.

The three wheelers ran until 1927 when production of all cars ceased. The firm continued to make vans and light trucks and was nationalised after World War Two by the East German Government. The factory now builds trucks and railway rolling stock.

THE MARQUE

Cycle-cars were produced by several European firms during the early days of motoring. The German cycle maker, Karl Gustav Hiller, designed and built (1907-27) a range of light vehicles of a unique design.

Though never mass produced, they were meticulously constructed and sold well in his native Saxony. Only one is known to have come to Australia.

In the 1907 model, a fan-cooled vee-twin engine, mounted on the front wheel forks, chain-drove the wheel. The tiller-controlled steering enabled the driver to sharply change the vehicle's direction. The passengers were exposed not only to weather but to direct engine noise and a few spots of oil.

Yet, Norman Hall, of North Balwyn, Victoria, who owns what may be the world's only surviving 8 HP Phanomobile, says it is extremely reliable and comfortable, providing it is not raining.

A spade-handle grip on the tiller controls the bands which operate the two-speed epicyclic gearbox (reverse gear is fitted). The accelerator and spark advance are also mounted on the tiller. The maximum speed is 20 mph (32 km/h). A single gauge shows the air pressure in the fuel and oil tanks. Both are pressurised by hand pump to force-feed the contents, the oil being fed to the engine by drip lubricator.

Phanomobiles were popular in Germany, especially before World War One and, no doubt, were keenly priced. The company had gained motorcycle experience before building the first three-wheeler in 1907. It developed twin

1910 PHANOMOBILE 8 HP

This unusual two seater tourer, with its elegant wooden frame and wickerwork body apparently came to Australia when new and was owned by a Mr Salvana, of Nunawading, Victoria.

In 1948 he sold the engine to a Mr N. Hunter for £10 ($20) and, two years later, sold Mr Hunter a trailer which was based on the Phanomobile chassis frame. The parts were later acquired by Bill Buchanan, one of Melbourne's well known old car enthusiasts, but he was not able to find sufficient technical data to commence restoration.

In 1960 the present owner, Norman Hall, bought the Phanomobile parts and undertook some extensive research. Over a six year period he completely rebuilt the car to the original specifications, making a new body which he lacquered and trimmed himself. In doing so he has produced a car which has won every major veteran car award for which it has competed.

MECHANICAL FEATURES

Engine: Air-cooled, twin-cylinder, mounted transversely over front wheel, approximately 990 ccs, rated at 8 HP developing around 10 BHP at a maximum speed of 500 rpm. Phanomobile special carburettor with Bosch magneto. The flywheel is at one end of the crankshaft, the gearbox at the other.

Gearbox: Two-speed epicyclic gearbox, chain driving front wheel.
Suspension: Two coil springs at the front, full-elliptic springs at the rear.
Brakes: Foot pedal actuated internal expanding and hand operated external brakes on rear wheels.
Steering: Tiller.
Wheels: Three wire spoked wheels, 4.00 x 19.
Dimensions: Wheelbase 8 ft 0 ins (2438 mm). Track 4 ft 3 ins (1295 mm). Overall length 11 ft 6 ins (3505 mm). Height 6 ft 0 ins (1929 mm).
Performance: Maximum speed when new — 20 mph (32 km/h). Normal cruising speed — 15 mph (24 km/h). Fuel consumption at highway speeds — 35 mpg (8 litres/100 km).

1910 S.C.A.T. With Self-Starter

THE MARQUE

The Societa Ceirano Automobili was founded in Turin, Italy, by Giovanni Ceirano with the object of producing around 120 cars a year. The marque is usually known as S.C.A.T., though Fiat, which bought the factory during World War One, refers to Scat in its official publications.

S.C.A.T. built 98 cars during its first year of existence, stretching its resources to the limit. Newton & Bennett Ltd., a major firm in Manchester, England, came to the rescue and invested heavily. George Newton joined the board and Newton & Bennett became British concessionaires for S.C.A.T.

The company built 276 cars in 1910 and completed a 22 HP racing car which won the Targa Florio road race.

By then the Italian company had launched a sensational new device — a self-starter. The compressed air unit was designed by R. O. Harper, an engineer attached to Newton & Bennett. It worked well and was fitted by S.C.A.T. to a 1908 model. The idea was quickly adopted by numerous other firms, eventually being replaced by the electric starter.

During 1912, S.C.A.T. again won the Targa Florio, with a car driven by Cyril Snipe, a nephew of a Newton & Bennett board member. S.C.A.T. won a third time in 1914.

S.C.A.T. was represented in Australia as early as 1908, with 14 and 22 HP four-cylinder models, priced from £235 ($570) for the chassis or £385 ($770) for a complete car. In 1910 a new model with an L-head monoblock engine joined the range; for that year only the wheelbase was 9 ft 6 ins (2926 mm).

S.C.A.T.'s were highly regarded. They had self-starters and one is believed to have been the first hire car in Sydney. One of the S.C.A.T.'s was probably the first car to be driven non-stop from Sydney to Melbourne — by a lady in 1916.

Unfortunately, the marque rates sketchy mentions in reference books. Most publications say that the company went out of business in 1914, but this is not so. S.C.A.T. had associations with the neighbouring Fiat factory during its first year, as Fiat supplied many of the components used in the early S.C.A.T.'s. Fiat acquired the factory during its expansion program at the start of World War One. Production continued until 1932 and S.C.A.T. was included as late as 1924 in the official list of new cars sold in Australia. It is likely, however, that the models were virtually deluxe Fiats.

After selling out to Fiat, Ceirano designed a delightful little overhead valve sports car named after himself, and Newton & Bennett became his concessionaires. He later joined Fiat as an engineer.

S.C.A.T. built roughly 2400 cars between 1906 and 1914, when the firm switched to the wartime production of buses and trucks. Eighteen pre-1914 cars are known to exist worldwide, but the 1910 model shown here is believed to be the only one of its type still surviving. There is a 1908 model in New Zealand and a 1911 in Victoria.

1910 S.C.A.T.

David Berthon, of Baulkham Hills, New South Wales, spent nine years rebuilding this rare car from a collection of rusted and damaged components. When he bought the parts from a fellow Veteran Car Club member, the late Brian O'Brien, the multiplate clutch was full of water, the gearbox seized and the rear axle totally unserviceable. There was no body and the engine had thrown a rod.

After some years of work David heard of some parts remaining from a dismantled 1910 car, most of which had been buried by a bulldozer working on a building site. The parts were rescued by a fellow club member and given to David, enabling him to complete a very authentic restoration.

David Berthon did most of the restoration work himself, apart from the major mechanical items. He hand built the body as a replica tourer of the type widely used in 1910 with body hardware from the dismantled 'spare' car.

The nine years' work was rewarded by an outright win in the inaugural Prestige Oblige Concours d'Elegance at the 1978 Sydney Motor Show. The S.C.A.T. was also named Car of the Year, 1978, by the V.C.C.A. (NSW).

MECHANICAL FEATURES

Engine: Four cylinder, side valve with L-head and monobloc cylinder block. Capacity 2724 ccs, rated at 18.6 HP. Water pump cooled, Zenith Brevette updraught carburettor, Marelli magneto ignition. Compressed air self-starter fitted. Engine No. N105.
Gearbox: Selective sliding, four speeds; reverse gate arrangement for the gear shift. Multi disc wet clutch.
Suspension: Semi-elliptic springs at front, three-quarter elliptics at rear.
Brakes: Internal expanding handbrake for rear wheels, external contracting transmission brake is foot operated.
Steering: worm-and-wheel with 40 ft (12.2 m) with 1½ turns lock-to-lock.
Wheels: Optional Newton patented detachable wire wheels, 815 x 105 mm.
Dimensions: Wheelbase 9 ft 6 ins (2926 mm). Track 4 ft 5 ins (1346 mm). Overall length 13 ft 9 ins (4191 mm). Height 6 ft 6 ins (2011 mm). Kerb weight 25 cwt (1273 kg).
Performance: Maximum speed when new — 55 mph (88 km/h). Normal cruising speed — 40 mph (64 km/h). Fuel consumption at highway speeds — 20 mpg (14.1 litres/100 km).

1910 Talbot Six

THE MARQUE

The early years were great times for Talbot in Australia. The first Melbourne-Sydney speed record of 25 hours and 40 minutes was established in 1907 in a 15/20 HP Talbot by Harry James and C. B. Kellow. A trio of Talbots proved invincible when the first Sydney speedway, Victoria Park, opened in 1908. Charlie East, who had tuned these cars, later became a nationally known speedster in his own right, starting his career with a record-breaking run in a Talbot.

The marque's most impressive feat was conquering the incredibly rough terrain between Adelaide and Darwin. The epic commenced late in 1907 when Harry Dutton and Murray Aunger set out in a 20 HP four-cylinder Talbot. They made remarkably good progress against appalling odds, until finally the rear axle broke down while the men were trying to extricate the car from a sea of mud, just 40 miles (65 km) short of Tennant Creek.

Dutton and Aunger hitched a lift to

Oodnadatta where they caught a train back to Adelaide. Undeterred, they prepared a 25 HP Talbot to repeat the journey. Setting out in June 1908, they battled through sand drifts and over dry river beds until they located the abandoned car which they repaired. The two vehicles proceeded to complete the historic trip to Darwin. The 25 HP model made the return journey in 67 days, suffering only three punctures and two broken springs. It was the most remarkable of all the early Australian motoring feats.

Talbots were made by Clement Talbot Ltd., of London, a wholly British firm established in 1903 to assemble the French built Clement range. Within a year the Talbot company was using a mixture of British and French components. In 1906, the first completely British car, a four-cylinder 20 HP model, emerged from an impressive new factory. A Six was introduced in 1910. The four-cylinder engine was improved and, in 1913, the 25 HP became the first four-cylinder car to cover 100 miles (160 km) in one hour.

After World War One, Talbot merged with Sunbeam and Darracq. The combined company went through some turbulent times, but Talbot regained its former glory in 1927 with the Roesch designed 14/45. Though Sunbeam interests dominated the firm, Talbot production continued until 1935 when the Rootes brothers gained control. In 1939 two famous names were merged in a new series of Sunbeam-Talbot sports models.

1910 TALBOT 6AS TOURER

The six-cylinder chassis reached Adelaide in July 1910 and was fitted with a local roadster body, made by Vivian Lewis. The car, now fully restored to the original condition, is owned by Dr F. C. Archibald, of Blackwood, South Australia. He bought it from Otto Breuninger, of Dulwich, SA. Mr Breuninger had been offended by criticism of the original restoration job and locked the Talbot in a garage where it ended up covered with furniture and grime.

Dr Archibald was able to purchase it for £195 ($390) in 1961. With Ron Bloyd, one of Adelaide's most knowledgeable restorers, Dr Archibald completely stripped the car, overhauling every component. The body work was entrusted to H. Mann, the trim to G. Eames.

The complete restoration took thirteen years. The engine, of French design, used metric threads with an odd pitch, so new bolts and studs had to be screw-cut on a lathe. When the engine was rebored, it revealed a blow hole in the casting, making it necessary to resleeve the cylinder. The original cast iron pistons were replaced by aluminium pistons. Badly worn cam and other gears were remade at considerable expense. The radiator was rebuilt, using 3200 new tubes made from sheet copper, the ends being swagged and cut and soldered to make a replica of the original honeycomb design.

The cam shaft consists of a shaft with five bearings and twelve cams, each keyed and pinned to the shaft. As some were worn, the cams were hard-chromed and reground to the correct profile to take the cam followers.

The work proved worthwhile. Since restoration, the tourer has done more than 3000 miles, proving a lively and extremely reliable performer, virtually trouble-free. According to Dr Archibald, it cruises effortlessly at 50-55 mph, returning 27 miles per gallon.

There is one other similar chassis in Australia, fitted with a Roi-de Belge bodywork. It is owned by J. Gloyn, of Bentley, Western Australia.

MECHANICAL FEATURES

Engine: Six cylinder, 3.6 litres, side valves, rated at 23.8HP, developing 35 BHP. Water-cooling with pump. Bosch magneto, Zenith Carburettor. Cylinders cast in three blocks of two.
Gearbox: Four-forward gears, straight cut teeth, mounted on square section shafts, with leather-faced cone clutch and large pressure spring between gearbox and flywheel.
Suspension: Semi-elliptics at front, semi-elliptics and transverse leaf spring at rear. Torque tube and two radius arms.
Brakes: Transmission brake on output shaft with cast iron shoes on a steel drum (now with bonded lining for safety). Internal expanding brakes on rear wheels.
Steering: Conventional with 1½ turns lock-to-lock.
Wheels: Rudge Whitworth knock-on hubs 880 x 120.
Dimensions: Wheelbase 10 ft 6 ins (3200 mm). Track 5 ft 1 in (1550 mm). Overall length 14 ft 8 ins (4470 mm). Height 6 ft 4 ins (1930 mm). Kerb weight 24 cwt (1222 kg).
Performance: Maximum speed when new — 60 mph (100 km/h). Normal cruising speed — 50 mph (80 km/h). Fuel consumption at highway speeds — 27 mpg (10.5 litres/100 km).

VETERAN CAR
NSW
010
AC

1911 A.C. Sociable Tri-Car

THE MARQUE

Designed by John Weller, this single-cylinder, three-wheeler was introduced in 1904 as the Autocarrier. The firm later changed its name to A.C. and was located at Thames Ditton, Surrey, United Kingdom. The original concept was as a business vehicle and parcel carrier but the three-wheeler proved so popular that in 1907 a passenger version was introduced. It was priced at a remarkably low £87 ($174) and around 1500 were built before production ceased in 1915.

The passenger version was called the Sociable to distinguish it from other cycle-cars in which the passenger travelled behind or in front of the driver. A.C. thought it would be 'sociable' if the passenger and driver sat on the same seat. At least five Sociables came to Australia; nineteen are known to survive in various parts of the world. Three Autocarrier models also exist.

During 1913 the firm started to build the four-cylinder Fivette, making only 475. After World War Two, a series of A.C. sports cars were launched, the best known model being the Ford-powered Cobra which sold well in the United States. In more recent years, A.C. has specialised in invalid carriages and equipment, but, in 1978, introduced a V-6 powered sports car.

1911 A.C. SOCIABLE

This quaint single-cylinder tri-car is one of a pair originally owned by Dr Bean for use during his daily rounds in Wallsend and Minmi, New South Wales. The cars were maintained for him by a local mechanic, and if one of his Sociables broke down, he simply sent for the other and told the mechanic where the ailing car could be found. Unfortunately little is known of the subsequent history of either A.C.'s.

The owner of the car pictured, Chris Broadbent, of Glendale, New South Wales, heard that a derelict A.C. was stored under a house, a short distance from his own home. He contacted the owner and learned that the engine was about to be fitted to a small boat. Chris arranged to find a more suitable marine engine and swapped it for the remains of the A.C.

An inspection showed that much of the original car was missing and that the engine was in poor shape. Fortunately, Chris heard that a Queensland enthusiast owned an 'A' type A.C. engine. It happened that Chris had the name plate and headlights from a steam carriage which the other man was restoring, so it was not difficult to effect an exchange.

Chris Broadbent started serious work on his A.C. in December 1965, completing the car in 1970 and having done most of this work himself. The Sociable is now the only fully restored model of its type in Australia and gained the title as the 'Most Unique Car' on its first Blue Mountains Rally. It has also toured South Australia, New South Wales and Queensland, taking part in five major rallies, covering a total distance, since restoration, exceeding 6000 miles (10,000 km).

The Sociable is extremely light. The engine drives the single rear wheel through a two-speed epicyclic gearbox built into the hub, pulling strong in top gear. A cruising speed around 25 mph (40 km/h) can be maintained on level roads. Extras, available when the A.C. was new, included front wheel brakes (A$12.00), a splash apron to keep the occupants dry (A$12.00) and a hood (A$13.00).

MECHANICAL FEATURES

Engine: Single-cylinder, 600 ccs capacity, rated at 4.5 HP, developing 5.5 BHP at 1200 rpm. An unusual engine it has both valves operated by a single cam. The valves have flat seats overlapping the ports; cross flow cylinder head, air-cooled by two fans; Chaudel Hobson carburettor and magneto ignition. Bore and stroke 90 x 102 mm.

Gearbox: Two-speed epicyclic built into rear wheel hub. No reverse. Geared to give a road speed of 32 mph at 2000 rpm. Chain drive to rear axle which revolves loosely in rear wheel hub, unless gear engaged.
Suspension: Semi-elliptics at front, one ¼ elliptic on each side of rear wheel.
Brakes: External contracting on gearbox, foot operated with ratchet to lock brake on when car is parked.
Steering: Hinged tiller, with one movement of lever from lock-to-lock. Turning circle very tight at 18 ft.
Wheels: Beaded edge originally fitted.
Dimensions: Wheelbase 6 ft 0 ins (1829 mm). Track 4 ft 6 ins (1372 mm). Overall length 9 ft 0 ins (2743 mm). Height 4 ft 0 ins (1220 mm). Kerb weight 4 cwt (204 kg).
Performance: Maximum speed when new — 32 mph (52 km/h). Normal cruising speed — 25 mph (40 km/h). Fuel consumption at highway speeds — 40 mpg (7.0 litres/100 km).

1911 Armstrong-Whitworth

THE MARQUE

Sir W. G. Armstrong and Whitworth & Co. Ltd. of Newcastle, England, set up as car manufacturers in 1904. Two years later they took over the ailing Wilson-Pilcher concern which, for five years, had been making a car with a four-cylinder horizontally opposed engine. Armstrong Whitworth changed the car's design and built a series of conventional four-cylinder models (and one six) until World War One started in 1914. Immediately after the War, Armstrong-Whitworth merged with the Siddeley-Deasy Company.

Siddeley Autocar Company had been formed in 1902 by Lord Kenilworth and, in 1909, had merged with a firm owned by Captain H. P. Deasy. When John Siddeley joined the Board of Directors, the firm became Siddeley-Deasy. After the merger with Armstrong-Whitworth, it was known as Armstrong-Siddeley. A series of 30 HP six-cylinder tourers was then produced under the brand of Armstrong-Siddeley.

Later still, the firm became Bristol-Siddeley Engines Ltd., manufacturers of Bristol and Armstrong-Siddeley cars and aircraft engines. In the automotive field the firm became noted for quiet pioneering rather than brilliant innovation. Production of Armstrong-Siddeley cars ceased in 1960. Bristol cars continued under the ownership of an independent company.

1911 ARMSTRONG-WHITWORTH TOURER

A well known Victorian pioneer motorist, Bill Till of Till Motor and Engineering, appears to have done a remarkable job selling the little known Armstrong-Whitworth tourer. Almost all of the surviving models (three complete, ten in parts) have been located in Victoria or in southern New South Wales.

Bill Till had some solid material for his sales pitch. The Armstrong-Whitworth was a large machine, moderately priced and noted for its eminently sensible design.

This 1911 version now owned by Jock McGowen of Hurstville, New South Wales has the manoeuvrability of a London cab, with a turning circle of only 30 ft (9.1 m), despite the fairly long wheelbase. Its quickly detachable wheels make short work of changing a punctured tyre, as each wheel slides onto a spline and is held in place by a large hexagonal nut.

The car was originally imported by the Sydney agents, Angus & Son, and fitted with a body of their own manufacture. In 1914 the car was sold to Mr Harry Davey of Parramatta. He used it for six years until the rear axle pinion collapsed, so he left it in a shed on his property at Mulgoa, New South Wales. The car remained there until 1937 when Jock McGowen and his late brother Frank bought it for £5 — a figure considered high at the time, as a Model T Ford in running condition could be bought for £10 ($20).

The brothers found a spare pinion in the car's tool kit, along with the original Owner's Handbook. They repainted the body, decarbonised the engine and then drove the car until World War Two started in 1939.

Having won second prize in the Parramatta 150th Year Anniversary Celebrations in 1938 (competing in the Edwardian Class), Frank set out to win more trophies. In 1947 he won the Sporting Car Club's Concours d'Elegance and the Razor Back Hill Climb. The brothers then decided to completely overhaul the car from the chassis upwards. They found some of the work more complicated than expected — the clutch, for example, consists of 30 driving and 29 driven plates.

Today, the 1911 Armstrong-Whitworth is in immaculate condition, completely original, apart from the seats, tyres and hood. Its most recent triumph was in winning the Lord Montagu Trophy.

MECHANICAL FEATURES

Engine: Four cylinder, 2.7 litres with side valves, rated at 17.9 HP, developing 25 BHP at around 2200 rpm. Thermo-syphon cooling system with fan in the flywheel White and Poppe sidedraft carburettor, Bosch Dual Magneto with 4 volt coil.
Gearbox: Designed by Wilson (of Wilson pre-selector fame), the box has four forward speeds and a 59 disc clutch running in oil.
Suspension: Conventional, with semi-elliptics at front, three-quarter elliptics with auxiliary dampers at rear.
Brakes: Footbrake operates on transmission, the handbrake on internal expanding drums on the rear wheels.
Steering: Worm-and-wormwheel, with 30 ft turning circle (9.1 m).
Dimensions: Wheelbase 9 ft 8 ins (2946 mm). Overall length 13 ft 6 ins (4115 mm). Height 7 ft 0 ins (2134 mm). Kerb weight 26½ cwt (1346 kg).
Performance: Maximum speed when new — 50 mph (80 km/h). Normal cruising speed — 35 mph (56 km/h). Fuel consumption at highway speeds — 18 mpg (15.7 litres/100 km).

DUNLOP CORD
VETERAN CAR
020

1911 Clement-Bayard

THE MARQUE

Adolphe Clement was a wealthy French businessman whose activities included making tyres, aircraft and cycles. He became involved in the car business in 1899, building Gladiators and all early cars bearing the name Clement were made in the Gladiator factory. Clement was also a director of Panhard Levassor, which is why a series of models carrying Clement-Panhard name plates were sold. He was one of the first men to appreciate the export market and his cars were built in Scotland (as Clement-Stirlings) and in Britain (as Clement-Talbots).

Though not an engineer himself, Clement employed excellent designers who introduced several promising ideas. Most Clements had shaft drive at a time when chain drive was easier to make and more commonplace. Some very potent racing cars were built, achieving appreciable success in competition. One memorable design was the 1908 racing Clement-Bayard with an enormous engine of 14 litres and a stroke of 185 mm. This engine had an overhead valve operated by an overhead camshaft, showing that the advantages of OHC design (now used by most high performance engines) was well known to the Clement factory.

Clement introduced the Clement-Bayard marque in 1903, after leaving Gladiator. Bayard was not a partner, but a sixteenth century folk hero from the French town of Mezieres where Clement had established his factory. Clement admired him so much that he later changed his own name to Clement-Bayard.

A range of new models was launched, including a 10 HP twin-cylinder light car and a larger 50 HP Four. About 1910 the company began to crystallise its designs, with a completely new four-cylinder 10-12 HP model. This featured a monobloc engine and a Renault-type radiator located between the engine and the instrument panel — an idea which Clement retained for some years.

Clement-Bayards were imported into England by a firm financed by the Earl of Shrewsbury and Talbot. When local production commenced the car was known as the Clement-Talbot.

The French company was at its best in the years 1907 to 1914 — the year that Clement himself retired from the concern. Models ranged from twin-cylinder voiturettes to an impressive six-cylinder tourer. The post-war years were not so happy and in 1922 Andre Citroen took over the plant. All Clement-Bayard activities were then transferred to Clement-Talbot in England. By that time, however, the whole of the English company had been purchased by another firm — A. Darracq and Company.

1911 CLEMENT-BAYARD 12-18 HP

James Munro and Company became agents for Clement-Bayards in 1910 and sold 200 cars in fifteen months. The chassis of this car reached Melbourne in 1911 and was fitted with a double phaeton body built by James Munro and Company. The complete car was purchased by Alwin Barnes of Boort, Victoria, for £445 ($890) for use on his property. It remained there until the 1960s when it was located by Adelaide enthusiast Reg Jamieson. It was taken to Adelaide by Bob Howie and acquired by Wal Reeves who completely restored it. Though several Clements of the same year and engine size are on show in European museums, this is one of only two of its type in the world with an original double phaeton body. The other is owned by Keith Carden of Sydney.

It has been beautifully restored and deservedly won the Sporting Car Club of South Australia's Award for 1970 as the 'Most Meritorious Restoration'. The brasswork alone is formidable. According to the present owner, John Grave of Adelaide, it normally takes nine hours to polish the bright metal — but if the brass is marked by rain spots, the job takes fourteen hours.

Despite its handsome line, the Clement-Bayard body is curiously constructed. The bonnet is a separate entity from the radiator, which in turn seems to be divorced from the main body. Neither the running boards nor mudguards appear to be integrated into the overall shape.

MECHANICAL FEATURES

Engine: Four-cylinder, side valve, 2.4 litre water-cooled engine with the block cast in two pairs and rated at 12 HP. HT magneto ignition system, Claudel Hobson carburettor and a rear-mounted radiator. No fan or water pump is fitted.
Gearbox: Quadrant type with four forward gears and a cone clutch.
Suspension: Semi-elliptic leaf springs at front, three-quarter elliptics at rear.
Steering: Conventional design with a tight turning circle of 25 ft (7.6 m) and ¾ turns lock-to-lock. Artillery wheels 815 x 105.
Dimensions: Wheelbase 9 ft 4 ins (2845 mm). Overall length 16 ft (4877 mm).
Performance: Maximum speed when new — 40 mph (64 km/h). Normal cruising speed — 30 mph (48 km/h). Mileage at normal highway speed — 30 mpg (9.4 litres/100 km).

1911 Ford Model T Town Car

THE MARQUE

Henry Ford did not originate the concept of mass production, but he certainly put the world on wheels. His Model T Ford (which surprisingly made its debut in England, not the United States) was introduced in 1908, twelve years after Ford had built his first car.

The newcomer was an immediate success and sold at a phenomenal rate. Some 15.5 million were cranked out during a nineteen year production run. More than any other car, the Model T transformed the social, business and economic life of major western countries.

Ford's success lay in his policy of building a basically simple, tough and reliable machine that was easy to drive and cheap to repair. To keep prices at bedrock, he fitted a minimum of accessories and comforts. A 2.9 litre four-cylinder engine drove a two-speed epicyclic gearbox. The light chassis had a transverse spring at each end. Though the whole car looked incredibly fragile, it often kept going over rough roads which defeated more expensive cars.

Ford offered practically no mechanical variations but his range included several body styles, the most expensive being the enclosed Town Car. Early Fords were hand painted in a variety of colours but when the company adopted spray painting to speed the rate of production, suitable paint was available in only one colour — black. That gave rise to the celebrated slogan — 'any colour you like, as long as it is black'!

1911 FORD TOWN CAR

Owned by Mrs Sally Kable of Hurstville, New South Wales, this most unusual Model T is the only known all-timber bodied Model T Town Car in Australia. Five are known to exist in America.

The Town Car was the most expensive Ford in 1911, selling for $US1,200 against $780 for the tourer. (This price came down sharply in later years as production rose to 9100 cars a day.) Ford hoped to sell the Town Car to wealthier motorists, but they continued to buy the more prestigious marques. However, the Town Car proved popular for taxi work, because of its relatively low price and cheap running costs.

The all-wood construction was probably the downfall of this particular design as structural weaknesses in the roof section and front pillars led to the early demise of the structure. After some years, Ford switched to steel cladding to stiffen the body, but sales never reached expectations. The Town Car was discontinued in 1918 and about 15 of the steel-clad Town Cars survive.

The timber body on this Model T is a modern replica built by Peter Kable as a faithful copy of the original. The six seater has an open front section and a landaulet type rear which can be opened or closed to suit the weather conditions. Unusual features include a jump seat in the rear and a leather-covered roof. The sliding windscreen can be vertical or slid upwards on rails to a horizontal position, close to the roof. The screen can be locked in any position between the vertical and horizontal axes. The rear doors have child proof locks.

It is not known when the original car came to Australia but after World War Two it was bought by Mr W. Barker from the estate of the late Mr Barlow of Newcastle, New South Wales. In 1964 it was acquired by Peter and Sally Kable and used for many years as a standard roadster. In 1976 Peter decided that their growing family required a roomier car. He personally constructed and painted the entire body, using drawings and photographs of original Model T Town Cars obtained from the United States.

MECHANICAL FEATURES

Engine: Four-cylinder, side valve, engine cast in one block. Capacity 2.9 litres, developing 22 HP at 1500 rpm. Cooling by thermo-syphon and fan. Kingston carburettor. Ignition is by low tension magneto and high tension coil.
Gearbox: Two-speed planetary type transmission, with reverse gear and a multi-disc steel clutch running in oil.
Suspension: Transverse leaf spring front and rear.
Brakes: Mechanical brakes with a contracting band operating on the transmission and expanding drum brakes on the rear wheels.
Steering: Planetary type steering, with only half a turn lock-to-lock but an unusually tight turning circle of 28 ft (8.5 metres).
Dimensions: Wheelbase 8 ft 4 ins (2540 mm). Overall length 11 ft 6 ins (3505 mm). Height 7 ft 0 ins (2133 mm). Kerb weight 17 cwt (865 kg).
Performance: Maximum speed when new — 40 mph (64 km/h). Normal cruising speed — 32 mph (51 km/h). Fuel consumption at highway speeds — 20 mpg (14.1 litres/100 km).

T FORD CLUB
VETERAN CAR
008

1911 Girling Parcel Carrier

THE MARQUE

A prolific British inventor, Albert H. Girling, achieved prominence in the brake industry after designing a new shoe to improve the stopping power of the Model T Ford. Within ten years his brake systems were being fitted by leading car designers around the world. Bert Girling also became involved with disc brakes in 1937, when he designed the brakes for a new tank.

Few people know that Girling's interest in brakes stems back to 1910. He designed his own parcel carrier and fitted a small internal expanding brake in the hub of the single rear wheel. He built twelve carriers between 1910 and 1912, and then took orders for 500 more at the 1912 London Motor Show. He could not finance full-scale production, so he sold the small concern and became manager of the Despatch Motor Company, the new builders of the carrier. The firm closed when the Ford Model T came on the market, as it sold in England for £115 ($230), against £98 ($196) for the Girling designed three-wheeler.

The entire project might have been lost to obscurity had Ron Stephenson, then living in Melbourne, not gone looking for Model T parts. In 1970, he investigated a pile of old parts left by a hot rod club under the home of John Hall of Lilydale, Victoria. Ron noticed a single-cylinder engine painted grey but without identification marks. Nearby was a friction type transmission, also grey, and various other mechanical and chassis parts, painted in the same way. Concluding that they came from the same vehicle, Ron swapped some antique phones and took the remains home.

It took fifteen months of research and numerous letters and phone calls before Jack Nelson, a Melbourne enthusiast, suggested that the single-cylinder, friction drive three-wheeler could be a British made Girling-Carrier.

Ron contacted the factory who replied, saying that their records held no information on a Girling car, but why not write to Mr Girling who was still alive? Within days of doing so, Ron Stephenson received an aerogram expressing tremendous delight that one of the Carriers had been found. Mr Bert Girling, then 88 years old, positively identified the bits. Using old photographs as a basis, he then painstakingly drew up plans for the restoration of the chassis and the body to original specifications.

The first letter started a long chain of correspondence in which Bert Girling and his brother Sidney (living in Canada) provided copies of every scrap of information they had on the original Carrier.

Ron Stephenson learned that Bert had designed the Carrier in 1910 and Sidney had machined all components. The brothers were then operating a garage at Woolwich, London. More than 500 orders for the Carrier were taken, including 110 from Australia, presumably for mail delivery. It is assumed that the one vehicle which came, was a prototype.

As progress on the restoration proceeded, Ron sent photographs and details to Mr Girling and always received an enthusiastic letter by return mail. Eventually he sent a photograph of the almost finished car. There was no reply. Some weeks later, Mr Girling's daughter wrote to say that her father had died, aged 90, but that Mr Stephenson was not disheartened. Bert Girling had seen the photograph and the family felt that his interest in restoring the old car had extended his life by many months.

1911 GIRLING-CARRIER

The design was obviously intended to be an extremely simple, economical and practical vehicle. A single-cylinder Girling-made 6 HP engine drove a single rear wheel through a friction transmission and shaft drive. The transmission control was notched to provide five forward speeds and one reverse.

The Carrier has extremely direct steering. A pair of semi-elliptic springs anchored in the centre allow each front wheel to rise and fall independently. An internal expanding brake, possibly a prototype of future Girling systems, is placed inside the rear hub.

The Carrier was designed to carry up to 5 cwt (255 kg), with a maximum speed of 18 mph and a cruising speed of 15 mph. The frame is made from timber, joined by malleable castings. Ron Stephenson finds the friction transmission very effective and trouble-free, possibly because of the low power. A single foot pedal brings the leather-faced friction wheel into contact with the flywheel.

MECHANICAL FEATURES

Engine: Single-cylinder, of 673 cc, rated at 6 HP. Air-cooled but some models of following year had water-cooled version.
Gearbox: Friction drive, with leather-clad drive wheel running at right angles to large wheel attached to engine crankshaft. Position of drive wheel is variable, thus allowing number of effective gear ratios, with five forward notches in selector mechanism and one reverse.
Suspension: Independent front wheel suspension with two transverse semi-elliptic springs. Quarter-elliptic spring at rear.
Brakes: Internal expansion brake built into rear wheel hub — possibly a prototype of later Girling patented brake system.
Steering: Very direct, tiller steering.
Wheels: 26 in diameter wheels.
Dimensions: Wheelbase 7 ft 0 ins (2134 mm). Track 4 ft 8 ins (1422 mm). Overall length 9 ft 0 ins (2743 mm). Width 5 ft 0 ins. Kerb weight 6 cwt (305 kg).
Performance: Maximum speed when new — 18 mph (29 km/h). Normal cruising speed — 15 mph (24 km/h). Fuel consumption at highway speed — 40 mpg (7.0 litres/100 km).

38

1911 International Buggy

THE MARQUE

The American-based International Harvester Company was well established in the horsedrawn farm equipment field when it began experimenting with motorised vehicles around 1901. At this time the company was based in Chicago, but when vehicle production commenced in 1906, a move was made to Akron, Ohio. Later the company returned to Chicago.

From the start, International Harvester Company saw farmers as its main clients, so the rather curious high-wheeler produced from 1906 to 1911 was designed primarily for rough roads. Its solid rubber tyres provided insurance against the inevitable punctures. The large diameter wheels rolled over large bumps with adequate ground clearance and the cart-like full elliptic springs insulated the occupants from the worst of the road shock.

By the standards of 1911, the appearance and mechanical design were remarkably old fashioned. A large capacity twin-cylinder, air-cooled engine chain-drove the rear wheels through a two-speed, epicyclic gearbox. Optional water-cooled engines were available but it is not known if the air cooling system was able to handle the worst of the summer heat.

The buggy was light in weight, ruggedly constructed and geared to provide a maximum speed of only 27 mph (43 km/h). The slow revving engine peaked at 750 rpm.

International made their own bodies which came in two styles. The more popular unit was the four passenger tourer photographed. Constructed entirely from timber, the body was designed so the rear seat could be quickly removed to provide the convenience of a 'pick up'. The alternative body was the Auto-wagon, a light truck built on the same chassis and intended mainly for farm use.

The under-floor engine is cranked from a handle at the side. Its features include an exhaust cut-out and a cam operated oiling system with flow control to the major lubrication points. The mechanically operated overhead valves have hair springs. Double chain drive to the rear wheels is employed.

During 1911 and 1912 International turned their hands to a more conventional design, with a four-cylinder tourer fitted with smaller wheels and pneumatic tyres. These apparently were not successful and thereafter the company concentrated on commercial vehicles, including a truck version of the high-wheeler.

A brief return to the passenger car field was attempted during the 1930s but it was not until the early 1960s that the company re-established itself as a car maker with a four-wheel-drive Scout.

1911 INTERNATIONAL

Owned by the Rainsford family collection, Springfield, South Australia, this unusual horeseless carriage first came to Australia in 1911. Its subsequent history is not known. The Rainsford family acquired the buggy in 1968 and fully restored it to its present condition, with Gordon Eames attending to the trim.

The car is fitted with the original International timber body, complete with detachable rear seat.

Other fully restored Internationals in Australia include George Green's 1909 twin-cylinder Buggy and Frank Nissen's 1912 model with its more orthodox appearance and pneumatic tyres.

MECHANICAL FEATURES

Engine: Twin-cylinder, air-cooled, 3.2 litres, rated at 20 HP. Overhead hair spring valves. Schebler carburettor and coil ignition.
Gearbox: Two-speed epicyclic unit with double chain drive to rear wheels.
Suspension: Full elliptic springs at each corner.
Brakes: External contracting bands on rear drums.
Steering: Gear-and-pinion with ¾ turns lock-to-lock.
Wheels: Large diameter artillery buggy wheels and solid rubber tyres.
Dimensions: Wheelbase 7 ft 1 in (2160 mm). Overall length 9 ft 6 in (2896 mm). Height 6 ft 11 in (2108 mm).
Performance: Maximum speed when new — 27 mph (43 km/h). Normal cruising speed — 20 mph (32 km/h). Fuel consumption at highway speeds — 25 mpg (11.3 litres/100 km).

1911 Martini Tourer

THE MARQUE

Several Swiss factories opened between 1895 and 1910 but most ceased producing cars during World War One. Martini alone kept going, building its last vehicle in 1931. In doing so, it was easily the most successful Swiss car maker.

The firm of Friedrich von Martini was first established in 1860 making textile machines and the Stutzer rifle which Martini himself designed. During the 1880s, Martini commenced making stationary engines to serve the textile industry. Initially they were fuelled by coal gas and later by petrol. Inevitably, Martini built a rear-engined experimental car, using one of his own engines. The date was 1897, but no attempt was made to produce the car in quantity.

Around the turn of the century, Adolf von Martini, son of the founder, realised that the demand for textile machinery was dropping but a growing number of cars were being imported. He put together a couple of experimental cars and a truck, and in 1903 secured the rights to build the French Rochet-Schneider under licence. This basic design was not unlike the Mercedes layout of the same year; all subsequent Martinis followed a similar pattern.

One hundred cars were built in 1903; a further 130 in 1904. The growing business encouraged the firm to establish a new factory at Ste Blaise, with an English company, headed by Captain H. H. Deasy, handling world distribution.

By 1909 production had risen to 260 chassis for the year, but financial troubles led to a complete reorganisation, with more modern production methods. The car-making division announced its first profit in 1911, thanks to a program covering 12, 15 and 18 HP models.

The outbreak of World War One saw a big increase in orders, especially from the Swiss army (which was not engaged in the conflict). However the peace-time years saw a flood of low priced imports from France, Germany and Italy. Martini could not compete against them. The firm was extensively reorganised in 1922 and became profitable after securing the rights to build the German six-cylinder Wanderer car. The success was short lived. In May 1931, production of Martinis ceased; three years later the company went into liquidation.

Martini built just under 4500 cars during its thirty years, but few survive. Two are in a Swiss museum, three are owned by a private collector in Ste Blaise, Switzerland, one is owned by Andy Beattie in New Zealand, and Australia has two or possibly three with only one having been restored.

1911 MARTINI 15.9 TOURER

Fitted with a London made body (by F. Curson) this exceptional example of a Martini was imported in 1911 by Henry Mitchell, of Summer Hill, New South Wales. He owned it for fifty years and after his death it passed to Colin Parker for a short time. The present owner, Robert McCarthy, of Haberfield, New South Wales, acquired the Martini in 1967. At that point the car still carried a 1934 registration label — indicating that that was the last year it had been road-registered. Mechanical restoration was done by Bob McCarthy and, apart from a new hood and paint job, the car is virtually original.

The medium sized tourer is completely orthodox in design, being powered by a 2.4 litre four-cylinder engine with a three-speed gearbox and leaf spring suspension. It cruises effortlessly at 30 mph (48 km/h) giving a very reasonable fuel consumption figure of 23 miles per gallon (12.3 litres/100km). The original owner may have used the car as a hire vehicle or light truck as he had heavy duty cantilever springs professionally fitted.

Martinis were sold in Australia from as early as 1908 when the 14/20 HP, the 16 HP, the 24/32 HP and the 40/50 HP models were offered, at prices ranging from £460 ($920) for the smallest model (chassis only) to £800 ($1600) for the 40/50, complete with four-seater touring body. The firm offered an optional four-cylinder 60/70 HP engine for an extra £150 ($300). This had a capacity of a massive 7.9 litres.

MECHANICAL FEATURES

Engine: Four cylinder, side valve, 2.4 litres, rated at 15.9 HP. Water pump cooling, Zenith carburettor, Bosch magneto.
Gearbox: Sliding selector type with three forward gears and multiple disc clutch and shaft drive.

Suspension: Semi-elliptic springs at front, cantilever spings at the rear, apparently fitted professionally for the original owner. Original specifications were for three-quarter elliptics.
Brakes: Internal expanding brakes on rear wheels, hand lever operated and external contracting transmission brake (foot pedal).
Steering: Worm-and-sector; very direct system with one turn lock-to-lock and 36 ft (11.0 m) turning circle.
Wheels: Wooden artillery type, 880 x 120.
Dimensions: Wheelbase 9 ft 3 ins (2819 mm). Overall length 13 ft 0 ins (3962 mm). Height 6 ft 3 ins (1905 mm). Kerb weight 21 cwt (1069 kg).
Performance: Maximum speed when new — 40 mph (64 km/h). Normal cruising speed — 30 mph (48 km/h). Fuel consumption at highway speeds — 23 mpg (12.3 litres/100 km).

1911 Mitchell Roadster

THE MARQUE

As a company, Mitchell had more right than most to enter the automobile business. Mitchell and Lewis were long established carriage builders, operating in Racine, in the American state of Wisconsin. In 1903 as a logical extension of its business, the firm developed a prototype horseless carriage. The rather orthodox design features a twin-cylinder air-cooled 7 HP engine, with chain drive to the rear wheels.

Rapid progress was made and, by 1906, the company was building successful 18 HP and 30 HP four-cylinder cars, the cylinders cast in blocks of two. In 1911, a completely new engine was announced, with a T-head designed by the French engineer, Rene Petard. The new car was sold in four-cylinder and six-cylinder versions.

Unlike most American companies, Mitchell manufactured the vast majority of components used in its car. Where other firms bought in proprietary engines, gearboxes, axles, steering boxes and other parts, Mitchell attempted to make every component themselves — an idea much favoured by Henry Ford. Mitchell experimented more than most American firms at the time and produced a V-8 as early as 1916. Unfortunately, the project failed. Another experiment broke the firm. In an effort to exploit the vogue for stream-lining, the company produced a 1920 model with a sloping radiator. The odd appearance quickly earned it the name 'drunken Mitchell' and even though the firm quickly reverted to the more orthodox shape, the damage was done, as large losses were incurred during 1920-21.

At one time Mitchell cars sold well in Australia and were assembled by Frederick Hugh Gordon in Sydney. His business was hard hit when the words 'drunken Mitchell' were bandied around, and very likely this is the reason why Gordon relinquished the Mitchell agency. Even before the new model, he had started to build his own Australian Sixes, the first of which appeared in 1919.

Mitchell sales never recovered, in Australia or overseas. In 1923 production ceased and the factory was bought by Nash.

1911 MITCHELL ROADSTER

This colourful roadster has spent almost all its days in Queensland. Its known history dates back to World War One when the car was used on Yarrawonga Horse Stud Station, where horses were trained for the cavalry. It seems that after the War, the Mitchell was traded in on a more modern vehicle. In the fashion of the day, one of the subsequent owners chopped down the bodywork and fitted a flat tray, producing a 'ute' long before the motor industry got around to it. After some time the converted Mitchell lay behind Charleville Motors where it remained for many years.

Queenslander, David McPhee, discovered and bought it during the 1960s. After some mechanical restoration, he sold it to John Akers. When it passed to the present owner, Ron Griffith of Ipswich, in 1970, the Mitchell was missing most of the body, the bonnet, side and rear lamps.

Ron Griffith and his son, John set about building a new body, a faithful replica of the original style, including the optional rumble seat. The original 26 inch wheels were beyond restoration but a set of slightly smaller Dodge wheels of the same era were found to be ideal. Suitable side and tail lights were located. Ron also fabricated a windscreen and top irons, only to discover at a later date that these items were optional equipment with new Mitchells, and his car had never been fitted with them!

Ron discovered that an engine bonnet from a 1909 Cadillac filled the bill and fitted perfectly. Immaculately restored, the 1911 Mitchell completed the 1978 International Rally without missing a beat.

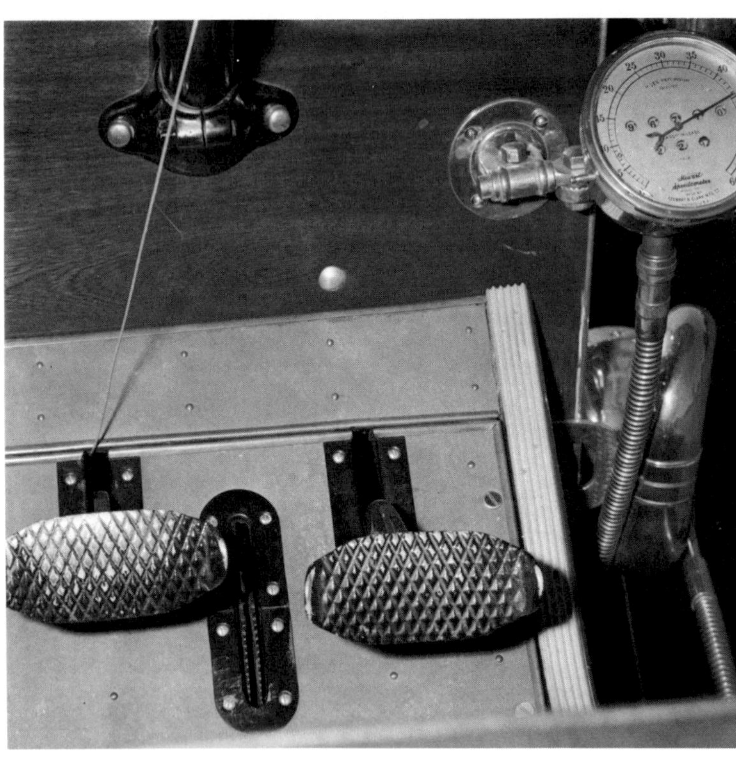

MECHANICAL FEATURES

Engine: Four-cylinder with overhead exhaust and side inlet valves. Water-cooled, with Holley carburettor and Bosch dual ignition. Its capacity is 4.6 litres rated at 30 HP.
Gearbox: Three forward speeds and cone clutch.
Suspension: Semi-elliptics at front, three-quarter elliptics at rear. No shock adsorbers.
Brakes: Internal contracting brakes on rear wheels.
Steering: Worm-and-sector.
Wheels: Timber spoked, size 500 x 24.
Dimensions: Wheelbase 8 ft 2 ins (2490 mm). Overall length 11 ft 11 ins (3632 mm). Height 7 ft ½ ins (2146 mm).
Performance: Maximum speed when new — 60 mph (100 km/h). Normal cruising speed — 40 mph (64 km/h). Fuel consumption at highway speeds — 24 mpg (11.7 litres/100 km).

1912 Buick Roadster

THE MARQUE

Though the Buick Motor Company was founded by David Buick, a plumber, its history belongs to William C. Durant, founder of General Motors and the most mercurial identity that Detroit has seen.

Born in Boston in 1861, Durant moved to Flint, Michigan, working in an ironmongery shop owned by an uncle. He did a powerful selling job to the J. Dallas Dort Company, carriage builders, and was offered a job there. He worked on carriage designs and then, at the turn of the century, helped Dort build two experimental light cars. Durant quickly realised where his future lay.

By 1904, he was ready to strike out on his own. Still in his early forties, he raised $10 million by selling stock in a new corporation. He then made take-over bids for the Flint Waggon Works and the struggling Buick company. Buick at the time was engaged in manufacturing a flat twin-cylinder engine, available to any car company wanting to use it.

A mediocre engineer but a financial wizard, Durant left the management of Buick to his engineers. After a flurry of wheeling and dealing, using Buick as the cornerstone of his power, Durant acquired control of several car companies and component suppliers. He merged the lot, forming General Motors Corporation.

Buick was a star attraction. Until 1907 the company built rather dull twin-cylinder tourers, but then it introduced a lively four-cylinder model which commanded immediate respect. In 1909 Bob Burman won the first ever Indianapolis Speedway Race, driving a hotted up Buick. A year later the firm announced that it had sold 30,000 cars in a twelve months period.

To stay on top, a new model was needed. The planetary transmission, then used in Buicks, was dropped in favour of a selective sliding unit. A new range of overhead valve engines was introduced, with 2.7, 3.3 and 5.2 litre capacity. The all-new 28 and 29 models were offered for $1250 in the United States, 'with all equipment'.

1912 BUICK MODEL 29 ROADSTER

When Bob Sullings, of Quirindi, New South Wales, first saw the Buick he now owns, it was on the floor of a tinsmith's shed, covered in silt, the residue of several floods. Bob bought the car virtually unseen. He made three trips with his utility, taking away the silt, before he could inspect the remains. The car was virtually complete apart from the body and hood which were missing.

Starting work in 1959, Bob spent two years restoring the mechanical components and building a replica body. Woodley's of Tamworth, New South Wales, did the trim.

The roadster has a fold-down white canvas hood, held at the front by leather straps. A two piece folding windscreen is secured upright by adjustable brass rods. A single door is on the passenger side, with the spare tyre mounted on the opposite running board. The original tool kit is still with the car. Acetylene gas headlights and kerosene side lights and tail lights complete the equipment.

An unusual feature is the total loss oil system which pumps through a sight glass on the instrument panel.

Though Bob Sullings has looked far and wide, he has yet to hear of a similar Buick in Australia.

MECHANICAL FEATURES

Engine: Four-cylinder 3.3 litres, overhead valve, rated at 25.6 HP developed at 750 rpm. Fan and pump water cooling system; Zenith updraught carburettor, magneto ignition. Square engine with 101 mm bore and stroke.
Gearbox: Three-speed selective sliding unit with gear lever and handbrake entirely enclosed in the dummy door on the right hand side of the body. Leather-faced cone clutch.
Suspension: Semi-elliptic springs at front, three-quarters elliptics at rear.
Brakes: Contracting and expanding drum brakes on rear wheels.
Steering: Turning circle 28 ft (8.5 m), with 2½ turns lock-to-lock.
Wheels: Artillery, with 875 x 105 tyres.
Dimensions: Wheelbase 9 ft 0 ins (2743 mm). Track 4 ft 8 ins (1422 mm). Overall length 12 ft 8 ins (3861 mm).

Performance: Maximum speed when new — 40 mph (64 km/h). Normal cruising speed — 30 mph (48 km/h). Fuel consumption at highway speeds — 25 mpg (11.3 litres/100 km).

A.C.M.C.
184

COBB & CO
VETERAN CAR
123

1912 Calthorpe Sport Roadster

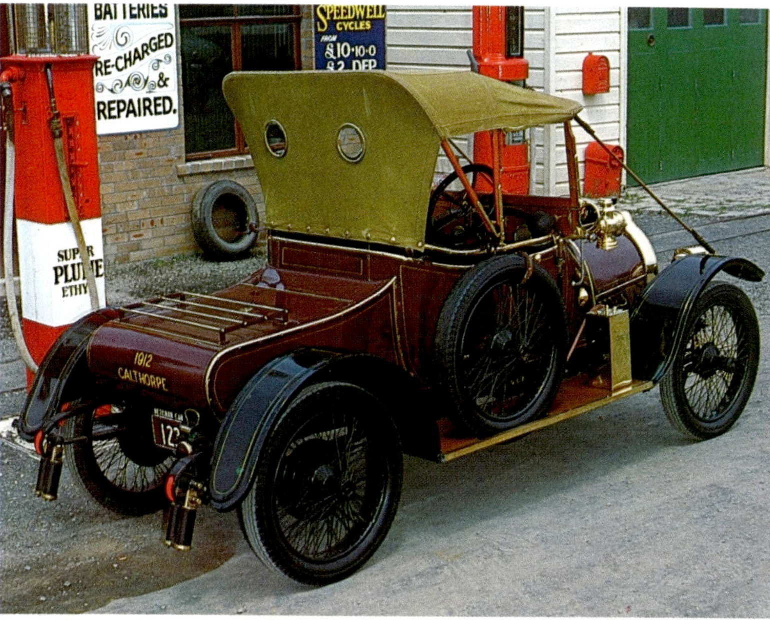

THE MARQUE

Any car guaranteed to complete 66 miles (106 km) within an hour in 1912 was something special. The British-built Calthorpe carried such a guarantee and, despite its relatively small engine, the 12/15 model had been clocked at a genuine 73 mph (117 km/h).

Though Calthorpe is one of the lesser known makes, it was one of the first British firms to enter European racing, with a team of four specially tuned tourers in the 1909 Coupés des Voiturettes.

The company had been founded in 1904 by George W. Hands, a cycle maker. Specialising in small cars from the start, Hands had his vehicles racing at Brooklands and making the occasional trip to a French racing track. His sports/tourer was one of the best British small cars available before World War One.

The sporting 12/15 was virtually a direct descendant of the original 1904 design, a small 10 HP car with shaft drive. The chassis layout was conventional throughout with a three-speed gearbox and leaf springs.

Calthorpe is, perhaps, better known for its 15.9 HP Grand Prix tourer with a beautiful Mulliner body, and also for the Minor, a beautiful little car built between 1913 and 1915. It, too, had a conventional design, with a four-cylinder 1.1 litre engine and a low price. Calthorpe later tried to introduce Britain's first £100 ($200) four-wheeler, using such components as noisy engine or axle which had been rejected from the more expensive models. The policy was a blueprint for disaster and was quickly dropped.

The Minor and the 12/15 were, however, excellent cars. The later 12/20, introduced after World War One, further expanded the company's business. The 12/20 was available in special sporting versions with a hotted up engine, including drilled connecting rods, light alloy pistons and specially balanced components. These engines were able to pull over 3000 rpm in top gear. It was an advanced engine with inclined side valves, a turbulent combustion chamber and positive crankcase ventilation.

According to John Matthews who worked with Calthorpe from 1912 to 1926, the company was best known for its handsome aluminium bodies. Most were made by Mulliner, a Birmingham body firm which George Hands eventually bought.

At one stage Calthorpe employed 1200 people in car production, building 50 cars a week. When Morris and others began producing more cars at lower prices, Calthorpe fell on hard times. George Hands sold his shares and launched his own light car, called the Hands. In 1923 he came back to Calthorpe and tried to retrieve the situation. A series of new models included a twin overhead camshaft six which originally was to have been built as a Hands. The Calthorpe six was never launched. As 1924 came to a close, all non-productive members of the staff were dismissed. The firm struggled on for a further two years but finally the creditors, which included George Hands, were paid off with completed cars.

Ironically, the Calthorpe factory then became a main service centre for Morris.

1912 CALTHORPE 12/15

Despite a production rate which once reached 70 cars in a week, few Calthorpes survive. Only three models similar to this one are known to exist; one in England, another in New Zealand and this car in Australia.

Its first confirmed owner was Mr C. Cowan, a dentist in Molong, New South Wales. He bought it in 1920, probably from a Mr R. Barr, of Cootamundra, who was the only New South Wales registered owner of a 12/15 HP Calthorpe in 1913.

Unfortunately, the dentist ran into financial difficulties during the Depression and the car was left to 'fallow' in his backyard. The flood of 1930 swept over it and so the car was sold at auction to a local orchardist, Mr B. J. Bennett. He converted it into a saw bench, with the engine over the back axle driving a front mounted saw blade. Fortunately, the other parts, including the body, were stored in a shed, so when Bob Baxter, of Sylvania, New South Wales, bought the saw bench for £20 ($40) in 1963, he recovered almost the whole car.

Bob completely rebuilt the chassis and body, restoring it to original condition. His handiwork won the 1967 C.V.V.T.M.C. Concours, the 1973 V.C.C.A. (NSW) Concours d'Etat and the 1973 V.C.C.A. (NSW) Concours d'Elegance.

MECHANICAL FEATURES

Engine: Four-cylinder F-head 1868 ccs capacity, rated at 11.9 HP. Thermo-syphon cooling, Zenith updraught carburettor, Eismann ignition.
Gearbox: Selective sliding transmission, three forward speeds. Hele-Shaw multiple disc clutch.
Suspension: Semi-elliptic springs at front, three-quarter elliptics at rear with shock absorbers.
Brakes: Handbrake operates transmission brake on tailshaft, footbrake operates internal expanding shoes in rear wheel brake drums.
Steering: Calthorpe design. Worm-and-wheel.
Wheels: Rudge-Whitworth wire wheels, 760 x 90.
Dimensions: Wheelbase 8 ft 6 ins (2160 mm). Track 4 ft 2 ins (1270 mm). Overall length 12 ft 0 ins (3657 mm). Scuttle height 4 ft 0 ins (1219 mm). Kerb weight 16 cwt (815 kg).
Performance: Maximum speed when new — 73 mph (117 km/h). Normal cruising speed — 37 mph (60 km/h). Fuel consumption at highway speeds — 25 mpg (11.3 litres/100 km).

VETERAN CAR
049

1912 Franklin-Air Cooled

THE MARQUE

H. H. Franklin Manufacturing Company firmly believed in air cooling from its inception in 1901. With no expensive radiators to make and no risk of water leaks, it conducted a series of publicity stunts to prove the advantages. On one occasion a car was driven across America in bottom gear to show that it would not over-heat. In 1908 a Franklin crossed the blistering desert between Los Angeles and Phoenix. Another broke the San Francisco — New York speed record.

Franklin used air-cooled engines from the first prototype to the last model built in 1933 and was the most successful manufacturer of this type of car until Volkswagen. The early models had a transversely mounted four-cylinder unit, coupled to a two-speed planetary gearbox. In 1905 the firm launched the design which served as a pattern for all future models. It featured an overhead valve six-cylinder engine, each cylinder being cast separately and finned for better cooling. The engine was mounted conventionally in a timber chassis frame, with full elliptic springing on all wheels but a notable absence of torque arms to locate the back axle.

The company retained the same basic chassis layout until 1927, using full elliptic springing to give a soft ride and long tyre life. The same basic engine design was also used, though it was later given a seven bearing crankshaft, alloy pistons and other refinements.

The Model D was built from 1911-13, featuring a bonnet similar to that of Renault (whose radiator was placed between the engine and the firewall). Further developments were introduced and, in 1922, more stylish bodywork was available, with open and closed models. This boosted sales to a record 11,000 cars for the year and attracted a rash of competitors.

In 1928 Franklin gained considerable mileage from the fact that aviator, Charles Lindbergh had bought a 26 HP sedan. However, sales were dropping sharply, reaching critical levels in 1930. Car production ceased in 1933 but the firm moved into the light aircraft and helicopter field with a range of air-cooled engines.

1912 FRANKLIN 'D' TORPEDO TOURER

Only three Model D Franklins are known to survive around the world, the one pictured being a star exhibit at Green's Motorcade, near Liverpool, New South Wales.

In 1912, when this car was built, the company offered two six-cylinder models, one with a 31 HP engine, the other with a 38 HP unit. The bigger version cost $2800 new in the United States, at a time when a five seat touring Buick cost $US1060 or a Packard 6 $US5500.

The 6 litre tourer offered a lively performance being able to accelerate from rest to 50 mph (80 km/h) in 24.5 seconds. Maximum speed when new was 60 mph (100 km/h), but fuel consumption was high.

This car was imported by Sydney department store owner Mark Foy for a Mr Wilson of Windsor, New South Wales. After Mr Wilson was killed in action during World War One, his brother ran the car until the mid 1920s, when it was stored in a barn.

It remained untouched until the late 1940s. At that time, the area was flooded and the elderly Mrs Wilson had to be rescued in a small boat by a young constable. She expressed her thanks by saying there was a car in the barn he could have. The constable was horrified to find his gift was delapidated and covered in cob webs and was glad to sell it to Hope Brothers, in nearby Richmond, for £10 ($20).

The car was returned to serviceable condition and competed in many vintage sports car events. It was then sold to Ampol Petroleum who used it in a stunt involving well known radio personalities Jack Davey and Bob Dyer. Jack bet Bob he could drive the old car from Sydney to Melbourne. He did, but in the course of the run the crash-type gearbox was extensively damaged. The car was then sold to Mr Gardiner of Blakehurst, New South Wales, and in 1955, after his death, it passed to George Green.

The Torpedo Tourer has an original aluminium body manufactured by Franklin. The mechanical restoration was done by George Green and James Kirby Ltd., but the trim is original. The car won the Concours at the Federal Olympic Rally.

MECHANICAL FEATURES

Engine: Six-cylinder, air-cooled, overhead valves, 6 litre capacity. Rated at 38.4 HP, developing 62 BHP at 2250 rpm. Franklin carburettor and Bosch magneto with coil and battery ignition for starting.
Gearbox: Selective sliding three-speed unit with shaft drive and off-set rear differential. Multiplate clutch running in oil.
Suspension: Full-elliptic springs on all wheels, slung from timber framed chassis.
Brakes: External contracting brakes on rear wheels, external contracting transmission brake.
Steering: Worm-and-nut with 42 ft (12.8 m) turning circle and two turns lock-to-lock.
Wheels: Wooden spoked wheels with 24 x 500 tyres (not original).
Dimensions: Wheelbase 10 ft 3 ins (3124 mm). Overall length 14 ft 6 ins (4420 mm). Height 8 ft 0 ins (2438 mm). Kerb weight 32 cwt (1629 kg).
Performance: Maximum speed when new — 60 mph (100 km/h). Normal cruising speed — 40 mph (64 km/h). Fuel consumption at highway speeds — 10 mpg (28.2 litres/100 km).

NAPIER
·53·

1912 Napier Tourer

THE MARQUE

David Napier and Sons Limited was one of Britain's long established engineering firms when Montague Napier, a former racing cyclist, took an interest in motor cars. He built his first car in 1898, then agreed to modify a 6 HP Panhard-Levasser for a fellow cyclist, Selwyn Francis Edge.

Edge was an Australian who went to London to join Dunlop tyres and who received his first taste of motor sport in the Paris-Toulouse race of 1900. After modifying the car, Montague Napier suggested he build a new engine and, slowly, the Panhard-Levasser became a prototype Napier. In 1900 the Napier Engineering firm was in the car business.

A reputation for robustness, quality and solid design quickly followed. S. F. Edge set up his own car selling agency, specialising in Napiers, and became the factory's main adviser. He successfully raced Napiers in the Paris-Toulouse event of 1900 and in the subsequent Gordon Bennett Cup in the United States. By 1910, the firm was making ten different types, ranging from a twin-cylinder light car to a 90 HP six-cylinder job. This large range enabled Napier to sell just over 800 machines during 1911. Edge left the company in 1912 but before doing so he organised the production of special 'Colonial' models which became available in 1910 for Australia and other countries with predominently rough roads.

The best known of these was the 1910 four-cylinder 15 HP model, unofficially known at the 'Anti-Clockwise Car', as the engine was reversed, placing the flywheel at the front. This was done so that the rather large flywheel was protected by the robust beam axle when the engine was passing over small rocks or clumps of earth. The 'Colonial' models also featured unusually good ground clearance, raised suspension and large wheels.

After World War One, Napier launched the T75 40/50 to compete with Rolls-Royce. Unfortunately for Napier the venture was not a success and production ceased in 1924. Thereafter the firm concentrated on aero engines.

COLONIAL MODEL T36 — 1912

Owned by Duncan Scott of Adelaide, the rare Type T36 shown on this page is

painted in Napier Green. A colour also known as British Racing Green, it was Britain's offical colour for the Gordon Bennett races. The six-seater tourer was partially restored by the owner in 1956 and has been regularly rallied ever since. Full restoration was completed in 1962-63.

It serves as an excellent example of the extraordinary durability of the Napier designs. The car was first registered in March 1912 for F. W. C. Catt of Leabrook, South Australia. It was later acquired by a farmer named Jones who converted it into a truck, and used it regularly on his farm in mid-northern South Australia. (Some of the body parts were found on his property many years later and used to restore the car). After its stint on the farm, the Napier was purchased by Messrs. McInerney Bros., of Jamestown, who were about to launch a trucking business. For some time the Napier hauled loads up to three tonnes, but finally the rear axle expired. The truck then became a stationary power unit, driving a timber saw, and was finally abandoned.

When Duncan Scott purchased the Napier as a wreck for £20 ($40) in 1953, he found the engine in exceptionally good condition. Even today, after many years of competing in veteran and vintage car rallies, it has the original engine bearings. Even the crankshaft has not required grinding.

MECHANICAL FEATURES

Engine: Six-cylinder, conventional layout of 4.0 litres, with a non-detachable L-head. It has dual magneto and coil ignition and full pressure-fed oil lubrication system by way of a drilled crankshaft and a full flow oil filter.
Gearbox: Sliding gear gate type with three forward speeds. The clutch is built into an oil type compartment in the gearbox and runs in light oil whereas the gears run in heavier oil.
Suspension: Conventional, with semi-elliptic springs on the front, three-quarter elliptics at the rear.
Brakes: Two wheeled brakes on rear wheel operated by the hand lever, plus a foot-operated transmission brake which also acts on the rear wheels.
Steering: Worm-and-sector with only 1¾ turns lock-to-lock, and a turning circle of approximately 40 ft (12.2 metres).
Wheels: The original Rudge-Whitworth wire wheels were converted from 880 x 120 to 500 x 24 to take the tyres available when the car was first restored.
Dimensions: Wheelbase 10 ft 4 ins (3150 mm). Track 4 ft 8 ins (1422 mm). Overall length 15 ft 6 ins (4724 mm). Height 6 ft 6 ins (1981 mm) with hood up. Kerb weight (chassis only) is 23 cwt (1171 kg).
Performance: Maximum speed when new — 70 mph (112 km/h) or more. Normal cruising speed — 60 mph (100 km/h). Fuel consumption at highway speeds — 16 mpg (17.6 litres/100 km).

1912 Rolls-Royce Limousine

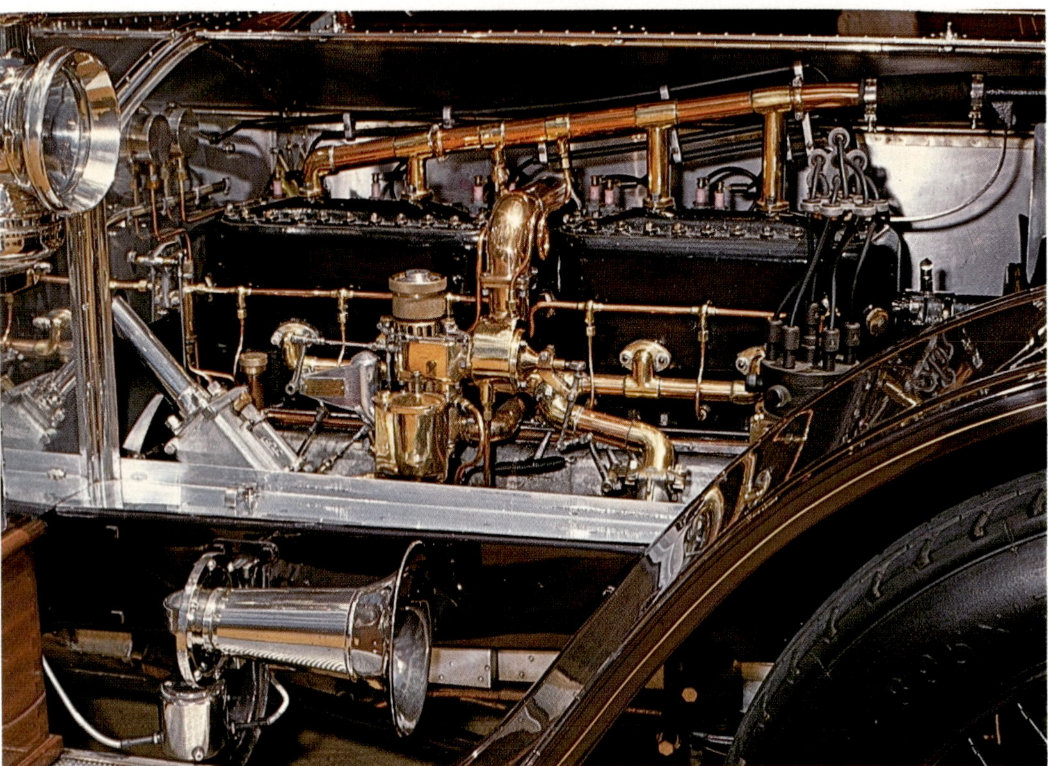

THE MARQUE

Motoring legends come in assorted shapes and sizes but few can top the reputation of the Rolls-Royce Silver Ghost. It was the quietest, most durable and most civilised car of its day.

Correctly called the 40/50 HP, the Silver Ghost was the first successful car built by the company. Henry Royce had made his first car, a twin-cylinder model, in 1904. A year later his small company was still struggling when he met the Hon. Charles Rolls, a wealthy sportsman, who also owned a successful car distribution firm. The two merged their interests, forming Rolls-Royce Ltd. Royce designed a series of three, four, six and even a V-8 model, but total production of all these models amounted to only 160 cars.

When the 40/50 appeared in 1907, it was an unqualified success. Because of its colour and quietness, the factory car was dubbed the Silver Ghost, though it was many years before the name was officially adopted. A total of 7876 Ghosts were built during a production run of 18 years. This includes 1700 made by Rolls-Royce in the United States and known as Springfield Ghosts.

Henry Royce's design set new standards of quietness and comfort, raising the status of Rolls-Royce from an obscure company in northern England to the acknowledged maker of the world's best car.

Rolls-Royce manufactured only the chassis, updating the design with detail improvements during the long production run. As a company, Rolls-Royce did not build any bodies until the Silver Dawn appeared in 1949.

Fifty Ghost chassis were made during 1907. Their reliability was established by a series of demonstrations which, coming from a less dignified firm, would be called publicity stunts. First, Charles Rolls matched the 40/50 against a 30 HP White steam car over a 2000 mile (3200 km) course in Scotland — he won hands down. The car then won a Gold Medal in the Scottish Reliability Trial. To silence any lingering doubts, a Ghost was driven day and night on a triangular course between Edinburgh, Glasgow and London. It was serviced every 1000 miles and suffered thirty punctures during the 15,000 mile run. Apart from this it made only one unscheduled stop, when a petrol cock shook loose, cutting off the fuel supply.

By the uncertain standards of the day, the car put in a remarkable performance. Officials of the Royal Automobile Club who observed the run testified that the car had averaged 15.7 miles per gallon. They pulled it apart and certified that it could be restored to 'as new condition' using about £3 ($6) worth of parts.

By 1925, when the Silver Ghost was replaced with the Phantom, Rolls-Royce had no peers in the luxury car field.

1912 SILVER GHOST WITH BARKER LIMOUSINE BODY

The pride of the extensive fleet of fine cars owned by the Rainsford family in Springfield, South Australia, this magnificent car reached Australia in 1912, fitted with an open-fronted limousine body made in England by Barker.

The body has since been completely rebuilt by the present owners, using all the original hardware and usable components of the original car.

Little is known about the car's early history. The Rainsfords purchased it from Sydney collector Laurie O'Neil, and it is believed to be the only one of its kind in Australia. Restoration was done by the Rainsford family, with trim by Gordon Eames. Their handiwork earned some of the top trophies awarded during a Rolls-Royce Owners Club Federal Rally, including the Age and Authenticity Trophy, the Best Silver Ghost and the outright Concours d'Elegance.

MECHANICAL FEATURES

Engine: Six-cylinder, side valve, 7.4 litre capacity, rated at 40/50 HP, developing 48 BHP at 1200 rpm. Honeycomb radiator, Rolls-Royce carburettor, dual coil and magneto ignition. Speed control by lever on steering wheel. Maximum 1700 rpm.
Gearbox: Three-speed sliding pinion type with torque tube drive. Gear ratios 3.3 to 1 in top, 6 to 1 in second, and 9.5 to 1 in first gear. Fabric-lined cone clutch.
Suspension: Semi-elliptic springs at front, three-quarter elliptics at rear.
Brakes: Internal expanding brakes on rear wheels mechanically operated.
Steering: Worm-and-nut type with 60 ft (18.3 m) turning circle and 2½ turns lock-to-lock.
Wheels: Dunlop wire spoked, 895 x 135.
Dimensions: Wheelbase 11 ft 11½ ins (3645 mm). Track 4 ft 8½ ins (1435 mm). Overall length 16 ft 1 in (4902 mm). Height 7 ft 0 ins (2134 mm). Kerb weight 38 cwt (1935 kg).
Performance: Maximum speed when new — 60 mph (100 km/h). Normal cruising speed — 45 mph (72 km/h). Fuel consumption at highway speeds — 12 mpg (23.5 litres/100 km).

ICES & SWEETS
C.O.R.
NSHIRE TEA
LUNCHES
TEA ROOMS
RGU·666

1912 S.P.A. Tourer

THE MARQUE

Running like a golden thread through the early history of Italian motoring is the name Ceirano. Several members of the family were engaged in vehicle design and manufacture, the best known being Ceirano, a famous designer, Giovanni who launched the S.C.A.T. and Matteo who built and designed the S.P.A., a name derived from Society Ligure Pietmontese Automobili.

Starting in 1906, S.P.A. was a successful attempt to produce a high quality Italian car, leaning more towards the sporting than the luxurious side of motoring. The first vehicles had four-cylinder engines — some 24 HP, others 60 HP. In 1907 a six-cylinder model appeared, followed three years later by L-head engines with integral gearboxes. Some notable competition successes included a class win in the Targa Florio.

The move towards a smaller line of vehicles commenced with the four-cylinder 14/16 tourer, followed by the 1912 16/20. Evidently it was popular as the company sold 500 cars that year. It then entered a variety of motor sport events, mainly those based on production

vehicles, and acquitted itself with some distinction.

The 16/20 was a quality car built on conventional lines, with modest dimensions and an excellent performance for 1912. The overhead valve engine developed around 35 BHP, providing a maximum speed of 50 mph (80 km/h).

After World War One, S.P.A. produced four and six-cylinder machines, moving into the luxury field, with some sporting and competition models. The Super Sports, launched in 1922 with a twin overhead camshaft 30/40 engine, featured such niceties as four wheel brakes, twin carburettors and dual ignition. It continued in production until 1926, by which time the company (like Ceirano) had been absorbed by Fiat. S.P.A. production ceased soon after Fiat took control.

Few S.P.A.'s survive. According to Bob Robinson, owner of the meticulously rebuilt 1912 model shown here there are probably only five fully restored S.P.A. cars in the world; three are in Australia.

Bob's own car is believed to be the oldest roadworthy S.P.A. in existence. Another rare car is a fabulous 1924 7-seater bought during the 1950s by Dr Paul Moni, of Queensland. It had been originally purchased at the London Motor Show by Mr Loftus Foote of Ipswich, Queensland. The six-cylinder DOHC tourer arrived with a range of tools and spare parts as lavish as the car itself. The owner drove it for 3108 miles, but never left sealed roads or went out in the rain. The car was then wrapped in a dust sheet, placed on blocks and locked in a garage, and when acquired by Dr Moni it was in virtually brand new condition.

It has since been acquired by Queenslander, Bernie Keeting, and still has barely 5000 miles on the clock.

1912 S.P.A. 16/20 TOURER

This impressive example of Italian craftsmanship reached Sydney in 1912 and was fitted with a locally made body, built by E. E. Agate. The original five seater touring body is still fitted.

The first owner, a builder named J. Noble, of Randwick, New South Wales, used the S.P.A. extensively, especially for shooting trips. He kept it until his death, when the car was acquired at auction by the late Jack Jeffery for £5 ($10). He later sold it to Gordon Nicol, then president of the V.S.C.C.A.

The present owner, Bob Robinson, of Gosford, New South Wales, bought the S.P.A. unrestored from Peter Crawford, of Hunters Hill, in 1962. He spent two years on mechanical and body restoration, then passed the car to Greg Daley-Greenacre for new leather trim.

The quality of restoration work is such that the car won the A.C.M.C. Restoration Trophy in 1964, the Best Veteran Trophy at Taree in 1974 and the Best Upholstery Trophy at Tamworth in 1976.

MECHANICAL FEATURES

Engine: Four-cylinder, overhead valves, capacity 2.75 litres, rated at 15/20HP, developing about 35 BHP. Water pump cooling with fan built into flywheel. Zenith carburettor and magneto ignition.
Gearbox: Four-speed gate change crash box with multi-plate disc clutch.
Suspension: Rigid front and rear axles with semi-elliptic springs at front and three-quarter elliptics at rear.
Brakes: Two wheel brakes, with foot pedal actuating transmission brake and hand brake operating rear wheel internal expanding brakes.
Steering: Irreversible worm-and-quadrant, with 34 ft (10.4 m) turning circle and one turn lock-to-lock.
Wheels: Rudge-Whitworth spoked wheels, size 440 x 23 beaded edge.
Dimensions: Wheelbase 9 ft 10 ins (3000 mm). Overall length 13 ft 5 ins (4089 mm). Height 6 ft 4 ins (1930 mm). Kerb weight 26 cwt (1324 kg).
Performance: Maximum speed when new — 50 mph (80 km/h). Normal cruising speed — 35 mph (56 km/h). Fuel consumption at highway speeds — 22 mpg (12.8 litres/100 km).

SPA
NSW
BR-981

1913 Aquila Italiana

THE MARQUE

Fabbrica Italiana d'Automobili Aquila was an Italian company which built remarkably advanced cars between 1906 and 1917. All of them, including a few six-cylinder racing machines, were based on a single design by Giulio Cesare Cappa.

Aquila means 'eagle' and Cappa evidently intended to combine grace with pace. He offered a choice between a 1.8 litre four-cylinder engine and a powerful 4.2 litre six.

The exact output of the four is not known but it is rated at 12/50 HP. The car's maximum speed of 55 mph (88 km/h) suggests that it was an unusually powerful engine for its size and era.

Whilst other engine makers were casting their cylinders singly or in pairs, Cappa cast the four-cylinders and the manifolds in a single unit. Another innovation was the use of a large alloy sump bolted directly to the chassis frame, providing additional stiffness. The crankshaft ran in ball bearings. Alloy pistons were used — a possible first for the industry.

Another advanced idea was a successful transaxle with a four-speed gearbox and differential built in the axle. The brake design was unusual, each rear wheel having a dual system with an external contracting band and separate internal expanding shoes.

Despite the advanced design, Aquila sales appear to have been limited. In an attempt to become better known, Aquila went racing. Cappa developed a very advanced six-cylinder engine with overhead valves actuated by two camshafts located high in the cylinder block, so as to keep the pushrod length to a minimum. Riley later adopted the arrangement for the highly successful Riley 9.

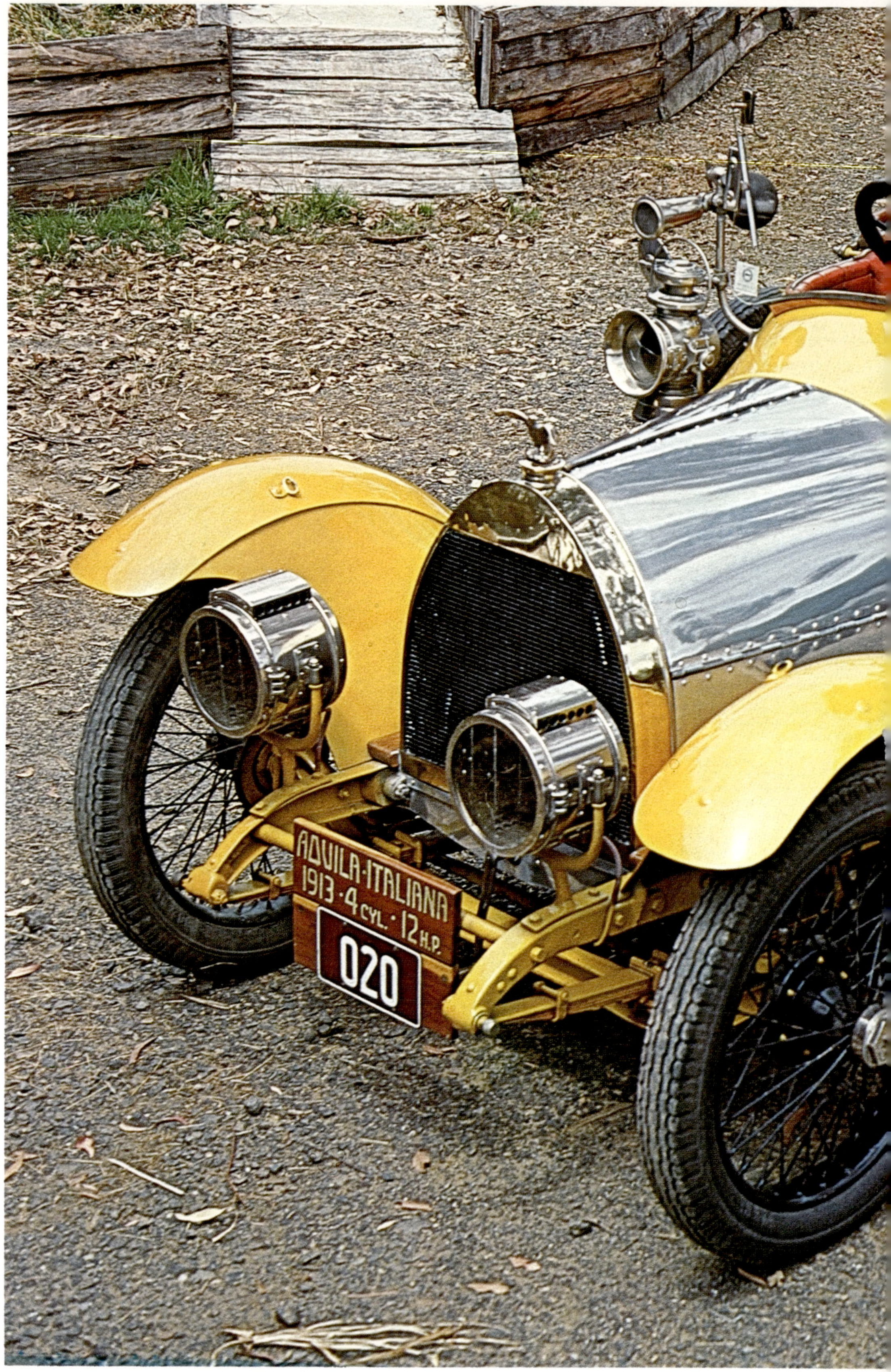

The same basic car was built from 1907 to 1917, but production ceased for three years from 1907 whilst Cappa sought a new financial backer, following the death of his original sponsor. When the plant closed he went to Fiat and designed the world's first supercharged engine. Between 1921 and 1924 he experimented with a series of blown engines based on standard production 403 and six-cylinder 404 units. These experiments provided

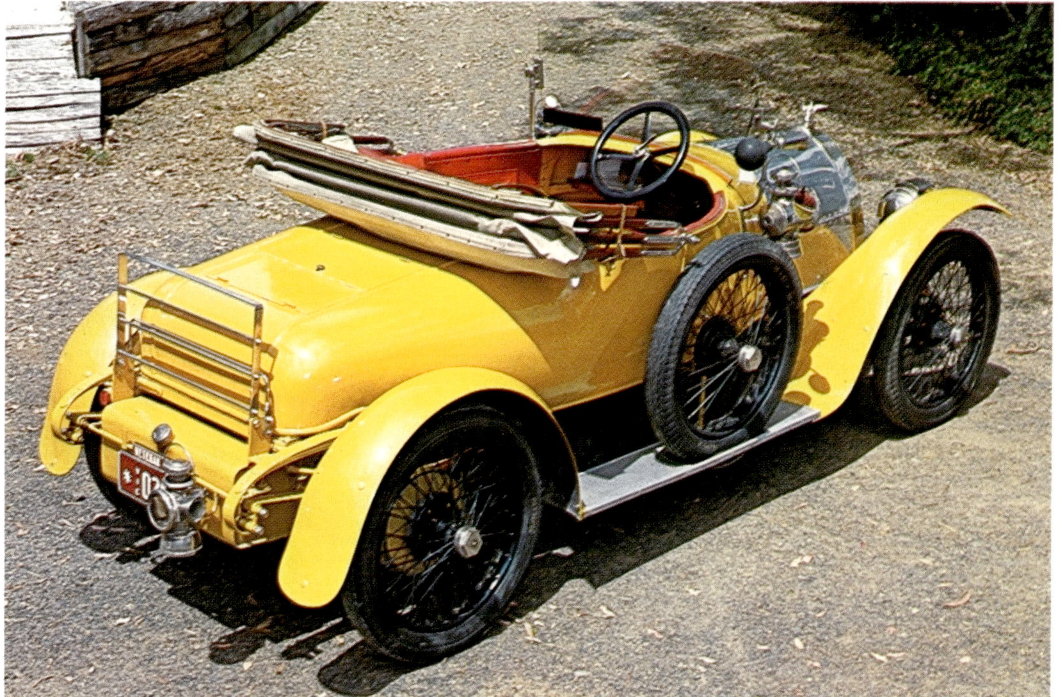

the basis of a new racing engine, the 405. This eight-cylinder unit developed 150 BHP at 5500 rpm. He then went to Itala and designed the six-cylinder Tipo 61.

Today, only one four-cylinder example of Cappa's unique Aquila is known to exist in the world. A six-cylinder racing Aquila is exhibited in the Turin Museum.

1913 TYPE K AQUILA ITALIANA

This sole surviving production Aquila, a delightful sports/roadster, was originally brought to Australia by the Italian consul who established a small agency for the marque.

In 1934 the car was acquired by Robert Fishburn, of Coburg, Victoria, who kept it until 1956, then gave the dilapidated car to a local kindergarten for the youngsters to play in. A year later the present owner, Frank Shield, of Diamond Creek, Victoria, bought the car from the kindergarten. By then little fingers had dismantled the easily removed accessories; however by raking through the grass, Frank was able to retrieve them.

He noticed that the car had been in a collision at some time as there are unmistakeable teeth marks in the steering wheel!

Commencing restoration in 1957, Frank had the car completely rebuilt by 1960. Harry Palmer was responsible for the upholstery. When finished, the Aquila won the V.C.C.'s Best Restoration of the Year, a gold medallion and an Award of Merit.

MECHANICAL FEATURES

Engine: Four-cylinder unit of 1.85 litres, rated at 12/50 HP. Side valve construction with engine block and manifolds cast in one piece. Water cooling; Zenith carburettor and Bosch magneto.
Gearbox: Four-speed gearbox built into rear axle; leather-faced cone clutch.
Suspension: Semi-elliptic springs at front, three-quarter elliptics at rear.
Brakes: Interior and exterior expanding brakes on rear wheels.
Steering: Worm-and-sector with only ⅞ turn lock-to-lock.
Wheels: Wire spoked wheels, 30 x 3½ ins.
Dimensions: Wheelbase 8 ft 6½ ins (2600 mm). Track 4 ft 6 ins (1400 mm). Overall length 12 ft 0 ins (3657 mm). Height 5 ft 2 ins (1575 mm). Kerb weight 13 cwt (916 kg).
Performance: Maximum speed when new — 55 mph (88 km/h). Normal cruising speed — 40 mph (64 km/h). Fuel consumption at highway speeds — 30 mpg (9.4 litres/100 km).

B·S·A
36699

1913 B.S.A. Tourer

THE MARQUE

Birmingham Small Arms grew out of an agreement with William III that arms would be produced in the city of Birmingham, in the industrial heart of Britain. By the beginning of the present century, B.S.A. was also producing pedal cycles and experimental motorcycle parts.

Unlike most firms which graduated from two to four wheels, B.S.A. built a complete car before making a complete motorcycle. Even so, in 1903 the firm was making an ingenious fully sprung motorcycle frame to sell to the neighbouring companies interested in motorcycle production.

The first Birmingham Small Arms four wheeler took to the road in 1907 as a prototype but it was, in fact, a direct copy of an Itala. A small number of similar cars were produced during the following year, but it was not until 1909 that the company officially declared its hand by exhibiting at London's Olympia Motor Show.

The 18/23 HP model was robustly but conventionally engineered, with a four-cylinder L-head engine, three-speed gearbox and a multi-plate clutch. It proved too heavy and was virtually redesigned by 1910. Extensive testing took place in Europe — a novel idea for a British firm then — and approximately 150 of the final designs were sold. Birmingham Small Arms also produced a smaller edition, a 14 HP model with a 2.9 litre engine and four-speed gearbox. It was also somewhat overweight, giving a very mediocre performance.

The Birmingham Small Arms management decided to enter the luxury car business and, following the publicity given to the 40 HP Itala which won the Pekin-Paris race, B.S.A. purchased an Itala. This was pulled apart and used as the basis of the new big B.S.A., a model freely known as the B.S.A.-Itala.

Production of the 40 HP car never got into full stride, because B.S.A. hit a bad patch and, for some months, looked like closing down. The owners managed to engineer a type of reverse take-over of Daimler U.K. (a separate concern from the German company), in which B.S.A. technically purchased Daimler, though Daimler executives controlled the resulting merger. Production of the 40 HP B.S.A.-Itala ceased and a new range of models were designed with Daimler-made sleeve valve engines, based on the Knight patent.

The first was a 13.9 HP Tourer with one of the first all-steel pressed bodies made in England. It was eventually to revolutionise automotive production. The 13.9 HP model also featured a three-speed gearbox built in unit with the rear axle. Its light design was an attempt to infiltrate the Model T market.

It sold for £325 in Britain and for a little more in Australia, where a handful or so were sold.

Production of B.S.A. cars ceased with World War One. It was not until 1921 that car production resumed, the newcomer being a light 10 HP model powered by a noisy air-cooled, twin-cylinder engine of 1.1 litres. It proved moderately successful and was followed by larger four and six-cylinder cars, fitted with Daimler sleeve valve engines.

The air-cooled twin was further developed and fitted to a fascinating front-wheel-drive three wheeler. This car was clearly intended to provide stiff opposition to Morgan who used a more simple chain drive to the rear wheel. Birmingham Small Arms tried to overtake Morgan, first with a four-cylinder engine, then by producing a light four wheeler. Morgan remained well ahead in sales figures.

Birmingham Small Arms next venture was the front-wheel-drive four-wheeled Scout. In a desperate attempt to find a sizeable market, the company also introduced a variety of new models, some being virtually cut-down Daimlers and Lanchesters. The Scout continued until 1937, and though it was listed in sales catalogues for three more years, it is unlikely that many were built after 1937.

Birmingham Small Arms ceased car production as orders poured in for military equipment. Daimler eventually merged with Jaguar and later became part of British Leyland.

1913 B.S.A. TOURER

This car has been in the hands of veteran car enthusiasts since the early 1940s and was purchased at auction in 1964 by the present owners, the Rainsford Family of Adelaide. It is currently on display at the National Motor Museum, Birdwood, South Australia.

Little is known of the car's early history, but it is fitted with an original pressed metal touring body and is one of two B.S.A.'s which are the oldest cars in Australia with this feature. The other, a 1912 model, is owned by the Craze family of Port Macquarie, New South Wales. The restoration of the chassis and body was done by Eric Rainsford, with G. Eames looking after the trim.

There are at least three similar cars in Australia, including one owned by Pat Kerr, of Fremantle, Western Australia.

MECHANICAL FEATURES

Engine: Four-cylinder Knight sleeve valve, capacity 2016 ccs. Rated at 13.9 HP with 75 x 114 mm bore and stroke. Water-cooled, with Zenith carburettor. Magneto ignition. Estimated maximum engine speed 2000 rpm.
Gearbox: Sliding pinion type with three forward gears. Leather-faced cone clutch. Gearbox is built in unit with the rear axle.
Suspension: Semi-elliptic springs at the front, single transverse spring at the rear. No shock absorbers.
Brakes: External contracting band brakes on rear wheels.
Steering: Worm-and-peg with only ¾ turns lock-to-lock.
Wheels: Wire spoked with 815 x 105 tyres.
Dimensions: Wheelbase 9 ft 4 ins (2845 mm). Overall length 13 ft 6 ins (4115 mm). Height 6 ft 7 ins (2006 mm). Kerb weight 11 cwt (560 kg).
Performance: Maximum speed when new — 45 mph (72 km/h). Normal cruising speed — 30 mph (48 km/h). Fuel consumption at highway speeds — 20 mpg (14.1 litres/100 km).

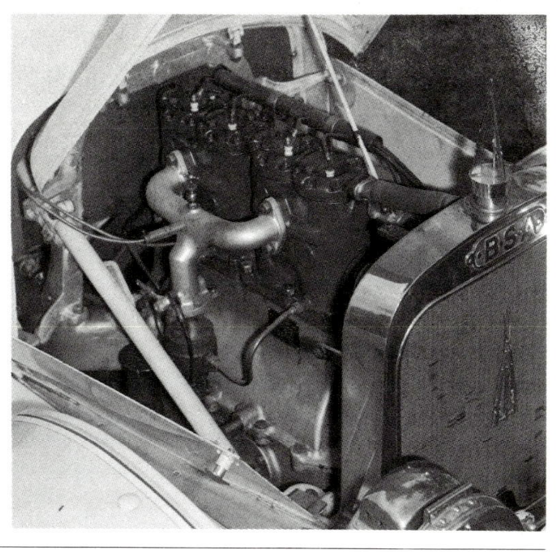

1913 Chalmers Raceabout

THE MARQUE

Chalmers built lively and robust cars between 1908 and 1924, and then became part of the Chrysler Corporation.

The firm had its roots in the Thomas-Detroit, one of the great American makes of the early days with one winning the 1908 New York to Paris race. Hugh Chalmers entered the scene in 1907, initially as a hard-hitting salesman for Thomas, but within a year he had sufficient control to commence calling the products Chalmers. The Thomas name continued for some years, but largely for special order cars.

Chalmers was an energetic and thoughtful innovator, introducing a self-starting system in 1912 and pushing sales to 20,000 cars a year by 1915.

The company was located in Detroit, Michigan, and became noted for its sporting designs, enhanced by high revving four and six-cylinder engines. The 4.0 litre 'four' in the 1913 Raceabout pictured revs to 3000 rpm, giving a road speed of 65 mph (104 km/h). That was unusually fast for a car selling at $1500 in the United States at the time, especially as a four-cylinder Stutz Bearcat cost more than $2000, with virtually the same performance.

This Model 16 Raceabout was one of the last four-cylinder models made by Chalmers. During 1914 two very successful sixes were produced and fitted in 115 inch (2921 mm) wheelbase cars. The firm also produced a larger 38 HP four, but dropped it after a while to concentrate on the sixes. The policy paid off and sales passed the 400 a week mark.

The Model 16 was mechanically advanced for its time, the cylinders being cast in a single block, with the three-speed gearbox directly behind. Due to a rigid crankshaft and a 3 inch (76 mm) diameter overhead inlet valve, the engine could rev cheerfully to high speeds for the day.

Chalmers were extremely popular in the United States, being both lively and reliable. One oddity was the use of a single pedal to operate the 40-plate clutch and foot brake. Pressing in the pedal for part of the way opened the clutch, further movement brought the rear wheel brakes into action.

Chalmers had some early racing successes, and sales reached their peak at the start of World War One. Sales flagged in the post-war months, so Chalmers came to an unusual arrangement with the rival Maxwell firm. Both marques were to be produced in the Maxwell factories, gaining the benefit of larger production, but Chalmers was to be in charge of the joint selling organisation.

The arrangement did not work, and Maxwell was soon in deep trouble. Walter F. Chrysler was called in to reorganize the company, reputedly at a fee of one million dollars. Within two years, Chrysler had taken over the joint organisation, renamed the Maxwell Four a Chrysler, and launched the Chrysler Corporation.

1913 CHALMERS RACEABOUT MODEL 16

Michael Bendeich, of Baulkham Hills, New South Wales, is lucky enough to own two 1913 Chalmers. Though many of the marques survive in the United States, few are in Australia.

The Model 16 illustrated was used for some years as a family car around Walgett, New South Wales. It was converted to a utility for carrying timber and eventually abandoned.

The car turned up in pieces during the early 1960s, and five years later the headlamps were found in a car dealer's yard.

Michael Bendeich rebuilt the chassis, then constructed a new body, a replica of the type offered by Chalmers as an alternative to the more orthodox tourer. Jack Leit was responsible for the trim.

With its monocle windscreen, cast metal boot scrapers on the running boards and exterior fuel tank, the Raceabout is an eye-catching example of the sportsters the young bloods of 1913 enjoyed. Strictly a fair weather car, it has no weather protection of any kind.

Restoration commenced in 1964 and was completed four years later. Subsequently the Chalmers won the Veteran Car Club's (NSW) annual award for the Restoration of the Year.

MECHANICAL FEATURES

Engine: Four-cylinder, 4.0 litre, rated at 25.6 HP, overhead inlet and side exhaust with 3 inch (76 mm) diameter inlet valve; water pump with cellular radiator, Stromberg carburettor, Bosch magneto, bore and stroke 4" x 4½". Maximum engine speed, around 3000 rpm.
Gearbox: Selective sliding gear with three forward speeds and reverse. Forty plates in clutch, shaft drive to rear. A single pedal operates both clutch (part pedal movement) and the foot brake (additional movement).
Suspension: Semi-elliptic springs on front, three-quarter elliptics at rear.
Brakes: Internal expanding drum brakes on rear wheels, with external contracting transmission brake.
Steering: Worm type with 35 ft (10.7 m) turning circle and 7/8 turns lock-to-lock.
Wheels: Felloes wood with steel, 23 inch (584 mm).
Dimensions: Wheelbase 9 ft 8 ins (2946 mm). Track 4 ft 8 ins (1422 mm). Overall length 13 ft 8 ins (4166 mm). Height 5 ft 0 ins (1524 mm).
Performance: Maximum speed when new — 65 mph (104 km/h). Normal cruising speed — 35 mph (56 km/h). Fuel consumption at highway speeds — 20 mpg (14.1 litres/100 km).

WATSON & CRANE PTY LTD
PLUMBER
SUPPLIES
P.C. ITEMS

FIRE STATION
WALK THROUGH TO
KOONGARRA
RAILWAY STATION
BATTERIES
RE-CHARGED
&
REPAIRED.
SPEEDWELL
CYCLES
FROM
£10·10·0

1913 Crossley Shelsley

THE MARQUE

In common with Hispano-Suiza and Vauxhall, Crossley helped establish the sports car as a vehicle in its own right, rather than just a fast touring car. The model pictured can accelerate from rest to 50 mph (80 km/h) in 19 seconds, potent motoring in 1913, especially as the top speed was 68 mph (109 km/h).

Crossley Motors Ltd. was an off-shoot of Crossley Brothers, makers of gas engines. It became involved in the car business when Charles Jarrott, the celebrated racing driver, asked J. S. Critchley (formerly of Daimler) to design a high performance touring car which Jarrott could market. The 22 HP 4.6 litre four-cylinder chain-driven design was shown to Sir William Crossley who agreed to manufacture it for Jarrott. The new car went on sale in 1905 and was quickly followed by a more powerful 40 HP model. Jarrott publicised it with a number of notable feats, including a drive from London to Monte Carlo in 37½ hours.

Another new model appeared for 1907. This 30/40 HP design had a conventional live rear axle and a radiator carrying the green cross which was to become Crossley's emblem.

The year 1909 saw the first small Crossley, a 12/14 HP design with four wheel brakes. The front brakes were coupled to the foot pedal, the rear to the hand lever, but over zealous braking caused all manner of problems as the front wheels would lock, causing loss of steering control. Crossley engineers never thought of coupling the four brakes with suitable compensation for the front and rear drums and the problems were never cured. In 1913, the front brakes were dropped.

The year 1913 was a notable year because the firm produced the prototype of a sporting car which was to make them famous — the Shelsley sports car. It derived this name because in 1911 the company had performed well at the famous Shelsley Walsh hill climb.

With the Shelsley providing an unusually good power-to-weight ratio, Crossley competed at practically every speed meeting and hill climb in Britain. One specially tuned model clocked 70 mph (112 km/h) at Brooklands. Another was entered in the 1914 Tourist Trophy but it failed to finish.

Had Crossley been content to use the Shelsley as the basis of a long line of sports cars, it would have prospered. Instead, the firm engaged in a bewildering array of activities, ranging from aero engine manufacture to military vehicles, from baby family cars to buses.

Crossley even tried to launch a rear engined six-cylinder sedan. It signed an agreement to manufacture 500 Bugatti Type 22's under licence but only 25 were made. Crossley flirted with the aircraft industry, with a temporary merger with Avro, and started to assemble Willys-Overland in Britain. But by 1926 the firm was heavily in debt as very few of its ventures paid off.

Crossley cars were solidly made, well engineered and popular with royalty. The Prince of Wales chose a fleet of Crossley 25/30s for his 1919 Australian tour. His father, King George V, had two Crossleys, including a specially-built six wheeler. King Alfonso of Spain and Crown Prince Hirohito of Japan also drove the British marque.

Crossley gamely tried to introduce a family Ten in 1932 (one actually won the Australian Rally Championship in 1935), but by 1937 production of all Crossley cars had ceased. In 1956 the commercial vehicle division closed as well.

Remarkably few Crossley cars have survived. The Shelsley is the most notable of the long line, but only five pre-1918 examples are known to exist.

1913 CROSSLEY SHELSLEY SPORTS

This car was bought second-hand in England in 1918 by a Mr Halford, of Cootamundra, New South Wales, and shipped to his home town. It stayed there until 1957 when the rather sorry looking old-timer was acquired by Sydney collector, George Green.

Investigation showed that it was a 1913 model, a 3 litre prototype of the Shelsley.

The car, now on display at Green's Motorcade near Liverpool, New South Wales, was restored by George Green personally. The body had been chopped in half at some time in its career, and was professionally rebuilt by W. S. Grice and Company, of Sydney.

MECHANICAL FEATURES

Engine: Four-cylinder 3 litre side valve design, rated at 15 HP, developing 38 BHP at 3000 rpm. Thermo-syphon water cooling with fan; Smith's 5-jet carburettor; magneto ignition.

Gearbox: Crossley-made crash box with four forward gears and cone clutch.

Suspension: Semi-elliptic springs at front, three-quarter elliptics at rear.

Brakes: Two wheel brakes, internal expanding on rear drums.

Steering: Conventional design, very direct with 1¼ turns lock-to-lock.

Wheels: Wire wheels 21 x 5.25 (originally 875 x 105).

Dimensions: Wheelbase 9 ft 6 ins (2896 mm). Overall length 13 ft 7 ins (4140 mm). Height 4 ft 9 ins (1448 mm). Kerb weight 24 cwt (1222 kg).

Performance: Maximum speed when new — 68 mph (109 km/h). Normal cruising speed — 45 mph (72 km/h). Fuel consumption at highway speeds — 19 mpg (14.8 litres/100 km).

1913 Delaunay-Belleville

THE MARQUE

Before World War One, knowledgeable motorists regarded the French built Delaunay-Belleville as the world's best car built in reasonable numbers.

Certainly the reputation of Rolls-Royce was rising fast, but Delaunay was producing handsome, reliable and refined cars at a much more attractive price.

When the Tsar of Russia took to motoring he asked Delaunay to build him three special machines. The firm responded in 1908-9, with a magnificent design, powered by a vast 11.8 litre six-cylinder engine. A compressed air starter was powerful enough to start the car in gear, so it could glide silently away from possible assassination attempts. These trappings of inherited wealth were not despised by Lenin and Trotsky when they seized power. They reputedly kept the three cars for their personal use.

Delaunay-Belleville were long established steam engineers and boiler makers. Ironically Louis Renault — later France's most successful car maker — learned his engineering skills at Delaunay's steam locomotive workshop.

The first car, announced at the 1904 Paris Salon, was an Aristocrat. Designed by former Benz engineer Marius Barbarou, it boasted a large four-cylinder engine with full pressure lubrication. It was quieter and more refined than its contemporaries. During the next three years, the company launched five different four-cylinder models, each an improvement on its predecessor. The company quickly moved into the carriage trade, aiming at the top echelon with a massive 8 litre six-cylinder model in 1908. Almost immediately, it was followed by four more six-cylinder models, the best known of which was the basis for the 'H' series, the company's best known model.

The great circular radiator — resembling a steam boiler — inspired some elegant body designs and Delaunay-Bellevilles were soon highly favoured by the world's wealthy men.

Between 1908 and 1914, Delaunay sold 3754 cars. Of these, 138 had engines of 8 litres or more, 524 had 6.5 litre units and some 2508 were four-cylinder models. Some interesting innovations were made, including the use of twin foot brakes, both on the transmission. The idea was the pedals should be used alternately on hills to prevent over-heating.

Delaunay also produced 'colonial' models with stiffened suspension systems and raised ground clearance, which helped to sell the marque in Australia. Notoriously tough and reliable, the French cars were widely used for staff transport and as ambulances during World War One.

After the fighting, the firm continued to produce a great variety of four and six-cylinder models. Though they streamlined the radiator, the designs remained curiously old-fashioned and the pre-war appeal was lost.

In retrospect, Delaunay's mistake was in offering a wide range of models instead of following the example of Rolls-Royce and putting all their efforts into one highly refined design.

During the 1930s, Delaunay made a further stab at the luxury car market by importing straight eight engines from the United States, but the demand was small and the marque lost its individuality. A six-cylinder model reappeared after World War Two, with a Cotal electric gearbox. Production continued on and off until 1950.

1913 DELAUNAY-BELLEVILLE 17 HP

This very active tourer originally came from Canberra and is one of only two mobile Delaunays in Australia. Both are owned by George Green of Sydney. Three other restored veteran Delaunay-Bellevilles are known to exist around the world.

The four-cylinder 'small' model was located on a property by the late Murdoch McDonald and restored between 1968 and 1970 by George Green and Max Walsh. It is now used to carry visitors on trips around the picnic area of Green's Motorcade, near Liverpool, New South Wales.

MECHANICAL FEATURES

Engine: Four-cylinder, side valve, approx. 3.75 litres capacity, rated at 17 HP, developing 26 BHP at 2500 rpm. Water pump cooled, originally fitted with Delaunay carburettor. Bosch battery/magneto. Full pressure lubrication, tubular connecting rods.
Gearbox: Four-speed conventional crash type with cone clutch.
Suspension: Semi-elliptic springs at front, three-quarter elliptics at rear with transverse platform spring.
Brakes: Metal-to-metal internal expanding drums on rear wheels, foot pedal operated transmission brake.
Steering: Worm-and-nut with 40 ft (12.2 m) turning circle, 2 turns lock-to-lock.
Wheels: Wire, 880 x 120.
Dimensions: Wheelbase 9 ft 9 ins (2972 mm). Overall length 13 ft 6 ins (4115 mm). Hood height 7 ft 0 ins (2134 mm).
Performance: Maximum speed when new — 55 mph (88 km/h). Normal cruising speed — 40 mph (64 km/h). Fuel consumption at highway speeds — 20 mpg (14.1 litres/100 km).

VETERAN C R
15

1913 Hillman Baby Car

THE MARQUE

Though Herbert Austin is considered the father of the British baby car, it can be strongly argued that Hillman conceived a four-cylinder baby car well ahead of Austin. The company tried to launch popular motoring in Australia as early as 1913 by offering the Melbourne-made James Munro body before Government legislation virtually forced car firms to fit Australian made bodies.

The story of Hillman's development from a hopeful Tourist Trophy contender in 1907 to part of the Peugeot UK organisation is told on page 132 dealing with the 1923 Hillman roadster. Here the discussion centres on the remarkable 9HP baby car that Hillman launched before the Rootes brothers gained control of the company.

Announced in June 1913, the single seater 9HP had an overall length similar to that of a modern Mini Minor. Unlike other small cars of the time, the Hillman had a four-cylinder engine to provide a full size performance. It was also robust, pleasant to drive and remarkably trouble-free.

Announcing that the Hillman would have a 1357 cc engine, the English Autocar called it a 'large car in miniature'. In an enthusiastic and detailed technical description, the Autocar commented on the ease of service and simplified frame construction. It added that the new car sold for £200 in England, complete with standard body, scuttle dash, acetylene lamps, an electric horn and tool kit.

Hillman's newly appointed Melbourne agent, James Munro & Co., was quick to have a local body ready. In an advertisement in the *Australian Motorist*, dated 2 November 1914, the 9HP was offered with a choice of English body at the equivalent of £285 ($570) or a 'colonial made' body for an extra £10 ($20). The difference was not mentioned.

The advertisement catalogued the competition successes the 9HP had gained in its short life. According to the advertisement, the 9HP held the class record at Brooklands for all distances from a half mile to ten miles. It said the 9HP had won a gold medal in the Royal Automobile's Club Reliability Contest, having made no involuntary stops. At the Brooklands midsummer meeting it has been placed first in the 2 mile sprint race, second in the 'long 75 mph handicap' and third in the 'short 75 mph handicap'.

There was also an extract from the English *Autocar* magazine describing one of the Brooklands handicaps, though which one was not specified. It ran: "This event ended in an astonishing win for the little Hillman. From the first its acceleration was perfectly extraordinary and it was fifty yards ahead of anything at the end of railway straight . . . and it came home a capital winner by a length. The Hillman's speed from a standing start is amazing considering the size of its engine — 66¼ mph."

This was indeed fast motoring for an 8.9 HP car, but the outbreak of World War One put an end to production. A similar car was later introduced with a 10 HP engine. When production eventually ceased in 1925 the engine size had grown to 1.6 litres.

Only two pre-war 9 HP Hillmans are known to survive — a pretty drophead coupé in the Rootes museum in Britain and this one in Melbourne.

1913 HILLMAN 9 HP

Fitted with a Munro body, this colourful roadster was first owned by a photographer named Colliver operating out of Shepparton, Victoria. During the late 1920s, a woodruff key in an axle shaft snapped and the car was laid up in a shed. It lay undisturbed until 1957 when the shed was demolished to make room for a new civic centre.

Well known veteran car enthusiast, Alec Ludeman, immediately bought the Hillman. After tidying it up, he rallied the car regularly until 1965 when the present owner, Allan Bathurst of Glen Waverley, Victoria, acquired it.

Allan completely restored the car to new condition, with Bob Kay retrimming the interior. It has competed in major rallies in three States, completing more than 18,000 miles (29,000 km) since restoration with complete reliability.

MECHANICAL FEATURES

Engine: Four-cylinder, 1357 ccs with side valve, rated at 8.9 HP. Thermo-syphon cooling without fan or pump. Solex side draught carburettor and Bosch magneto ignition.
Gearbox: Three-speed selective sliding gearbox mounted in centre of chassis with shaft drive to a worm wheel differential. Leather-faced cone clutch. Gate change gear shift.
Suspension: Semi-elliptic springs front and rear.
Brakes: Foot actuated external contracting drum at rear of gearbox. Hand lever operates internal expanding shoes in rear wheel drums.
Steering: Worm-and-sector.
Wheels: Sankey detachable steel wheels, 710 x 90.
Dimensions: Wheelbase 7 ft 9 ins (2362 mm). Track 4 ft 0 ins (1219 mm). Overall length 10 ft 10 ins (3302 mm). Kerb weight 12½ cwt (636 kg).
Performance: Maximum speed when new — 50 mph (80 km/h). Normal cruising speed — 40 mph (64 km/h). Fuel consumption at highway speeds — 25 mpg (11.3 litres/100 km).

VETERAN CAR
014

1913 Little

THE MARQUE

As its name implies, the American-built Little was one of the smallest cars of its day. It was, however, named after William H. Little, formerly a foreman with Buick. The single seat roadster has an overall length of 10 ft 10 inches (3.3 m), roughly the same as a Mini Minor. Though it had a relatively large 20 HP four-cylinder engine, it was unusually small by American standards, being only slightly longer than a friction-drive Metz, which has the same wheelbase, track and steering system.

The Little was born because William C. Durant was thrown out of General Motors, the company he had founded. In May 1911, Durant announced that he was establishing a new factory with racing driver Louis Chevrolet. He said he would produce a new high priced car 'whose distinctive feature will be an engine perfected during the winter by Chevrolet and assisted financially by Durant.'

What the press release did not reveal was that the wily Durant had also formed another company, with a contract to build the new Chevrolet. It was also to produce a new small car, the 'Little Four'.

Durant made this double move because Louis Chevrolet was insisting that any car bearing his name would be a luxury model. Durant knew that the real future lay in the mass production of a competitor for the Model T Ford.

The Republic Motor Company, which either distributed or built the Little, claimed to have 6½ acres of floor space. Its production rate is not known, but the four-cylinder Little was sold ex-factory at the remarkably low price of $US690, against $US350 for a single-cylinder Brush or $US950 for a four-cylinder Mitchell or Buick. The company emphasised the low price, its slogan being 'The Car You Want at a Price You Can Afford to Pay.'

Introduced in 1911, the Little had a 20 HP engine, with a 90 inch (2286 mm) wheelbase, a two-speed gearbox and rack-and-pinion steering. Its single seat roadster body was available in two colours — grey and black.

In 1911 the company introduced a larger car with a 3.7 litre six-cylinder engine but few were built. The Little operation had proved successful and Chevrolet was becoming such a big money spinner that Durant was able to use the company to regain control of General Motors. He immediately merged the Little operation with Chevrolet and production of Little cars ceased.

1913 LITTLE

Probably the only complete and driveable Little in Australia, the model is rare even in the United States where fewer than twenty examples of the Durant-inspired design are known to survive.

H. V. McKay, farm machinery manufacturers, imported Littles to Australia and sold them through a network of dealers. They sold at least 37 by 1917. The earliest known owner of this car was Nadin Iverack of Western General Store Merchants, Coolamon, New South Wales. He later sold it to Norman Stow of Temora, New South Wales, who tried to sell in at auction in 1923 but failed because the engine would not start. He then cut the car in two and a Mr Ray Schultz of Temora bought the motor, gearbox and half chassis for use as a stationary power plant. The back half of the chassis and the body were sold separately and never found.

The present owners, Alan and Raema Carpenter of Canberra acquired Mr Schultz's half car. They later heard that parts of another Little were near Bogan Gate, New South Wales, and more bits at Darby's Falls, near Cowra. Later still they found the complete body which belonged to the second car in a farm shed some 40 km away. Other parts were located at Tocumwal and Grenfell, making it possible for Alan, Ian Wise and Les Robinson, with some professional help, to rebuild one complete Little. Bill Jeffs of Wagga made the trim and Bill Phillips of Canberra the hood.

MECHANICAL FEATURES

Engine: Four-cylinder, side valve, 2.3 litre capacity, rated at 20 HP. Cylinders cast in pairs with flywheel at front of engine. Thermo-syphon cooling, splash lubrication, Marvel updraught carburettor. Battery and magneto ignition.
Gearbox: Selective sliding, two gears with 6 in (152 mm) diameter cone clutch faced with asbestos. Shaft drive to semi floating rear axle.
Suspension: Quarter-elliptic springs in the front, three-quarter elliptics at rear.
Brakes: Internal and external operating on rear wheel drums. Service brake operates by foot pedal, emergency brake by hand lever.
Steering: Rack-and-pinion steering with 40 ft (12.2 m) turning circle and ¾ turns lock-to-lock.
Wheels: Artillery type 30 x 3½ originally with Goodyear clincher tyres.
Dimensions: Wheelbase 7 ft 6 ins (2286 mm). Track 4 ft 8 ins (1422 mm). Overall length 10 ft 10 ins (3300 mm). Height 6 ft 6 ins (1980 mm). Kerb weight 10 cwt (510 kg).
Performance: Maximum speed when new — 46 mph (73 km/h). Normal cruising speed — 32 mph (51 km/h). Fuel consumption at highway speeds — 25 mpg (11.3 litres/100 km).

QLD
VETERAN
157

1913 Metz Friction Drive

THE MARQUE

The Metz Company of Waltham, Massachusetts, United States, produced 42,647 cars between 1909 and 1922, when production ceased. The firm began when C. H. Metz took over the Waltham Manufacturing Company which had been making cars since 1902. He had the design department discontinue Waltham's buckboard design and build a completely new car. With a 12 HP twin-cylinder engine, it featured friction drive transmission and twin chains to the rear. The new car was sold both in kit form for home assembly and as a built-up vehicle ready for the road.

In 1911, Metz brought out a more powerful model, with a four-cylinder engine and improved friction drive, selling for only $US495 assembled. The company's chief engineer, a former Ford man, designed the new 22 HP engine which bore a strong resemblance to the Model T unit.

The most unusual feature was the friction drive, the Metz being advertised as 'The Gearless Car — No Clutch to Slip, No Gears to Strip'. The basic principle was the use of a large alloy drive wheel at right angles to a smaller cast-iron driven wheel whose position could be varied in relation to the centre of the drive wheel. The closer the driven wheel came to the outer rim of the drive wheel, the higher the effective gear ratio. Moving the driven wheel across the centre of the drive wheel gave reverse.

The driven wheel was pressed against the machined face of the drive wheel when drive was engaged. Compressed paper, bolted in sections to the rim, was the original friction material, and, under normal conditions, lasted for about 2000 miles (3200 km). It could be replaced in about 1½ hours. Some owners extended the friction material life by using special leather and, today, a variety of materials, including neoprene and polyurethane sheet, is used.

In 1913 three Metz cars were entered in the Glidden Eight Day Endurance Contest. Thirty one starters left Minneapolis, travelling to Glacier National Park. The three Metz made perfect scores and were joint winners. In Australia in the same year, Dr F. R. Crouch won the Sydney to Melbourne Reliability Trial in a Metz. His was the lightest car in the event, but scored maximum points.

Despite such successes, Metz sales were poor. The transmission worked well when properly adjusted, but as the friction material became worn, the transmission wheels had to be brought closer together. If this adjustment was not done, the drive would slip, causing flat spots. The Metz was, and still is, a difficult car to drive; the foot pedal controls (especially the left pedal) being different from normal.

In 1916 the car was given a larger 25 HP engine, but this proved to be the company's last friction-drive model. In 1919 a conventional design powered by a Rutenber six-cylinder engine with a standard gearbox was announced. To overcome a rather poor reputation, the car was sold as a Waltham. Production ceased a year later.

1913 METZ MODEL 22

Now owned by Mr Walter Que of Gympie, Queensland, this friction drive roadster was retrieved from a property in the Jambin district of Queensland. It was a shearer's car and regularly used to travel from place to place shearing sheep. The guards and some components came from a different wreck found in Coonabarabran, New South Wales. The chassis was overhauled by the present owner but the engine required no attention. The body, built by Walter Que and Ian Rawlinson, is a replica of the original American roadster. The unusual curved windscreen is made from perspex, the original being celluloid. It looks great but in heavy rain the air flow carries the drops over the screen and it falls on the occupants like a bathroom shower.

Mr Que commenced restoration in January 1976. Mrs Myrtle Que completed the trim just in time for the 1978 International Rally. They found that though the car has a maximum speed of 48 mph (77 km/h), it is happiest cruising around 35 mph (56 km/h).

MECHANICAL FEATURES

Engine: Four-cylinder, side valve. Manufactured by Metz but similar in design to Model T Ford. Rated at 22 HP. Thermo-syphon cooling with fan incorporated in the flywheel.
Gearbox: Friction drive. Six notches in engagement lever provide six forward gears, plus one reverse. No clutch pedal but a drive pedal is pushed to engage drive wheel with its counterpart. Compressed paper was original material on drive wheel rim, but leather or polyurethane now used.
Suspension: Full elliptic springing front and rear.
Brakes: Foot pedal operated expanding drum braking on rear wheels only. A second foot pedal works the external contracting transmission brake.
Steering: Rack-and-pinion working on quadrant principle, with 1½ turns lock-to-lock. It has a 40 ft (12.2 m) turning circle.
Wheels: Wooden spoked, 30 x 3½ ins.
Dimensions: Wheelbase 7 ft 6 ins (2286 mm). Overall length 10 ft 6 ins (3200 mm). Height 6 ft 6 ins (1981 mm). Kerb weight 9.8 cwt (500 kg).
Performance: Maximum speed when new — 48 mph (77 km/h). Normal cruising speed — 35 mph (56 km/h). Fuel consumption at highway speeds — 30 mpg (9.4 litres/100 km).

1913 Vinot & Deguingand

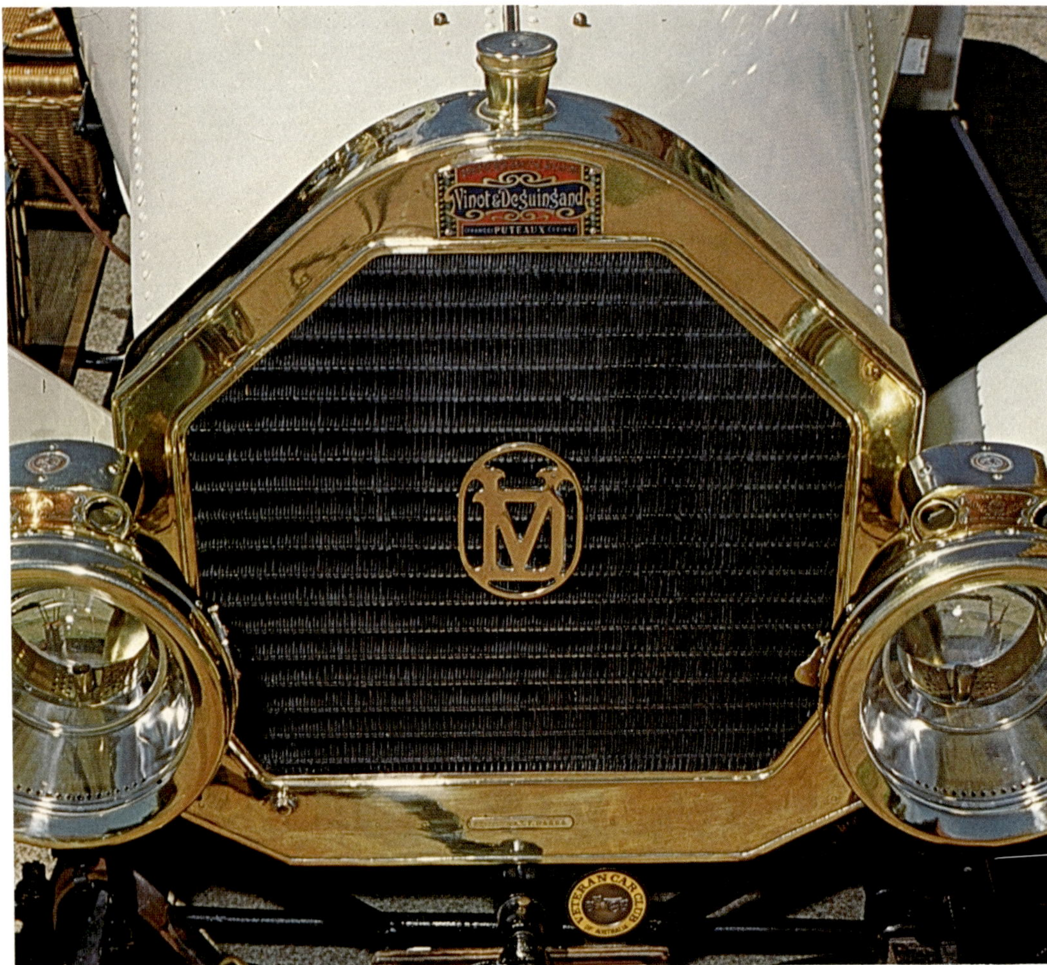

THE MARQUE

Vinot & Deguingand cars very quickly became known as Vinots, possibly to save the English the embarrassment of trying to pronounce the last name.

The firm was established in 1901 in Paris, near the Renault factory and they built fast, well-constructed cars which were also sold in England as La Silencieuse. It is also said that the first Enfield four wheelers, manufactured in England in 1901, were in fact locally assembled Vinots with an Enfield name plate.

The first production Vinots were powered by a 1.5 litre vertical twin engine with the fashionable automatic inlet valve. It also had a complex and unusual gearshift, which remained in production until World War One. In this device the lever is lifted vertically and moves in three planes to change from one ratio to another. The gearbox itself was in a cylindrical case.

Another unusual feature for 1901 was the use of a pressed steel chassis frame. A primitive belt and chain transmission was initially used but by 1903 the firm had adopted the more conventional side chain drive. A less progressive step was a change back to a timber chassis frame but two years later they reverted to steel frames.

From 1905 Vinot built a 10 HP twin, a 3.3 litre four (rated at 14 HP) and a larger engined 18 HP four. The two bigger models were equipped with four-speed gearboxes with the vertical change mechanism.

In 1905 the company had a brief but successful fling at motor sport. That year the Tourist Trophy race was held at the Isle of Man, mainly because motor racing required a special permit if held on mainland Britain. Rolls-Royce entered two cars in the race. One was driven by Charles Rolls. Minerva was strongly favoured to win but an Arrol-Johnson, driven by John Napier, was conceded to have more than a chance.

Some 42 cars took part but Rolls' car broke down almost immediately with gearbox trouble. After one lap, Napier's Arrol-Johnson was leading, followed by the second string Rolls-Royce driven by Percy Northey. Third place was held by Norman Littlejohn in a 14 HP Vinot. That was the order in which the cars finished the four lap 208 miles (333 km) race.

In 1906 Vinot introduced its first six-cylinder model with a giant 6.5 litre engine rated at 40/65 HP. Two years later the company switched from chain to shaft drive, introducing a new light car, the 10/14 HP. In 1909 Vinot took over the French Gladiator firm (founded by Darracq). A twin line of cars then began emerging from the Vinot factory, sharing many components, but not the unusual gearshift.

The year 1911 saw a more modern design — the 15/20 with a monobloc engine of 2.6 litres with pressure lubrication. This model continued until after World War One, but Vinot found it could not stay in the same league as its rivals, especially Renault and Peugeot. Production of Gladiators ceased soon after the war. Though Vinot introduced an attractive light weight with a 1.8 litre overhead valve engine, the firm began sinking into deep financial trouble. By 1926 it was so heavily in debt the factory closed down.

1913 VINOT & DEGUINGAND MODEL AO

This car reached Australia in chassis form and was fitted with a Melbourne-made body by Drought & McGlone.

Apart from being used by a reputedly legless fuel merchant in the Deniliquin,

New South Wales district for many years, little is known about its history. The present owner, Bill McCarthy, of Haberfield, New South Wales, bought the derelict chassis in 1969 from Malcolm Elmslie, of Gordon, New South Wales, who had owned it for about ten years.

The chassis was rebuilt by Bob McCarthy and Reg Jones, and a replica of the original roadster body was made by Bob McCarthy and Peter Wards, with trim by Fred Thompson. Their handiwork earned the Len Sheen Concours d'Elegance Junior Trophy at Vaucluse House in 1975 and the senior Concours at the same venue in 1978.

Vinot cars were sold in Australia from 1908, the first model offered here being the big 40/65 HP six, selling at a chassis only price of £850 ($1700), which put it in a similar price bracket to Mercedes.

In 1910, well known speedster Syd Day set a Sydney-Melbourne record in a 25 HP Vinot, covering the 573 miles (917 km) in 20 hours and 10 minutes.

MECHANICAL FEATURES

Engine: Four-cylinder, monobloc with tubular connecting rods and side valves, 80 x 130 mm, capacity 2610 ccs. Rated at 15/20 HP. Water pump cooling, Zenith carburettor and Bosch magneto.
Gearbox: Cylindrical case four-speed unit with vertical gate change and cone clutch. Shaft drive.
Suspension: Semi-elliptics front and rear, with rear mounted Le Telesco shock absorbers.
Brakes: Handbrake operates internal expanding drums on rear wheels, foot pedal actuated external contracting transmission brake.
Steering: Worm-and-sector box with 36 ft (10.9 m) turning circle and one turn lock-to-lock.
Wheels: Wire spoked, 23 inch, formerly 880 x 120 B.E.
Dimensions: Wheelbase 9 ft 3 ins (2819 mm). Overall length 13 ft 0 ins (3962 mm). Hood height 6 ft 0 ins (1829 mm). Kerb weight 20 cwt (1018 kg).
Performance: Maximum speed when new — 65 mph (104 km/h). Normal cruising speed — 40 mph (64 km/h). Fuel consumption at highway speeds — 22 mpg (12.8 litres/100 km).

1913 Wolseley Torpedo

THE MARQUE

Wolseley Tool and Motor Company had its roots deep within the Australian sheep shearing industry. Frederick York Wolseley was the son of a distinguished British Field Marshall, Viscount Wolseley. The young Wolseley came to Victoria to manage a sheep shearing property for a settler named Caldwell.

Realising the potential of mechanical clippers to speed sheep shearing, Wolseley spent twenty years experimenting. In 1887 he finally formed the Wolseley Sheep Shearing Machine Co. Ltd. in Sydney. His early machines were troublesome, and he hired Herbert Austin, another Englishman who had come to Australia on a working holiday. When Wolseley took his entire business to England in 1889, Austin went with him as chief engineer.

Because sheep shearing is a seasonal business, the company looked around for other work. Austin designed and built a prototype car in 1885. The company considered manufacturing it, but the three-wheeled, air-cooled machine did not perform well. Austin designed a second car and in 1899 — the year when Frederick Wolseley died — a third one.

This proved a success, winning numerous awards and setting the company up as the first British firm making cars in reasonable numbers. Austin left the concern in 1905 to found his own car making company, and J. D. Siddeley joined Wolseley as chief engineer. Siddeley introduced many improvements including a new engine with vertical cylinders, whereas Austin had favoured horizontally opposed cylinders. In 1910 Siddeley designed a 2.2 litre four-cylinder engine with pressure lubrication, which became the basis of a series of successful Wolseleys.

The 1913 model which cost £460 in Britain, was a pace setter in its day with full electric lighting. Its effective self-starting system used compressed air, maintained in a small tank supplied by an engine driven compressor. Wolseley's success was very real. In the 1913 Olympic Motor Show, some 65 exhibitors of British cars shared an annual output of 26,238 vehicles, an average of about 400 each. Wolseley did better than most. The company had built only 323 cars in 1901, 692 in 1906 and 1300 in 1911. But at the 1913 Show, Wolseley forecast total sales of 3000 for 1914.

Unfortunately, the company went into decline during the 1920s and was virtually bankrupt when acquired by the energetic William Morris in 1927. It became part of the BMC group in 1953 and later a division of British Leyland.

1913 WOLSELEY C-6 TORPEDO TOURER

This extremely original car was first sold with its Wolseley-made touring body to a wealthy European living in Malaya. He had a large collection of cars and hardly touched the Wolseley. In due course it went to Mr Choo Cheeng Khay of Kuala Lumpur, who also spent little time in the car. When Singapore fell in 1942, Mr Choo found it confiscated by the Japanese Imperial Army, and issued with a notice saying that it was to be used only by Senior Staff. Apparently they too had little use for the Wolseley. When it was finally acquired by Mr Tom Wilson in 1953, the car had travelled only 2500 miles since new.

Tom Wilson dismantled the mechancial parts, checked them all, repainted the body and then used the car extensively for his personal and family use, travelling extensively throughout Asia. He won numerous Concourse and hill climbing events and, in 1969, migrated to Australia bringing the car with him.

In 1974 the 1913 Wolseley was purchased by Jim Cooper Snr and his son Jim, of Bexley, New South Wales. It has since proved a most reliable competitor in numerous veteran and vintage car events and came fourth in the 1978 V.C.C.A. Blue Mountains Rally, a tough test for an old timer as it encompasses some of the steepest main road hills in New South Wales.

MECHANICAL FEATURES

Engine: Four-cylinder 3.07 litres capacity, side valves, rated at 16/20 HP, with honeycomb radiator and water pump. A taper needle type S.U. carburettor, magneto ignition, maximum engine speed 1200 rpm. Full electric lighting.
Gearbox: Selector gate change in right hand position, with four forward gears and multi-disc clutch.
Suspension: Semi-elliptic leaf springs at front, semi-elliptics with unusual scrolls at the ends for rear springing.
Brakes: The handbrake operates internal, self-energising expansion brakes on rear wheels; the foot pedal operates on a brake countershaft
Steering: Worm-and-sector steering with unusually large turning circle.
Dimensions: Wheelbase 10 ft 4 ins (3150 mm). Overall length 14 ft 6 ins (4420 mm). Height 5 ft 0 ins (1524 mm).
Performance: Maximum speed when new — 60 mph (100 km/h). Normal cruising speed — 45 mph (72 km/h). Fuel consumption at highway speeds — 20 mpg (14.1 litres/100 km).

V.C.C.
1913

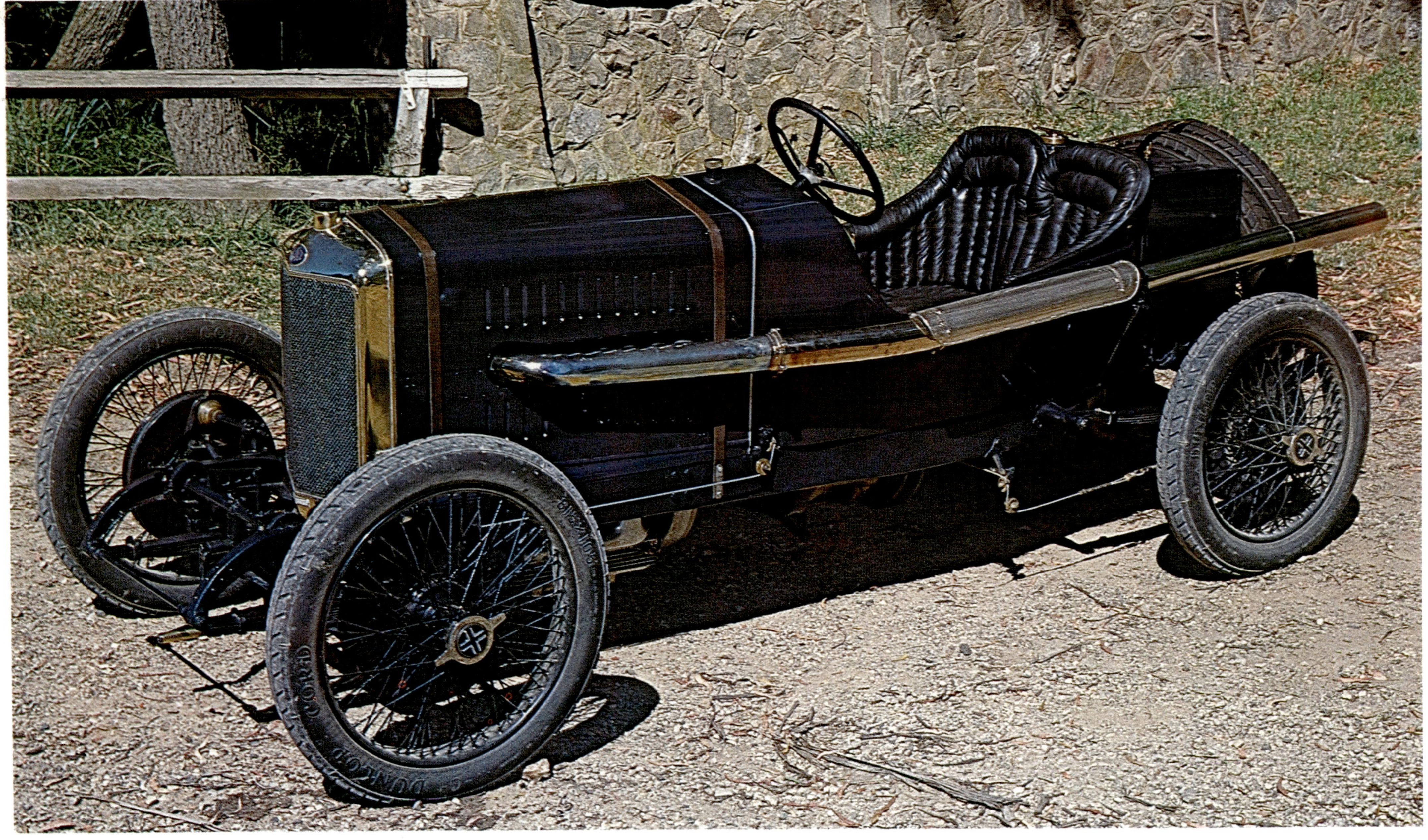

1914 Delage Grand Prix

THE MARQUE

Like many firms, Delage built its first car using a single-cylinder De Dion engine. Quickly realising the commercial potential of motor sport, the French firm started racing in 1906, taking second place in the French Coupés des Voiturettes. Two years later they won the event. By 1911 the firm was ready to tackle Grand Prix racing with the Type 'X'. In 1913 the Type 'Y' followed and for the French Grand Prix at Lyons in 1914 a trio of Type 'S' machines were produced. Only one of them survives — the car on these pages.

It is of exceptional interest because of its amazingly advanced concept, twin overhead camshafts, desmodromic valve action, four valves per cylinder, four wheel brakes and five-speed gearbox — all in 1914!

Over the years, the company built a fascinating variety of engines. During the 1920s they campaigned a successful 2 litre V-12 GP car, as well as a massive 10.5 litre V-12 which developed 280 BHP at 3200 rpm, providing a timed maximum speed of 143 mph (229 km/h) in 1924. The 1½ litre straight 8 of 1926-27 was probably their most famous Grand Prix car.

Delage produced a very good line of sporting machines but ran into financial difficulties during the 1930s. The founder, Louis Delage, was forced to sell to Walter Watney in 1935 and Watney subsequently resold to Delahaye in 1937. In 1954, the firm became part of Hotchkiss.

1914 DELAGE TYPE 'S'

This meticulously restored racing car is the sole survivor of three identical machines designed by Arthur Michelat

for the 1914 French Grand Prix. They were driven by factory drivers Paul Bablot, Albert Guyot and Arthur Duray, but only one finished the race.

Later that year an American millionaire, Harry Harkness, who wanted to go racing, sent his chauffeur to Europe for suitable equipment. The clouds of World War One had already descended and the American was able to snap up and ship home the three Delages. One of the cars driven by Barney Oldfield, a colourful driver of the early American racing scene, finished in 6th position at Indianapolis in 1916, lapping the brick circuit at 94.35 mph (151 km/h). The three cars raced with success from 1916 to 1918 at Sheepshead Bay Speedway where one was destroyed in a spectacular crash. Later Oldfield acquired the two surviving cars and took them around American showgrounds staging racing stunts.

In 1925 Oldfield sold one, or possibly a composite of two cars, to Australian, George McCarey who raced it at the inaugural meeting of the Maroubra Speedway in Sydney. He also raced it at Aspendale, Victoria.

Later, well known speedster Jack Burton bought the Delage but eventually it ended up on a used car lot and was purchased by the late Ken Hume. It made some spasmodic appearances at motor sport events, including a run at Rob Roy Hill Climb Victoria, during the late 1940s before it was acquired by the late Lex Davison.

For 28 years it stood untouched, a bare chassis with many mechanical parts frozen solid. In 1974, 10 years after Lex's death, Mrs Diana Davison commissioned Jack Nelson of Romsey near Melbourne, to commence the mammoth restoration job. Using photographs of the original three cars, Jack made a new body, keeping every detail as authentic as possible, down to the leather-clad glovebox where presumably the old timers stored their goggles.

In the middle of the four year restoration the car changed hands. Melbourne barrister, Stuart Murdoch, the new owner, instructed Jack Nelson to complete the work, making the car suitable for vintage hill climbs and sprints.

The Delage Type 'S' is incredibly advanced, with its twin overhead camshaft engine, four wheel brakes and five-speed gearbox. During their racing days, one of the trio was officially timed at 106 mph (170 km/h), making it one of the fastest cars of its time. It also held the 10 mile record at Sheepshead Bay at 97.8 mph (157 km/h). Today it is perhaps the most distinguished vintage competition car in Australia.

MECHANICAL FEATURES

Engine: Four-cylinder 4.4 litres rated at 21 HP, developing 110 BHP at 2750 rpm. Twin overhead camshafts with desmodromic valve action. Water pump cooling (no fan). Bosch magneto. Four valves per cylinder, ball race main bearings, 94 x 160 mm bore and stroke.
Gearbox: Delage five-speed crash box with 3rd gear direct, 4th and 5th over-drive ratios. Helle Shaw multi-plate clutch.
Suspension: Semi-elliptic springs front and rear.
Brakes: Perrot-type front brakes, conventional rear. Handbrake operates all four wheels, foot brake operates a transmission brake of 400 mm diameter.
Steering: Worm-and-sector with 1⅝ turns lock-to-lock.
Wheels: Rudge-Whitworth, front size 820 x 120, rear 815 x 105 mm.
Dimensions: Wheelbase 9 ft 2 ins (2743 mm). Track 4 ft 7 ins (1400 mm). Overall length 12 ft 4 ins (3760 mm). Height 4 ft 0 ins (1219 mm). Kerb weight 21.6 cwt (1100 kg).
Performance: Maximum speed when new — 106 mph (170 km/h). Normal cruising speed — 70 mph (112 km/h). Fuel consumption at highway speeds — 12 mpg (23.5 litres/100 km).

1914 Delahaye Seven Seater

THE MARQUE

Emile Delahaye, a railroad engineer, exhibited his first car at the Paris Exhibition of 1895. Production commenced in 1896 and a year later he moved the factory from his native Tours to Paris, the centre of the young but flourishing French motor industry.

Delahaye was one of several marques competing in the 1896 Paris-Marseilles-Paris road race. A contemporary report described his design as having a "studied elegance and a great wheelbase". It was, however, very similar to the German designs of the day, with a rear-mounted twin-cylinder engine, driving the wheels through a two-speed belt system. Delahaye entered two cars, one was leading the race at the end of the first day, but a trio of Panhards then took the lead and finished in front.

A production Delahaye also took part in Britain's first sprint meeting held in 1897. Racing over public roads in Essex, the French car clocked the fastest time, covering a measured mile at an average speed just under 27 mph (43 km/h).

In 1901, Emile Delahaye retired from the company, having sold nearly 1000 cars, all with belt drive. The new manager introduced chain drive and, in 1907, a shaft driven design followed. From then on the company specialised in simple orthodox but extremely reliable machines. Its one venture into the unconventional was a V-6 produced from 1912-14. Most Delahayes built before World War One had a four-cylinder engine with two bearing crankshaft.

The cars produced after World War One were dependable but dull. However, in 1933 a fresh breeze swept through the firm, bringing an advanced overhead valve six-cylinder design. It had independent front suspension, an optional Cotal electric gearbox and a choice of several stunning body styles. This design also led to the magnificent Type 135 Sports, a remarkably fine sports car which ranks as one of the most desirable of collectors' cars. In the same year (1935) Delahaye bought the ailing Delage concern and began to specialise in elegant coachwork.

The competition Type 135 was born in 1936, with a 3.3 litre engine producing 160 BHP. A Bugatti just won the 1936 French Grand Prix with the Delahaye team taking the next four places. The company also won the 1937 Monte Carlo race and, in the following year, scored an outright victory at the Le Mans 24 Hour race.

In 1939 the English *Autocar* magazine staged a special race to determine the fastest standard equipped sports car on the market. A Delahaye Type 135 romped home, lapping the Brookland's circuit at 127 mph (203 km/h), leaving a 2.9 Alfa and a 4.0 Darracq in its wake. Delahaye won the Monte Carlo race again in the same year.

The post-war years proved disappointing. The French company was building fast and expensive machinery at a time when money was short. In 1950 they sold a mere 483 cars. By 1951 production had dropped to 77 and, though the company won the Monte Carlo for the third time, the end was in sight. In 1954 Delahaye merged with Hotchkiss and its car factory became a truck manufacturing centre.

1914 DELAHAYE TYPE 43

A Frenchman, Henri Moreau, of Darling Point, New South Wales, imported this Type 43 early in 1914 for use in his perfumery business. He was recalled to France when World War One commenced.

His car was bought by a Mrs Tabley, of Tamarama, New South Wales, as a surprise present for her husband, who ran a gold-stamping business. He drove it for three years but apparently experienced over-heating problems as he had a Mr Steinbohm install a larger radiator. He also had the original royal blue colour changed to a biscuit-yellow, the blue apparently being hard to keep looking clean.

In 1918, the car was sold to a Mr Cox, of Newtown, New South Wales. A builder, he used the car extensively for some years, first as a tourer, and then, with the rear part of the body off, as a utility. Reputedly, the Delahaye outlasted two Ford Model T trucks and was used until 1942.

The present owner, Arthur Garthon, of Hurstville, New South Wales, heard from George Sevenoaks that the Delahaye was in Mr Cox's back garden, and he purchased it in 1955. Fortunately, the thoughtful owner had also preserved the rear part of the body, along with the hood bows, one side lamp, rear seat and Stephney wheel.

This made it possible for Arthur to make a thoroughly original restoration. Despite its many years of hard work, the Delahaye still has the factory pistons, valves, clutch facing and trim.

It was the only 16/20 brought to Australia and is believed to be the only fully restored Type 43 in the world.

MECHANICAL FEATURES

Engine: Four-cylinder, 2950 ccs, side valve design, rated at 16 HP. Water pump cooling, Claudel carburettor, Bosch magneto. Two bearing crankshaft with full pressure lubrication.
Gearbox: Four-speed sliding pinion with gearshift on right-hand side and leather-faced cone clutch.
Suspension: Semi-elliptic springs at front, three-quarter elliptics at rear.
Brakes: Handbrake — internal expanding shoes on rear brake drums. Footbrake — internal expanding on transmission.
Steering: Worm-and-sector with only 1⅛ turn lock-to-lock.
Wheels: Wooden artillery, 880 x 120.
Dimensions: Wheelbase 10 ft 7 ins (3226 mm). Overall length 14 ft 4 ins (4172 mm). Height 7 ft 0 ins (2134 mm). Kerb weight 30 cwt (1527 kg).
Performance: Maximum speed when new — 50 mph (80 km/h). Normal cruising speed — 40 mph (64 km/h). Fuel consumption at highway speeds — 18 mpg (15.7 litres/100 km).

DUNLOP
1914
VETER.
066

VETERAN CAR
201
12

1914 Hispano-Suiza Alfonso X111

THE MARQUE

Hispano-Suiza's Alfonso XIII is often credited as being the world's first production sports car, being directly derived from the 1910 Coupé de l'Auto. Certainly cars with sporting characteristics were produced well before the 1912 Alfonso but few, if any, could match its performance and splendid road manners.

The Alfonso is a relatively small machine of orthodox design employing technical excellence to achieve lively and refined motoring.

Soon after the turn of the century, a young Swiss engineer Marc Birkigt teamed up with a wealthy Spaniard, Senor Mateu, to launch Hispano-Suiza (a name meaning Spanish-Swiss). The original factory was in Barcelona but later a French factory was established and a curious twin-company developed with Marc Birkigt designing all cars built by both firms.

When Hispano-Suiza first tried its hand at racing, the French Sizaire-Naudin concern had no trouble out-pacing them. When studying the regulations for the Coupé de l'Auto, Birkigt found that the engine bore was limited to 64 mm but there was no restriction on the stroke. He had always favoured long stroke engines, because of their flexibility, so he designed an engine with a 180 mm stroke. When the opposition matched this, he extended the stroke to 200 mm. The opposition went further — to 260 mm — but the engines were so troublesome that the durable Hispano-Suiza unit stayed on top.

In 1912 Birkigt adapted the Coupé de l'Auto car as an entirely new road-going machine, the Alfonso XIII. It was named after the King of Spain who was given one by his wife. He became so attached to the car that he had a succession of them.

Initially the engine was of 80 x 180 mm design, having one of the longest strokes of any production engine.

The Alfonso was unquestionably the best remembered Hispano-Suiza design, but it was overshadowed by the radically new H6B luxury limousine, launched in 1916 as a challenge to the Rolls-Royce Silver Ghost. The H6B is now regarded as one of the great designs of the era, but the Alfonso remains the most interesting machine built by Hispano-Suiza.

The last new Hispano-Suiza was produced in 1933, but the range of V-12 and six-cylinder models continued until World War Two, with a few cars assembled after the War. The factory was also renowned for its aircraft engines, marine engines, trucks and buses and was purchased by the ill-fated Pegaso venture during the late 1940s.

HISPANO 15T ALFONSO XIII

Parts for more than a dozen Alfonso cars have been located in Australia, indicating the popularity of the model. Some cars were raced and one is reputed to have been tuned to clock 95 mph (152 km/h). The makers claimed a top speed of 77 mph (123 km/h) for the standard Alfonso, but one was officially timed at Brooklands at 86 mph (137 km/h).

This 1914 model is rare, being one of only ten built with an engine bore of 85 mm, giving a capacity of 4.1 litres.

It was brought to Australia for a Mr McPhillamy of Forbes, New South Wales, but apparently off-loaded in Aden for World War One, arriving in Australia four years later. After some years the McPhillamy family traded it on a new car, but bought the Alfonso back again as they were unhappy with the way it was being treated. It was stored for some years in a shed. When a bush-fire burned down the shed damaging the car, they pushed the remains into the Lachlan River.

Mr Alan Wilson of Forbes rescued it during the 1940s and cleaned the remains, a job which involved removing a number of large frogs from inside the cooling system.

In 1969 the present owners, Bill Burrows and Jim Sandy of St. Ives, New South Wales, took over the restoration. They built a new timber decked body, overhauled the mechanical parts and made new trim. The Alfonso has since travelled several thousand miles, cruising at an easy 50 mph (80 km/h). Compared with most pre-1939 cars, it handles effortlessly.

There are at least four road-going Alfonso's in Australia, with four more in the course of restoration. A further twelve models (six in museums) are known to exist in other parts of the world.

MECHANICAL FEATURES

Engine: Four-cylinder, twin overhead camshafts, capacity 4088 ccs, rated at 16.9 HP, developing 72 BHP at 2300 rpm. Centrifugal water pump, 3-jet Hispano carburettor, magneto ignition.
Gearbox: Four-speed unit built integrally with engine. Exceptional smooth and easy change from right hand gear lever. Leather-faced cone clutch.
Suspension: Semi-elliptic springs front and rear, full double-acting Hispano-Suiza hydraulic shock absorbers.
Brakes: Rod actuated internal expanding drum brakes at rear operated by hand with transmission brake working from foot pedal.
Steering: Worm-and-sector, with 41 ft (12.5 m) and 1¾ turns lock-to-lock.
Wheels: Beaded edge size 815 x 105.
Dimensions: Wheelbase 8 ft 8 ins (2642 mm). Track 4 ft 0 ins (1220 mm). Overall length 13 ft 6 ins (4115 mm). Height 3 ft 10 ins (1168 mm). Kerb weight 17 cwt (865 kg).
Performance: Maximum speed when new — 86 mph (137 km/h). Normal cruising speed — 60 mph (100 km/h). Fuel consumption at highway speeds — 19 mpg (14.9 litres/100 km).

1914 Rolls-Royce Alpine Eagle

THE MARQUE

A brief history of the Rolls-Royce Silver Ghost 40/50 HP is given earlier with the description of the 1912 Rolls-Royce limousine. Just as the 40/50 HP was never correctly known as the Silver Ghost, so the sporty Alpine Eagle carried an unofficial name. Alpine Eagle was the name coined after a modified Silver Ghost with a special light weight 'Continental' body had won the 1913 Austrian Alpine Trial, then considered Europe's toughest test for a production vehicle.

The name became widely used. An article on a similar car to this one, published in the English magazine, *Autocar* (June 1915), said: "The 'Alpine Eagle' type R-R chassis has certain features differing from the standard four-speed type to render it more suitable for Alpine touring. For instance, the radiator is larger, holding 12 gallons of water, the brakes are larger and the frame has a tie-rod under each side member to stiffen it to resist the stresses imposed by high speed work on bad roads."

There is little doubt that the engines were modified too, developing around 65 BHP at 1600 rpm, compared with 48 BHP at 1200 rpm for the standard unit. Known as 'Eagle' engines, they were revving up to 2600 rpm, against the recommended 1700 rpm for the standard engine of the same year.

Apart from two attempts at the Tourist Trophy on the Isle of Man, (Charles Rolls winning the second attempt in 1906), the factory did little actual racing. It competed with distinction in numerous trials and, in 1911, recorded the magic 'ton' (100 mph) at Brooklands, with a special racing body. Basically, though, the Silver Ghost was a refined touring car and its competition activities were confined to endurance events.

In 1912 a wealthy enthusiastic owner, James Radley, entered his Ghost in the Austrian Alpine Trial. It was one of the first of the modified Ghosts with a three-speed gearbox, an innovation thrust on Henry Royce because some owners disliked using the overdrive fourth gear in the manner he intended. The colourful James Radley was daring to the point of eccentricity, and the British motoring press gleefully sent a photographer and reporter to record his progress.

The shattering news was published that Britain's pride and joy had come quietly to rest on a one-in-four gradient known as Katschberg and could not proceed until two of the occupants had stepped out. The news stunned the factory, especially as several relatively cheap cars had sailed up the hill.

Being a matter of honour, Royce entered a team of four cars in the 1913 event having sent out a small team to inspect the hill and report on the necessary modifications. The specially prepared cars (including a private one for Radley) were fitted with a four-speed gearbox, a pepped up engine, appropriate gear ratios and light weight touring bodies.

The cars dominated the event, with Radley the star driver. An amazing man, he had driven from Paris to Vienna non-stop for the event, then accepted a bet that he could not drive from Vienna to Klagenfurt and back (640 km) between sunset and sunrise. He did, collected the stake money, snatched a few hours' sleep, and set off in the gruelling Alpine Trial.

Radley held an impressive lead of 40 minutes at the end of the first day, but was almost disqualified during the second day when he swept past the official car on the feared Katschberg hill — overtaking the official car was against the rules. After two more days of slithering icy bends and steep mountain passes, Radley came home an easy winner, well ahead of the Rolls-Royce factory drivers.

All Ghosts with similar chassis specifications and a Continental touring body were immediately called 'Alpine Eagles'. Most bodies were built by Vanden Plas (who then had factories in Britain, France and Belgium). Though ostensibly a fast tourer, the Alpine Eagle was the closest thing to a sports car that Rolls-Royce had ever built up until the time they purchased Bentley.

All Silver Ghosts are rare and valuable, with the Alpine Eagle an exceptional collector's piece. As a point of interest, James Radley sold his winning car for £1450 ($2900) immediately after the trial to Jeremy Bacon who drove it daily until 1934 when he accepted £100 ($200) from a local garage. During the 1950s, the ex-Radley Alpine was restored to its former glory and today is worth quite a considerable amount on the market.

1914 ALPINE EAGLE 40/50

This rare example of a genuine Rolls-Royce Alpine with an original Belgian Vanden Plas body was built for the Duke of Westminster in 1914. World War One broke out later that year and the five seater Alpine became a staff car.

After two years of hard service, it followed the fate of many Silver Ghosts and became an armoured car, carrying very heavy protective steel plates. It saw active service with the Duke in Palestine and had its original body refitted after the War.

The car appears to have been shipped to Australia about 1930. For the next twenty years it was used as a station hack in New South Wales, turning up in 1959 in Mildura, Victoria, dilapidated and damaged. The present owner, Gavin Sandford-Morgan, of Walkerville, South Australia, commenced restoration in 1969, finishing one year later. He handled the mechanical work himself, with help rebuilding the Torpedo touring body from George Loveday. The trim was restored by Tom Butterfield.

MECHANICAL FEATURES

Engine: Six-cylinder, 7.4 litre capacity, side valve, rated at 48 HP, developing about 65 BHP at 1600 rpm. Water pump cooling, Rolls-Royce carburettor, Bosch magneto and R-R trembler coil, distributor ignition.
Gearbox: Conventional selective sliding pinion gearbox with four forward gears and cone clutch. Torque tube drive.
Suspension: Quarter-elliptic springs at front, cantilever springs at rear.
Brakes: Rod actuated internal expanding drum brakes at rear.
Steering: Worm-and-nut with 45 ft (13.7 m) turning circle and 2½ turns lock-to-lock.
Wheels: Dunlop wire spoked, 895 x 135 mm.
Dimensions: Wheelbase 11 ft 11½ ins (3645 mm). Track 4 ft 8½ ins (1435 mm). Overall length 16 ft 0 ins (4877 mm). Kerb weight 34 cwt (1730 kg).
Performance: Maximum speed when new — 70 mph (112 km/h). Normal cruising speed — 60 mph (100 km/h). Fuel consumption at highway speeds — 10-12 mpg (23-28 litres/100 km).

RNS 555
72

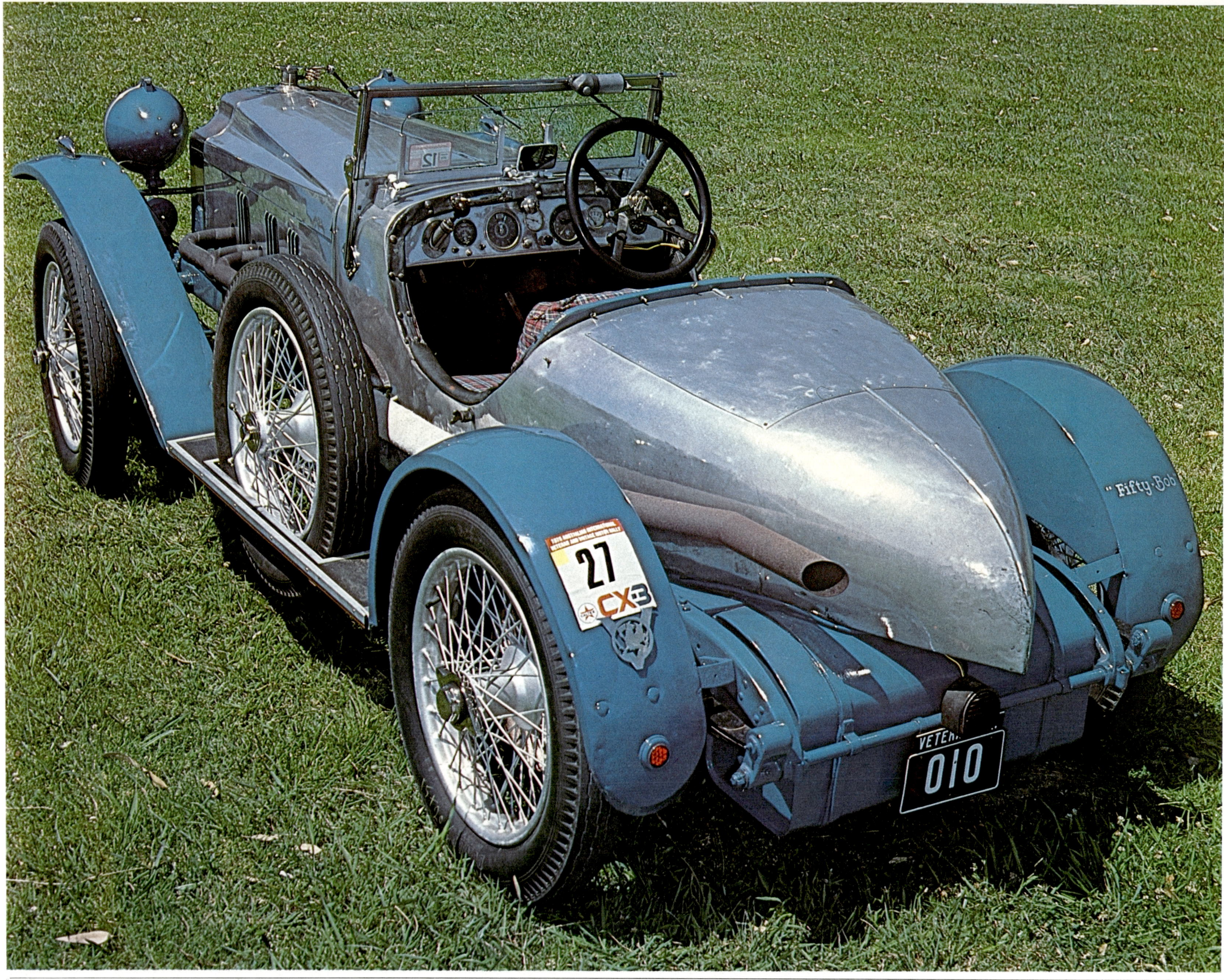
27
"Fifty-Bob
010

1914 Vauxhall 'Fifty Bob'

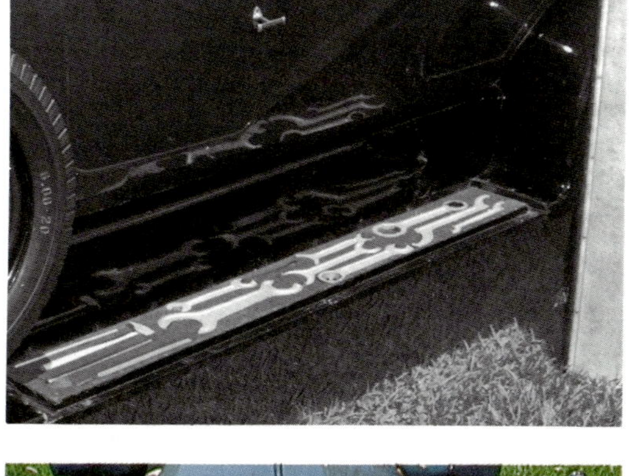

1914 A-TYPE SPORTS

After Edkins' death in 1930, 'Fifty Bob' was bought by one of his mechanics, Les Campbell, who used it as a hack. Around 1937 it was acquired by Bill Chadwick of Bathurst, who used it regularly for long trips. In 1948, with his family growing in number, he exchanged the two seater for a four seater Bentley owned by Jack Jeffery. Jeffery sold it to Ted Ansell who spent two hectic years driving in a variety of competition events.

In October 1950, Sandy Holmes, who had been on the lookout for a Bugatti, bought the Vauxhall for £225 ($450). For the next thirteen years it was almost his everyday car, used for his honeymoon, work and holidays. He also visited several States competing in veteran car events, and in 1956 won the Best Performance prize in the Veteran Car Club's first Blue Mountains Rally.

'Fifty Bob' has done an estimated 800,000 km since new. It is now owned by Martin, Sandy's son, and leads a comparatively quiet life.

THE MARQUE

Vauxhall was a British marine engineering firm whose first car appeared in 1903. Until it was purchased by General Motors in 1925, Vauxhall made some of the most attractive touring cars to come out of Britain. The Prince Henry sports car and the later 30/98s were the 'stuff that make legends'.

The man who did most to put Vauxhall on the Australian map was a former sheep station manager, Boyd Edkins. After some years working on the land in Queensland, Edkins joined the motor trade in Brisbane and, in 1912, established a Vauxhall distributorship in Sydney. Originally called Motor House, the firm was later renamed Boyded.

Edkins was a very competitive and skilful driver. When arch rival A. V. Turner started showing him a clean pair of exhaust pipes, Edkins cabled the Vauxhall factory asking for a suitable car. It happened that Laurence Pomeroy, the famous designer, was bench-testing an engine from an 'A'-type Vauxhall. The whole car had been returned by a customer who complained bitterly about the lack of performance. Testing the engine, Pomeroy found a casting defect. He machined the block and made a few modifications which not only fixed the trouble but boosted the power output to 68 BHP, the most the company had ever achieved from an 'A' type motor.

Meanwhile, the unhappy customer had been given a new car, so Pomeroy fitted the modified engine (which had been built in 1912) into a standard Model A 16/20 chassis and shipped it to Edkins, apparently without charge. It arrived in 1915.

The car was an immediate success, going far harder than other A-type Vauxhalls and giving Boyd an endless string of victories. Its chassis number was A210 which, in the currency of the day, sounded like £2/10/- or 'fifty bob'. The car has been 'Fifty Bob' ever since.

Though Vauxhall literature has referred to it as a Prince Henry model, it is not. The Prince Henry was a modified Model A, with a high performance engine, some rounded sections in the front of the chassis frame (presumably for stiffness) and a handsome Vee radiator. Only 43 Prince Henrys were made in 1914. 'Fifty Bob' appears to be a composite between a standard Type A and a true Prince Henry.

The 1913-14 Prince Henry was developed from the 25 HP 'D' type, but the earlier Prince Henry was developed from the 'A' type in 1912.

Whatever its nomenclature, Boyd Edkins exploited 'Fifty Bob's' power to the full. In March 1916 he drove 'Fifty Bob' from Melbourne to Sydney in under 17 hours, knocking 2 hours off the record. He then raced the Brisbane-Sydney express, but was stopped by a storm damaged road near Parramatta. At that time he was an amazing three hours ahead of the record.

'Fifty Bob's' career came to a peak in 1919-20 when Edkins was almost invincible in a cross section of motor sport. At the time the car had an attractive four seat touring body but in 1924 the chassis was shortened and the body removed for Maroubra speedway racing. A light weight alloy body was fitted — and has been on the car ever since.

At the end of 1924 Boyd Edkins received a letter from Vauxhall saying that the company was giving him a brand new 30/98 as a tribute to his success in racing and selling Vauxhalls. He gratefully accepted the car — but continued to drive 'Fifty Bob' as much as possible.

MECHANICAL FEATURES

Engine: Four-cylinder side valve, five main bearings and head integral with the block. Engine develops 68 BHP at 2500 rpm. Capacity 3.0 litres, bore and stroke 90 x 120 mm. Bosch ignition and Claudel-Hobson carburettor. Two plugs per cylinder.
Gearbox: Four-speed gearbox, with 3 to 1 axle ratio and a Hele-Shaw clutch.
Suspension: Semi-elliptic springs all round. Each spring very flexible with 13 thin tapered leaves.
Brakes: Fitted with four wheel brakes of Perrot design, taken from a Sunbeam.
Steering: Worm-and-wheel in an aluminium steering box, with ¾ turn lock-to-lock.
Wheels: Rudge-Whitworth knock-off type, 5.25 x 21 inch tyres.
Dimensions: Wheelbase 8 ft 10½ ins (2705 mm). Front track 4 ft 9 ins (1448 mm). Overall length 12 ft 6 ins (3810 mm). Height 4 ft 5 ins (1346 mm). Kerb weight 23½ cwt (1196 kg).
Performance: Maximum speed when new — 90 mph (144 km/h). Normal cruising speed — 60 mph (100 km/h). Fuel consumption at highway speeds — 22 mpg (11.7 litres/100 km).

33 x 4½ BARNET GLASS
35
041

1919 Australian Six

THE MARQUE

The first serious attempt to mass produce cars in Australia was the Australian Six, a Sydney based venture which assembled (and later substantially manufactured) cars from 1919 to 1930. More than 900 Australian Sixes were sold but only four are known to survive.

Before the firm went bankrupt with massive debts, it had shown that Australian made cars could be successfully exported but that local car makers could not compete in price against imported vehicles without tariff protection or a subsidy. The venture lost £1000 ($2000) on every car built, at a time when its work people were earning around £5 ($10) a week.

The new car was launched in 1919. By the end of that year, an advertisement in a trade journal claimed that the Australian Sixes were selling faster than the factory could build them. The claim was exaggerated, as only 49 were produced that year.

The man behind the project was Frederick Hugh Gordon, who obtained the distribution rights for the American built Mitchell. When sales began to decline, he decided to launch a car of his own, tailor made for local conditions. The true origins of the Australian Six are not known, but it is probable that it began as a modified version of the American 'B', a car built in 1918 by American Motor Corporation.

Gordon had visited America and placed orders for sufficient components to assemble 150 Australian Six chassis in Sydney. After assembly commenced, the factory found it had to modify many parts, including the radiator which

over-heated in hot weather. It also had to switch to Grant-Lees gearboxes as the original unit was proving unsatisfactory.

The Australian Six was initially advertised at £495 ($990), but within three years the price had almost doubled. One reason was that the erratic supply of imported parts and the associated engineering costs had forced Gordon to have many of the components made locally. The lower production volume made these parts much dearer than the imported equivalent. As the car's price rose, sales dropped. Gordon tried to boost sales by establishing two speed records, but by 1924 he was forced to pull out of the venture.

The engineering firm of Harkness and Hillier, a major creditor, took over. It continued assembly of the chassis, using a range of locally made bodies, including coupé and touring styles. To reduce costs the new management moved to smaller premises. They also switched to a more powerful Ansted engine with overhead valves. They engaged in a variety of motor sport events, including a successful attack on the Melbourne-Sydney speed record. An Australian Six with a specially tuned engine clocked 80 mph (128 km/h) but this did little to stimulate sales. During 1930 the last six cars were built and the factory closed.

1919 AUSTRALIAN SIX ROADSTER

Simon Kelleher, who is the grandson of Frederick Gordon, saw his first Australian Six in 1966. He acquired a derelict model which had been on blocks in Queanbeyan for 27 years, and restored it. Then at Dareton, Victoria, he located the wreck which formed the basis of the roadster shown on opposite page. It had been owned by a Mr Schadwick who brought it in 1946 for £140 ($280) from a Mr Hayes, of Albury, New South Wales.

Simon Kelleher took over the car in 1967 and had a new body professionally built, based on a photograph showing a businessman's roadster on the original Australian Six assembly line. The major restoration work was done by Albert Michel, of Narellan, New South Wales.

MECHANICAL FEATURES

Engine: Six-cylinder, American built Rutenber of 3.7 litres developing 45 BHP at 2400 rpm. Detachable L-head cylinder head, side valve, water-cooled with Zenith carburettor and Westinghouse ignition. Features include a Westinghouse starter, plus an engine-driven air pump for inflating the tyres.
Gearbox: Grant-Lees crash type with three forward gears driving an imported Columbia differential. Multi-plate Borg and Beck clutch.
Suspension: Orthodox with semi-elliptic springs at the front and rear.
Brakes: Two separate systems — one internal expanding, one external expanding. Both operate on 15 inch diameter (380 mm) drums.
Steering: Worm-and-sector. 24″ disc wheels, large turning circle.
Dimensions: Wheelbase 10 ft 2 ins (3099 mm).
Performance: Maximum speed when new — 60 mph (100 km/h). Normal cruising speed — 45 mph (72 km/h). Fuel consumption at highway speeds — 12 mpg (23 litres/100 km).

1920 Isotta-Fraschini

THE MARQUE

Isotta-Fraschini, the Italian car firm, was founded in 1899 by Cesare Isotta and Vincenzo Fraschini who had acquired the rights to assemble and sell Renaults. Within three years the young firm launched its own design. In 1904, a new factory was built in Milan and the firm developed an unswerving belief in the future demand for large, powerful and very expensive machines.

The influence of Ettore Bugatti is evident in some early designs, as Bugatti was engineering consultant for Lorraine-Dietrich, the French firm which acquired a controlling interest in Isotta-Fraschini.

Like many firms of the day, Isotta raced. It scored important victories in the Targa Florio and the Coppa Florio, plus numerous successes in the United States where the marque flourished.

In 1910, Isotta-Fraschini joined the ranks of the motoring immortals by producing the KM model. Probably inspired by Bugatti, the design featured four gigantic cylinders, overhead camshaft, with 16 valves, and an unbelievable power for the day — 140 BHP at 1800 rpm. Equally interesting was a successful system of four-wheel brakes developed by Oreste Fraschini, brother of Vincenzo. They were the first to be fitted to a production car.

During World War One, the company developed an entirely new model, the Type 8, featuring the world's first straight eight engine to go into production. The prototype was built in 1916, but it was not until 1919 that Type 8's began to reach the public. Designed by chief engineer Giustino Cattaneo, it had a 5.9 litre engine developing 75.9 BHP at 2200 rpm, with overhead valves, an aluminium crankcase and cast iron cylinder block. The crankshaft is machined from one massive billet of forged steel.

The Type 8 continued until 1924 and was replaced by the Type 8A, with an even larger engine (7.4 litres) and power assisted four-wheel brakes. It ran until 1931 when the Type 8B was announced.

By then the Depression had decimated the number of people able to pay $10,000 or more for four-wheeled luxury cars. As fewer and fewer cars were sold, Isotta Fraschini concentrated on marine and aircraft engines. The last Type 8B was built in 1935.

After World War Two, the company tried to return to the auto field with the rear engined V-8 Type 8C, but the concern quietly folded in 1949.

Though little known today, Isotta-Fraschini once ranked with Rolls-Royce and Hispano-Suiza. In 1929 the firm printed a list of its top clients, which included His Holiness the Pope, a queen, king, empress, princes, princess, maharajahs, the Aga Khan, Benito Mussolini, plus assorted dukes, duchesses, barons, counts and viscounts. Prominent American owners included Clara Bow, Rudolf Valentino, William Hearst and Jack Dempsey.

Only 83 Isottas are known to survive; eight are in Australia.

1920 TYPE 8 TORPEDO TOURER

Originally imported in 1920, this magnificent road machine was fitted with a large touring and camping body by the Sydney agents, Phizackerly & Co. Made from aluminium panels, the body had a

large and most comprehensive tool kit built into the running board. Another unusual feature was a 25 gallon fuel tank, necessary because the heavy car (2½ tons) returns only 8 miles per gallon. The fuel consumption was probably the reason why the Type 8 was laid up on blocks before World War Two, and remained unused for twenty years.

Prior to that it had only a few owners. The new car had originally been sold to a buyer in Grafton, New South Wales. It went through two other hands before being laid up in Armidale, New South Wales. In 1957 it was acquired by Lyndon Hardman and restored by him, with help from the trim firm, Blencowe & Son, Armidale.

MECHANICAL FEATURES

Engine: Straight eight and 5.9 litres with 9 main bearings and tubular con-rods. Engine rated at 38 HP, developing 75.9 BHP at 2200 rpm. Overhead valves, two side draught Zenith carburettors and Bosch magneto.
Gearbox: Crash type with three forward gears and centre ball control. Multi-plate dry clutch.
Suspension: Semi-elliptics front and rear, the rear springs being unusually long and wide.
Brakes: Rod operated internal expanding brakes on four wheels. The handbrake also operates on the four wheels. The drums are finned.
Steering: Very direct with 1¼ turns lock-to-lock.
Wheels: Michelin disc, 6.50 x 20 ins.
Dimensions: Wheelbase 12 ft 1 in (3683 mm). Overall length 16 ft 10 ins (5131 mm). Height 5 ft 9 ins (1753 mm). Kerb weight 44¾ cwt (2278 kg).
Performance: Maximum speed when new — 70 mph (112 km/h). Normal cruising speed — 50 mph (80 km/h). Fuel consumption at highway speeds — 8 mpg (35 litres/100 km).

1921 Alfa Romeo G1

THE MARQUE

Henry Ford's name has been linked with other famous cars. He once explained to a group of pressmen that he had arrived in a Rolls-Royce 'because there was no Ford available so I took the next best car'. On another occasion he said: 'I raise my hat when I see an Alfa Romeo go by'.

And well he might, for the Italian company has long been noted for its stirring designs, the fruity chirp of its exhaust and the sheer magic of road manners.

Surprisingly, the Italian company owes its birth to a Frenchman, Alexandre Darracq, who founded a small shop on the outskirts of Milan to assemble his French built cars. Three years later the factory was taken over by Anonima Lombarda Fabbrica Automobili (A.L.F.A.) and by 1910 the company had launched its own range of 15/20 HP and 20/30 HP cars.

An imaginative and energetic new manager, Nicola Romeo, was appointed in 1914 and within four years had acquired a controlling interest. He added his name to the factory's products, and they were not confined to cars. The firm produced a bit of everything: compressors, rock drills, railroad equipment, tractors, air brakes and machines for the building industry.

But it was cars that made Alfa Romeo a legendary name around the world. Its competition successes were the envy of the entire industry. According to Lawrence Pomeroy, the celebrated British automotive historian, Alfa Romeo won 58 'Great Races' in Europe between 1909 and 1953, compared with 34 by Mercedes, 33 by Bugatti and 21 by Ferrari. Alfa's most famous racing model, the P2, won its first Grand Prix in August 1924, but it was partly derived from a car almost unmentioned in the factory's official history. The Type G1 was born in 1921 and raced by Antonia Ascari, Ugo Sivocci and Giuseppe Campari. Between them, they collected a whole string of victories at a time when the racing world had scarcely heard of Alfa Romeo.

1921 ALFA ROMEO G1

This is the only known survivor of a batch of 52 Type G1's built in 1921. One was ear-marked for Enzo Ferrari, then an Alfa factory driver. Seven came to Australia, but little is known about the car's racing history, if in fact, the model had one.

The early days of this survivor are also sketchy. It is believed that a grazier originally imported the chassis for £850 ($1700) and had a body fitted. He took the car to his property, Cressy Station, near Winton, Queensland, but had little time to become acquainted with it. He was declared bankrupt. Rather than lose his beloved car, he placed it under the care of a neighbouring grazier named McKenzie, on Lorraine Downs.

McKenzie put the car on blocks where it stayed untouched for 25 years. Around 1947 two lads on the property fired up the big Alfa and had the time of their lives charging around the paddocks.

The rough treatment eventually caused the rear axle pinion to snap, and when the car was later found the pinion was missing. The car was then converted into a stationary power source, driving a water pump, its body taken off, the tail shaft cut and the wheels chopped down. The car was then 26 years old — but its speedometer showed only 1000 miles.

In 1964 a mechanic, Roger Young, was asked to replace the rather thirsty Alfa set-up with a more modern Buick engine. He did so and when told that the Alfa would be dumped, advised Don Roberts, a well-known Queensland enthusiast. Don and George Roberts, with Dave Fiechtner, heard that some of the car's parts were in the local tip. With the aid of the car's headlights they located the wheels the same night.

The remains were acquired in 1965 by the present owner, Ross Flewell-Smith, of Ipswich, Queensland. Ross was fortunate in that he found some parts from another G in Wangaratta, Victoria, which helped him complete his restoration. These parts came from a similar Alfa imported by a grazier named Saxton.

Over a ten year period, with the aid of drawings from the factory in Milan, Ross completely rebuilt the car to its present magnificent condition. The trim was done by Keith Albury of Brisbane.

The restoration has been so successful that the car won the Queensland Vintage Car Concours in 1977 and was awarded first place in the historic Mille Miglia Memorial Run, conducted by Alfa Romeo, Australia in March 1978. During this event, the big red Alfa was timed at 86 mph (138 km/h).

MECHANICAL FEATURES

Engine: Six-cylinder, side valve design, non-detachable heads, with two blocks of three cylinders, offset from the centre line. Cam ground pistons and priming cup on each cylinder. Capacity 6.33 litres, rated at 35.7 HP, developing 70 BHP at 2100 rpm. Smith carburettor now fitted in place of original Zenith unit; magneto ignition, water pump cooling.
Gearbox: Straight cut crash-type four-speed unit with multi-plate dry clutch and open shaft drive to rear axle with separate torque arm.
Suspension: Semi-elliptic at front, very long twin cantilever springs at rear.
Brakes: Hand operated internal expanding on wheels, with foot pedal acting on transmission brake.
Steering: Worm-and-wheel, with one turn lock-to-lock.
Wheels: Sankey, 895 x 135 mm.
Dimensions: Wheelbase 11 ft 2 ins (3404 mm). Overall length 15 ft 0 ins (4572 mm). Height 5 ft 0 ins (1524 mm). Kerb weight 30 cwt (1527 kg).
Performance: Maximum speed when new — 86 mph (137 km/h). Normal cruising speed — 60 mph (97 km/h). Fuel consumption at highway speeds — 10-12 mpg (23-28 litres/100 km).

1921 Mercedes Targa

THE MARQUE

The companies founded by Gottlieb Daimler and Karl Benz were fierce rivals until they merged in 1926. Both men had built motorised vehicles in 1885-86 and, quite independently, did more to make the modern car a reality than any other men in history.

In a sense they also pioneered motor sport. The Daimler-engined Peugeot and the Benz-built Victoria started things off in the 1894 Paris-Rouen race and Mercedes remained actively engaged in motor sport until 1955.

The first Mercedes, which left the Daimler assembly lines in 1901, was not a true racing car, but it decisively won all the major events in the Nizza Speed Week, then the most strenuous and difficult racing contest in the world. In 1911, a 4.5 litre Mercedes racing car gained a triple victory in the French Grand Prix, the winner completing the 750 km course at an average speed of 104 km/h.

Following the death of his father in 1900, Paul Daimler became chief engineer. About the same time, French financier and sportsman, Emil Jellinek, acting as general agent for Daimler in France, commissioned some specially built Daimler cars for sale in France and Austria. He asked that they be called Mercedes, after the name of his daughter. (Jellinek's wife was Spanish). The cars and the name proved popular, and within a few years all German-built Daimler cars were known as Mercedes models.

Daimler and Benz continued their rivalry into the 1920s. In 1921 the two firms threw their might against each other at the Avis track and the 10/30 Benz sports car came first. But Mercedes made amends at the Targa Florio Race of the same year, with its 28/95, which came second to a much modified Fiat. Another works driver, Count Masetti, used a Mercedes Grand Prix car to win the Targa Florio in 1922.

The 28/95 sportster was a most interesting design. Its power plant, a massive 7.3 litre six, was derived directly from the DF80 aircraft engine, developed in 1912 and extensively used in World War One.

Mercedes had planned to produce the 28/95 as an unusually powerful touring

car in 1915, but World War One intervened. According to the official factory history, the first 28/95 was built in 1914, but sales of the vehicle were delayed until after the War.

With the 28/95, Paul Daimler began experiments in automotive super-charging, following the company's aircraft practice, using twin-bladed Roots blowers. The Targa was fitted with a 120 BHP blown engine for the 1922 racing season, the blower being housed at the rear left hand side of the engine.

The engine itself has three pairs of steel cylinders, with 105 mm x 140 mm bore and stroke, giving a capacity of 7.4 litres. It developed 95 BHP at 1800 rpm, more in racing tune. Overhead valves formed in the shape of a Vee are actuated by an overhead camshaft, with a full hemispherical combustion chamber.

1921 28/95 TARGA

It is doubtful if any car in Australia can top this superb machine for its looks, thunderous performance and starkly elegant appearance. The owner, Ted Lobb of Grenfell, New South Wales, knows none of the car's history other than that it was imported in 1923 by Myer, then the Mercedes agents in Bourke Street, Melbourne.

In recent years, the 28/95 was discovered abandoned on a property near Moree, New South Wales. It was later acquired by Jack Jeffery in the mid 1950s. The next owner was C. B. Jacquet of Rowena, New South Wales. Ted Lobb acquired the car in 1976 and entrusted the restoration to Rod Warriner, one of Melbourne's most meticulous and talented restoration engineers. Rod carried out the mechanical restoration himself and, with a colleague named Syd Ward, built a full replica body, based on drawings supplied by the curator of the Mercedes-Benz museum at Stuttgart. The curator also authenticated that this extremely rare car is a genuine 1921 28/95 Targa. The only other one known to exist is on display at the Harrah Museum in Nevada.

Superlatively restored, the Targa gave Gwen and Ted Lobb a spirited and trouble-free ride in the 1978 International Rally.

MECHANICAL FEATURES

Engine: Basically a DF80 aircraft engine designed in 1912, it has six cylinders, 7.4 litre capacity, overhead valves; rated at 41 HP, developing 100 BHP at 1800 rpm. Maximum engine speed 2300 rpm. Twin Mercedes carburettors, magneto ignition.
Gearbox: Four-speed gearbox, separate from the engine. Double cone clutch.
Suspension: Semi-elliptic springs front and rear.
Brakes: Four wheel brakes, internal expanding type.
Steering: Worm-and-sector.
Wheels: Rudge knock-off wire wheels, 21 inch tyres. Originally 935 x 135 beaded edge tyres were fitted.
Dimensions: Wheelbase 10 ft 0.6 ins (1930 mm). Overall length 14 ft 2 ins (4318 mm). Height 4 ft 2 ins (1270 mm). Kerb weight 29 cwt (1476 kg).
Performance: Maximum speed when new — 100 mph (160 km/h). Normal cruising speed — 70 mph (112 km/h). Fuel consumption at highway speeds — 6 mpg (47 litres/100 km).

NSW
OB-091

1921 Spyker Torpedo

THE MARQUE

Spyker, the Dutch firm is best known as the maker of the world's first front-wheel-drive car, a racing vehicle which appeared in 1902. But Spyker also made extremely fine touring cars. Had Government policy permitted some kind of tariff protection, the small but extremely talented firm might have emerged as the Rolls-Royce of Europe.

The company was well established as a carriage maker when it built its first car in 1896. The development of some twin-cylinder models commenced, but meanwhile Jacobus Spyker, the younger of the two brothers running the firm, laid down plans to build a revolutionary racing car which he hoped to use in the 1903 Paris-Madrid Race. The concept was staggering. Not only did the four-wheel-drive system employ the basic principles later followed by Willys and others, but the car had the first six-cylinder engine, the first wind-cheating, vee-shaped radiator and the first four-wheel brake system.

Unhappily it was not a success, proving unreliable, possibly because of its weight. The massive 8.7 litre engine developed a modest 40 BHP at 1400, enough to provide a maximum speed of 46 mph (75 km/h), which was not race material, even in 1903. The four-wheel-drive car is now part of the fabulous collection owned by Dutch industrialist, Max Lips, and was never considered good enough to actually race, though it made several appearances in motor shows. The company offered it for sale, along with more conventional two-wheel-drive 32/40 HP models.

Spyker went on to build a series of extremely well engineered orthodox cars. The promotional literature, which came with the 1921 Torpedo shown on page 126 mentions the firm's 'famous success on the Pekin-Paris Race' and goes on to describe an impressive endurance feat witnessed by the Royal Netherlands Auto Club. Between November 1920 and

January 1921, a stock Spyker 30/40 HP model covered 18,600 miles (30,000 km) in 36 days on public roads, averaging over 35 km/h. Only £2 ($4) was spent on replacement parts during the run and, afterwards, the Royal Auto Club found the car was in 'a most excellent condition'.

Spyker made a range of bodies for their six-cylinder chassis in 1921, including a cabriolet and landaulet. They describe the Torpedo as an 'open tourer representing the highest possible achievement in respect of comfort, appearance and road worthiness. Its hood can be operated by one person.'

A unique feature of all Spykers was the use of heavy gauge aluminium for the body, mudguards, bonnet and running boards. This is why so many were broken up during World War Two for use by the German military industry.

Spyker built aircraft, aircraft engines and cars, but in 1926 the Dutch Government allowed the unrestricted entry of low priced American cars,

putting Spyker out of business. A liquidation auction followed and the remaining eighteen cars, all unassembled, were sold off. Today only three six-cylinder Spykers are known to survive in the world.

Ironically, the company's sales literature carried a rather guarded promise. It said that the car was 'guaranteed for life, provided the chassis is sent once every two years to one of our works for inspection and left at our disposal for purposes of effecting all such work as we deem necessary on the owner's account'.

1921 TORPEDO 30/40

Though Spykers were made in Holland, they were distributed overseas by the British Spyker Company of Holland. The local selling agent was Edmunds Brothers & Co., of Melbourne.

In 1921 a Mrs Mitchell purchased this Torpedo new as a wedding present for her second husband, a Mr Baysley, of Mullengandra Station, New South Wales. The car was fairly extensively used and, in 1933, was put in storage where it remained until 1960.

It was sold to the late Jack Jeffery. Two years later it was acquired by the present owner, Owen Bourke, of St. Ives, New South Wales, who completely restored the car to its original factory condition. Brian Hawke looked after the body and paint work. The original leather trim was in sound condition and retained. The five year restoration was completed in 1967.

The rebuilt car proved a remarkably pleasant and reliable performer, competing in the 1970 and 1978 International Veteran and Vintage Rally. The engine is German, not Dutch, built by Mayback, and is virtually a scaled down WWI aircraft unit, developing 72 BHP from 5.7 litres. The gearbox is believed to have been made in France.

MECHANICAL FEATURES

Engine: Six-cylinder 5.74 litres, built by Mayback in Germany, rated at 30 HP, developing 72 BHP at 2200 rpm. Spyker carburettor, 95 x 135 mm bore and stroke, dual magneto and coil ignition.
Gearbox: Four-speed conventional design with enclosed propeller shaft and spiral bevel drive. Single plate dry clutch. Unusual gate change with 2nd and 3rd at the top of the H pattern.
Suspension: Long semi-elliptic springs front and rear.
Brakes: Rear wheel brakes with internal expanding shoes, rod operated.
Steering: Conventional design.
Wheels: Wire spoked detachable, size 700 x 21.
Dimensions: Wheelbase 11 ft 5 ins (3470 mm). Track 4 ft 9 ins (1440 mm). Overall length 16 ft 8 ins (5100 mm). Kerb weight 44 cwt (2250 kg).
Performance: Maximum speed when new — 80 mph (128 km/h). Normal cruising speed — 50 mph (80 km/h). Fuel consumption at highway speeds — 12 mpg (23 litres/100 km).

STUTZ
STUTZ

1921 Stutz Tourer

THE MARQUE

Harry Stutz was a clever component manufacturer who owned an engineering factory in Indianapolis, United States of America. In 1911, having heard that a 500 mile race was to be run at the nearby oval test track, Stutz designed and built a racing car within five weeks. It came eleventh.

Realising that the buying public has a remarkable weakness for remembering facts, Stutz launched replicas of the racer with the slogan 'The Car That Made Good in a Day'. Few buyers checked on the dubious feat of scrambling into eleventh place in a virtually unknown event, and Stutz found ample buyers.

In 1913 he turned to full time car manufacture. He designed one of the best remembered American cars of all time, the Bearcat. For $US2000 the buyer had a choice of four or six-cylinder engines in a sportster that was little more than a chassis with mudguards. As one observer put it: 'Everything which did not rust, including the passengers, was out in the open.'

The rakish machine clocked 80 mph (128 km/h) which pleased Stutz so much that he designed a 100 mph (160 km/h) racing version with twin overhead camshafts and four valves per cylinder. The four valves per cylinder and separate camshafts for the inlet and exhaust valves continued with the production engines, but for them Stutz used a less expensive T-head.

By 1919 Stutz was tired of the business and sold it. The new owners began concentrating on orthodox, conventional tourers, using the engine and trans-axle designs bequeathed by Stutz. Later they switched to conventional gearboxes and more powerful engines. By 1932 the factory was boasting the famous DV32 with an eight-cylinder engine producing a remarkable 161 HP. Even this was not enough to ward off the gloom of the Depression and, in 1934, the company crashed.

Many thousands of Stutz were made; few survive.

1921 STUTZ FOUR

Doug Grant, of Carlton, New South Wales, made a rare find in 1967 with the discovery of a pair of identical 1921 Stutz tourers on a property near Clifton, Queensland. They had been imported by George Anderson and his brother for use in adjoining properties and were still there.

The cars had suffered badly with the years, one being converted into a utility around 1930, then later abandoned. The other had been pulled apart and its seats and other parts used around the homestead.

Doug Grant acquired the bits and worked for eighteen months, often sixteen hours a day, seven days a week, building one factory-fresh Stutz from the two wrecks.

The finished job is magnificent, differing from the 1921 design in having neoprene oil seals. The 'close coupled' touring body is original, though a few panels were too rusty to salvage. The shade of red paint is also correct. Stutz offered this model in two colours only, red and blue, and Doug was able to obtain a sample colour from Ed Brubecker, a nephew of Harry C. Stutz. He owns a large collection of Stutz cars and keeps them in fuel and oil by working as a musician.

The design has several interesting features. The front bumper is spring-loaded to absorb minor bumps. The three-speed gearbox is built into the back axle. A valve mounted on the steering column cuts off the fuel supply, providing maximum engine braking for crash stops, in theory but not always in practice. The electric system has an ingenious buzzer which would sound off if a short circuit occurred.

The 1921 Stutz has covered a great deal of ground since restoration was completed in 1968. The large capacity four-cylinder engine provides unusually brisk acceleration and a timed maximum speed of 82 mph (131 km/h). By the standards of the day, the road holding and handling are excellent.

MECHANICAL FEATURES

Engine: Four-cylinder 5.9 litres, twin cam, side valve. Rated at 30.6 HP developing 88 BHP at 2400 rpm. Water-cooling, Stromberg updraught carburettor, twin ignition system. Unusual features include four valves per cylinder and four bolts per connecting rod big end.

Gearbox: Stutz-made three-speed selective sliding gearbox built into back axle. It has a 14-plate multi-disc clutch. Spiral bevel drive.

Suspension: Conventional leaf springs, with Timkin beam axle at front and three-quarters floating rear axle. Adjustable Hartford shock absorbers.

Brakes: Large 18 inch (457 mm) diameter rear brakes drums with two sets of shoes, one for service brake, one for parking brake.

Steering: Worm-and-gear with 1½ turns lock-to-lock.

Wheels: Houlke wire wheels, size 23 inch.

Dimensions: Wheelbase 10 ft 10 ins (3300 mm). Track 4 ft 8 ins (1422 mm). Overall length 16 ft 0 ins (4877 mm). Height 5 ft 7½ ins (1714 mm). Kerb weight 36 cwt (1833 kg).

Performance: Maximum speed when new — 82 mph (131 km/h). Normal cruising speed — 55 mph (88 km/h). Fuel consumption at highway speeds — 16 mpg (17.6 litres/100 km).

1922 Essex Model 'A'

THE MARQUE

An off-shoot of Hudson Motor Car Company, Essex was introduced in 1919 as a low cost line to compete with Chevrolet. The first Essex, the only one with a big four-cylinder engine, is now recognised as the best of the marque, as it had character as well as a lively power-to-weight ratio. The 2.86 litre Four featured automatic spark advance and a Ricardo F-head with overhead inlet and side exhaust. A lock-up type gearbox was offered as an extra. Fitted with a Hudson carburettor, the Essex gave better than average fuel economy.

By 1922, the two-door coupé and its sedan counterpart were top sellers, retailing for $US1295 at a time when a similar looking Chevrolet 4 cost $1325 or a six-cylinder Buick coupé $1795.

In Australia the marque was inextricably linked with Norman 'Wizard' Smith, the best known speedster of the day. Smith had joined the Essex Sydney agents, Dalgety and Co., at the time they accepted the new franchise. He drove a specially tuned Essex Model 'A' in a series of convincing wins in reliability trials and hill climbs and caused a minor sensation when his Essex covered a

measured mile at a speed of 93 mph (148 km/h). Within a year, Smith had won all major car trials in New South Wales — a feat which caused his rivals to dub him 'Wizard', the name he was known by for the rest of his life.

City-to-city speed records were fashionable in the 1920s. Smith established the first of many after hearing that his old tutor, A. V. Turner, had broken the Melbourne-Sydney record. Wizard took the trusty Essex, and after hitting speeds as high as 80 mph (128 km/h) on the dusty, rutted roads, knocked 68 minutes off Turner's run. He went on to establish new records between Brisbane-Sydney, Adelaide-Melbourne and Hobart-Launceston and, more than anyone, helped put Essex on the Australian map.

Essex's popularity was short lived. In 1924 the company decided to follow some rivals into the six-cylinder field. Their new models became less exciting and in 1933, Hudson replaced the Essex brand with a new name — Terraplane.

Surprisingly few Essex Model 'A's survive, there being seven known examples in Australia.

1922 ESSEX 'A' ROADSTER

Owned by Barry and Wilma Pusey of Valentine, New South Wales, this immaculate example has a custom-built body. It was made by the Sydney firm of Smith and Waddington, for the original owner, Dr Joseph McElhone.

The chassis was shipped from Hudson in Detroit to Sydney where the body was fitted. A well known sportsman (he later established the McElhone foundation for sport), the doctor used the Essex to win several side bets. One bet was won by climbing Knobs Hill in top gear — the first car to do so.

Dr McElhone used the Essex for four years, then sold it to Mr Eric Schiller Vogele of Port Macquarie, who christened it 'Elizabeth', the name it still carries. After 39 years, the car was purchased by a young man, Neville Unicorm of Cardiff, New South Wales. Barry Pusey acquired it in 1970 and, in eighteen months, restored it to its present condition.

It has since won a variety of awards, including the Best Vintage Car in the 1973 Australian Hub Rally, the Best Vintage in the 1974 Twin City Rally and for three consecutive years it was named as the Most Appealing Car at the annual Antique and Classic Motor Club Shoal Bay Rally. After competing in rallies in South Australia, Queensland, Victoria and New South Wales, the 1922 Essex has clocked up more than 32,000 miles (51,000 km) since its restoration.

MECHANICAL FEATURES

Engine: Four-cylinder 2.86 litres overhead inlet and side exhaust valve, rated at 18.2 HP, developing 55 BHP at 2800 rpm. Thermo-syphon water cooling. Hudson carburettor with pneumatic operated piston, splash oil system and coil ignition.
Gearbox: Sliding quadrant change with three forward gears and cork lined multi-plate clutch running in oil.
Suspension: Conventional semi-elliptic leaf springs front and rear.
Brakes: External contracting drums on rear wheels only.
Steering: Worm-and-gear system with 1½ turns lock-to-lock and 39 ft (12 m) turning circle.
Wheels: Artillery 24 ins.
Dimensions: Wheelbase 9 ft 0½ ins (2756 mm). Overall length 14 ft 3 ins (4343 mm). Kerb weight 23 cwt (1171 kg).
Performance: Maximum speed when new — 60 mph (100 km/h). Normal cruising speed — 45 mph (72 km/h). Fuel consumption at highway speeds — 27 mpg (10.5 litres/100 km).

NSW
RP·097
246
CX3

1923 Hillman Roadster

THE MARQUE

Hillman cars were born of a strange partnership between cigar-chomping Norfolk-suited English gentleman, William Hillman, and a brilliant young French designer, Louis Coatalen. Hillman owned a small but successful engineering shop; Coatalen gained his experience with Darracq in France and later designed a succession of Sunbeam, Talbot and Darracq cars. He cemented his friendship with Hillman by marrying his daughter.

Hillman was so keen to have a car bearing his name that he entered the 1907 Tourist Trophy race on the Isle of Man, even before the car was built.

But built it was, and in a hurry, with the guiding genius of Louis Coatalen. It was too much to expect victory from a brand new machine but Coatalen, driving the car himself, at least created a minor sensation by leading at the end of the first lap and setting a lap record in excess of 60 mph (100 km/h).

Delighted, Hillman set up a new factory in Coventry, the home of the British motor industry. His first production machine, a 25 HP four-cylinder tourer, was orthodox in design and it sold well, but Hillman decided to concentrate on small, low powered cars suitable for families of limited means. In 1910 he produced his first small car, a 12 HP landaulette. This was followed by a baby 9 HP light weight which kept the factory busy until World War One.

Having set his course, Hillman produced a new light car for the post-war years, an 11 HP model which stayed in production until the late 1920s. In many ways this was the pathfinder for the Austin and Morris baby cars which followed. Whilst they attracted large sales, Hillman did not, and he was forced to move up-market with a Hillman 14. Later, in 1928, he tried the luxury car field, with an overhead valve 2 litre straight eight, a distinguished and attractive car.

It was about this time that two energetic brothers, William and Reginald Rootes, owners of Britain's largest distribution firm, acquired control of Hillman and the neighbouring Humber company. The two factories were merged to form the Rootes Group. The Hillman division was instructed to continue a series of light cars, leading to a long succession of Minx models, whilst Humber pursued its traditional role in the luxury field.

After World War Two the Rootes Group fell on hard times and was eventually acquired by Chrysler, the name being changed to Chrysler U.K. In 1978 Peugeot of France bought the former Rootes factories and reverted to the name of Talbot, a name once associated with the Rootes Group.

1923 HILLMAN 11 HP ROADSTER

Little is known about the origins of this delightful little Hillman. Evidently it came to Australia when new, as it is fitted with a very pretty Australian made roadster body with room for an extra passenger in the dickey seat.

The present owners, Lyndon and Des Hardman, of Armidale, New South Wales, acquired the Hillman at a local property. During the early 1970s it was thoroughly restored by the late E. R. Hardman, with new trim fitted by Blencowe & Son, of Armidale.

The car is of orthodox design with a small side valve engine driving the rear axle through a three-speed crash box. An unusual feature is the location of the gear shift lever on the driver's right, between the seat and the body. Rolls-Royce and some other firms later adopted this position.

MECHANICAL FEATURES

Engine: Four-cylinder, 1593 ccs, side valve, rated at 10.4 HP, developing 20 BHP at 2000 rpm. Thermo-syphon cooling. Zenith side draught carburettor with high tension magneto.
Gearbox: Three-speed gate crash with lever inside body on driver's right. The leather-faced cone clutch has a rather aggressive action.

Suspension: Semi-elliptic springs front and rear.
Brakes: Internal expanding rod-operated brakes on rear wheels.
Steering: Worm-and-sector, with only 1 turn lock-to-lock.
Wheels: Beaded edge Sankey wheels 710 x 90.
Dimensions: Wheelbase 8 ft 8 ins (2642 mm). Overall length 12 ft 0 ins (3658 mm). Height 5 ft 3 ins (1600 mm). Kerb weight 15 cwt (764 kg).
Performance: Maximum speed when new — 55 mph (88 km/h). Normal cruising speed — 47 mph (75 km/h). Fuel consumption at highway speeds — 35 mpg (8 litres/100 km).

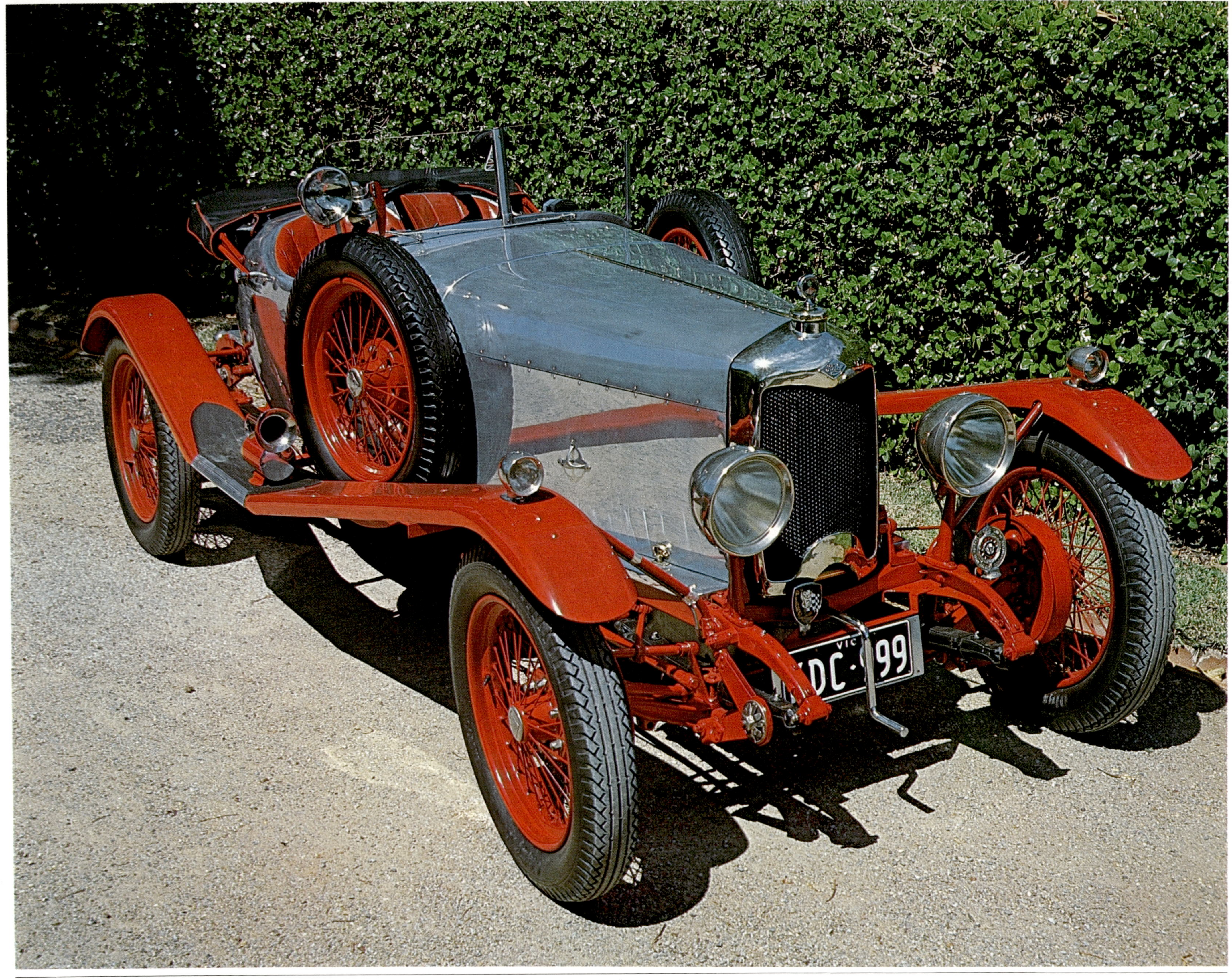

1923 Riley Redwing Sports Car

THE MARQUE

Riley was a prosperous family business even before it moved into cycle-making. Then in 1899, Percy Riley, son of William who founded the company, built a quadricycle with a 2½ HP De Dion engine. It was exhibited at Britain's National Cycle Show.

William Riley was against moving into car manufacture, so three of his sons established their own business, the Riley Engine Company. They developed a four-wheeler and, after a few years, father agreed to unite the two businesses under the name Riley (Coventry) Ltd.

His sons — Victor, Stanley, Percy, Alan and Cecil — enthusiastically took control of the new firm. Three of them were keen competition drivers and achieved some notable successes during the early days. At the time, wheel manufacture, not cars, provided the main business. The Riley patented centre-lock detachable wheel was bought by nearly two hundred firms, including Mercedes, Rolls-Royce, Hispano, Panhard and Renault. But in 1913, Percy, the engineering genius of the family, designed the first four-cylinder Riley, and the company was moving towards its great days.

Immediately after World War One, the brothers laid plans to export cars to countries as far afield as Australia, India and South Africa. Percy updated the pre-war model and designed a new engine which proved to be one of Britain's better units. Percy was one of the industry's first men to discover the importance of valve overlap and his study of camshaft designs led to a high revving engine which produced considerable power for its weight. The new unit was seen at its best in a racy looking sports car with a stark but astonishingly appealing body designed by Stanley Riley.

The car created a sensation when revealed in 1922 and lived up to its looks by winning numerous gold and silver medals in reliability trials. It also won its class at Brooklands, being timed at speeds above 80 mph (128 km/h). The engine could safely rev to 4200 rpm.

The original prototype had polished aluminium bodywork, flanked by bright red mudguards which ran from the front to the back of the car. The eye-catching colour scheme gave birth to the name by which the car was later known. The Red Wing — sometimes called Red Winger — cost £520 in Britain in 1922, but the price had fallen to £398 by 1928.

The very narrow body made it necessary for the passenger's seat to be staggered slightly behind the driver's seat to provide a little more elbow room.

The Red Wing remained in production from 1922 to 1928 by which time the famous Riley Nine had been introduced. This new car led to Riley's greatest days. Unfortunately, Percy Riley could not produce a third triumph and, by 1938, the company was in serious financial trouble. It was sold to the Nuffield organisation which, in turn, became part of British Motor Corporation and later British Leyland.

Production of cars with the Riley name plate ceased in 1969, but most enthusiasts agree that the last 'real' Riley was built in 1957.

1923 RILEY REDWING

Only two genuine Riley Redwings are believed to still exist. Possibly twelve two-seaters and some four-seaters came to Australia but this sole surviving two-seater, a 1923 model, remains one of the rarest cars in Australia. It was bought in 1968 by Ray Black, of Elwood, Victoria, after having lain on blocks at Mt. Eliza for many years.

Ray and Dennis Wallace spent nine months restoring it. The biggest problem was the aluminium body which had oxidised over the years. Even so, all the metal and most of the original timber frame have been retained.

After restoration, the car competed in the 1970 International Veteran and Vintage Rally, covering the 1200 mile (1920 km) route through New South Wales and Victoria with remarkably little trouble. It has won numerous concours events, including first prize at the 1970 Motor Show for a pre-1930 car.

MECHANICAL FEATURES

Engine: Four-cylinder side valve, 1.5 litres, rated at 10.8 HP. 1½ inch S.U. carburettor, HT magneto, 3 main bearings.
Gearbox: Four-speed crash box with cone clutch, centre gear lever open prop shaft to rear axle. Geared to pull 3500 rpm in top gear, equivalent to 70 mph (112 km/h).
Suspension: Semi-elliptic springs front and rear, adjustable friction shock absorbers.
Brakes: Four wheel internal expanding front and rear, full compensation and easy adjustment rod operation. The front brakes were fitted in 1925.
Steering: Worm-and-wheel, Marles design, 1½ turns lock-to-lock.
Wheels: Detachable six bolt wire wheels, 27 x 4.40.
Dimensions: Wheelbase 9 ft 0 ins (2743 mm). Track 4 ft 4 ins (1321 mm). Overall length 13 ft 0 ins (3962 mm). Height 3 ft 6 ins (1067 mm). Kerb weight 14½ cwt (738 kg).
Performance: Maximum speed when new — 70 mph (112 km/h). Normal cruising speed — 50 mph (80 km/h). Fuel consumption at highway speeds — 35 mpg (8.0 litres/100 km).

1924 Berliet Tourer

THE MARQUE

A talented engineer, Marius Berliet commenced building cars in a small workshop in Lyons, France, as early as 1895. His first product was a rear-engined buggy. After six years of working almost alone, he acquired an engineering company called Audibert-Lavirotte and commenced building a range of orthodox but solid machines that in many ways were ideal for France's rural areas. They used the classic chassis layout, introduced by Mercedes, and which even then was the logical pattern for the future.

By 1906 Berliet had a reputation for building very fast, very durable machines. His four-cylinder models ranged from a relatively small 22 HP tourer to a massive 80 HP job. Though designed as a full road going machine, not a racer, the 80 HP was entered in the 1905 Tourist Trophy in Britain. It came fifth. Berliet tried again in 1906 with Paul Bablot, a French racing driver, at the wheel, and came a creditable second, behind a Rolls-Royce (one of the few times that Rolls-Royce has ever raced).

This success inspired the American Locomotive Company to acquire the manufacturing rights for the United States, and this is why subsequent Berliets, including the modern trucks, carry a locomotive emblem.

In 1908 Berliet moved into the six-cylinder field, with a series of well powered but rather dull touring cars. The four-cylinder line continued to be more popular than the sixes.

After World War One, the company introduced the new VB model, with a 3.3 litre side valve engine and three-speed gearbox. In 1924 they introduced an OHV version of the engine, along with a four-speed gearbox and front wheel brakes. Prior to this, however, the firm had produced an interim model, the VM, with the two-wheel brakes, a side valve engine and four-speed gearbox. Most of these were built in 1923.

Berliet ceased building passenger cars

in 1939 and, in post-war years, concentrated on trucks. In 1967 the company was acquired by Citroen. When Citroen merged with Peugeot, the Berliet division was sold to Renault and is now part of the State owned Renault Group.

BERLIET 1924 VM

Fitted with a local body made by T. J. Richards, of Adelaide, this robust looking tourer was originally sold for £795 ($1590) to the Hicks family of Adelaide. Seven new Berliets were sold in South Australia between 1924 and 1927.

This particular car was used until World War Two, then placed on blocks. After more than ten years, it was serviced and the wheels cut down to 16 inch size to take the only tyres available at the time.

By then, the Berliet belonged to the original owner's daughter. After her death, it passed to George Thomson, an Adelaide car dealer who, in 1968, sold it to Alan Morris, of Mildura, Victoria. Three years later, with the speedometer showing 21,000 original miles, the car passed to Sydney collector Frank Illich. He later sold it to the present owner, Brian Hill, of Kyle Bay, New South Wales.

The car was driveable but dilapidated. After twelve months of hard work, it was back on the road, repainted in its original olive green, with black guards, gold lines, new hood and the original leather re-stitched.

A set of 19 inch wheels were obtained from Kevin Field, of Adelaide, who owned a similar, but not identical, Berliet. The restoration was finally completed in November 1976. Prior to this the 3.3 litre engine probably had never had its head off.

More recently a set of original wire wheels were obtained. Two came with a Berliet front axle converted to a box trailer, and three from western Victoria. These were all beaded edge 8.20 x 120 wheels in good condition. After sand-blasting, painting and fitting them, the car was almost totally original.

Several Berliets survive in Australia. Apart from those mentioned, there are two unrestored examples in South Australia, one in New South Wales and one in Victoria.

MECHANICAL FEATURES

Engine: Four-cylinder, side valve, capacity 3.3 litres, rated at 22 HP, developing 26 BHP at 2800 rpm; conventional cooling system; Zenith Lyon side draught carburettor, Nilmelior magneto, bore and stroke 90 x 130 mm.
Gearbox: Conventional design with four forward speeds and multiplate dry disc clutch.
Suspension: Semi-elliptic springs at the front, cantilever rear springs.
Brakes: Expanding internal drum on rear wheels, and internal expanding transmission brake.
Steering: Conventional worm-and-wheel box. Turning circle 46 ft (14 m).
Wheels: Rudge 72 wire wheels fitted with 4.40 x 23 inch tyres.
Dimensions: Wheelbase 10 ft 3 ins (3130 mm). Overall length 14 ft 3 ins (4343 mm). Height 6 ft 7 ins (2000 mm). Kerb weight 30 cwt (1527 kg).
Performance: Maximum speed when new — 55 mph (88 km/h). Normal cruising speed — 45 mph (72 km/h). Fuel consumption at highway speeds — 13 mpg (21.7 litres/100 km).

1924 Buick Tourer

THE MARQUE

David Buick was a plumber who made his money making bath tubs. In 1901 he could see a great future for the automobile but unfortunately never reaped his rewards, for he went bankrupt during the Buick Car Company's first year of operation. The marque survived, mainly by manufacturing a twin-cylinder overhead valve motor which sold well to other car firms.

In 1904 an enterprising company promoter named Billy Durant gained control of Buick, reforming it with $10 million in borrowed money. The twin-cylinder engine and a car built around it improved in sales and Durant introduced production line methods borrowed from Oldsmobile. He also acquired other firms and, in 1908, merged them into a single entity called General Motors Corporation. Two years later Durant over-reached himself financially and was sacked from General Motors. He made a spectacular comeback by acquiring Little Motor Company, changing its name to Chevrolet, then using it as the basis of a bold take over operation to gain control of General Motors once again.

As founder company for General Motors, Buick always did well, at times outselling Chevrolet. In 1926 for example, Buick sold 280,000 cars, even though many of its lines were twice as dear as the equivalent Chevrolet. The man who pushed Buick to the top was Walter P. Chrysler (who later founded his own company). When Chrysler joined Buick, the output was a leisurely 15 cars a day. Within two years the figure was 150 cars a day. He was appointed president of the company, at a salary of $500,000 a year. He resigned, a millionaire, in 1920.

By that time Buick's reputation for building tough and dependable cars was established. The firm had its first four-cylinder model in 1907 and the B25 tourer, introduced in 1914, came with electric starting and headlamps.

That year the company marketed its first six, but the four-cylinder models remained the stronger seller. In 1924, the range was completely revised, the four-cylinder Model 35 being fitted with four wheel brakes and a new engine with detachable cylinder head. The former rounded radiator was discarded in favour of a squarer unit said to give the car 'a Packard look'. The four-cylinder tourer was priced from $935 (in the United States), whereas the six cost an extra $600.

The factory realised that the more powerful six was the engine of the future and dropped the four. By 1931, straight eight engines were in production.

However, an earlier experiment to produce the low priced Marquette had failed, costing the company sufficient money to send most firms broke.

Buick continued — and remains one of General Motors leading divisions.

1924 BUICK TOURER MODEL 35

Unlike most American cars sold during the 1920s, this stylish looking tourer arrived in Australia with a Detroit-built body. The equipment included wire wheels and wind deflectors on the windscreen pillars. The American price at the time was $US965, against $US490 for a Chevrolet tourer.

Little is known about the car's early

history, except that it spent many years in the Hay district of New South Wales. The present owner, Kevin Bennett of Condell Park, New South Wales, bought the car from J. Simmons of Kirribilli, New South Wales, in 1972. He spent five years on restoration, doing much of the mechanical work himself, with A. Hebblewhite doing the new trim. The work was finished in 1978.

The completed car more than satisfied some of the country's top concours judges. It won the Best Restored Car at the Buick Car Club's 1978 meeting; was named Grand Champion at the prestigious C.V.V.T.M.C. Warwick Farm annual meeting in the same year and won the Restoration Trophy presented by the Antique and Classic Motor Club.

MECHANICAL FEATURES

Engine: Four-cylinder, overhead valve, 2.8 litres, rated at 18.23 HP, developing 35 BHP. Marvel Updraught carburettor, Delco generator and combined starter motor. Splash lubrication.
Gearbox: Crash type three forward speeds with back-to-front gear change and multi-plate dry disc clutch.
Suspension: Conventional semi-elliptics front and rear, three-quarter floating rear axle.
Brakes: External contracting brakes on all four wheels.
Steering: Worm-and-split nut with 36 ft (11 m) turning circle.
Wheels: Wire wheels 23 ins. size.
Dimensions: Wheelbase 9 ft 1 in (2768 mm). Overall length 13 ft 4 ins (4064 mm). Height 6 ft 2.5 ins (1892 mm). Kerb weight 24 cwt (1218 kg).
Performance: Maximum speed when new — 50 mph (80 km/h). Normal cruising speed — 40 mph (64 km/h). Fuel consumption at highway speeds — 18 mpg (15.7 litres/100 km).

NSW
JGK·000

1924 Kissel Golden Bug

THE MARQUE

Kissell Motor Car Company was founded in 1906 by Louis P. Kissel, owner of a successful factory making agricultural equipment and stationary engines. Unlike most car makers, Kissel had the equipment to manufacture almost every item of his cars within his own works.

The first was a 35 HP four-cylinder model called the Badger subsequently re-named the Kissel Kar. When Louis Kissel died in 1906 his four sons took over the firm. They embarked on an expansion plan which made the firm a highly respected manufacturer of well built, beautifully styled cars.

The guiding hand behind the curvacious lines of the speedster which made the firm famous was a German artisan, J. Frederick Werner. He had built coaches for European royalty before coming to America, and then had subsequently become chief designer at Kissel's.

The firm never reached great heights in a production sense. In 1924, when the Golden Bug speedster was flourishing, the firm employed only 1000 people yet they were still making almost all of the car, including the body. The lack of quantity was made up for by quality. The range of body types included a brougham, phaeton, speedster, tourer, coupé and sedan, all powered by Kissel's own 4.4 litre six developing 65 BHP at 2500 rpm.

At the time, the speedster sold in the United States for $3075, which was more than a Type 37 Bugatti with a comparable performance.

The company was well known for its innovative body ideas, including one built in 1918 with a removeable hardtop, so it could double as a phaeton for summer and a closed car for winter. Earlier still, the firm had pioneered the use of a curved windscreen in 1914. It also built a roadster with two extra seats which pulled out like drawers, one on each side. Many of their models, including the Golden Bug speedster, had provision for a set of golf clubs strapped against each rear guard.

The idea for the Golden Bug originated when Kissel's New York agent, Conover T. Silver, suggested that the firm produce a sporting two seater. Two experimental models were built in 1917 and the first production example, named the Silver Special, came out in 1918.

An improved model was announced for 1919. At the same time the factory standardised the body colour as chrome-yellow. The car became known as the Golden Bug — partly because of its colour, but also as a cute reference that it was a step up from the previous 'Silver' model.

The two-seater body was beautifully styled. Though the car's performance was not astonishing, it accelerated well, with a maximum speed of 75 mph (120 km/h). Initially it had a 4.3 litre engine, but later the stroke was extended to give 4.7 litres.

In 1924 Kissel offered four wheel Lockheed hydraulic brakes as an option. They followed with a 100 mph (160 km/h) straight eight model, but competition from other firms badly eroded its market. Sales went downhill rapidly. In 1931 the firm joined with Moon to form New Era Motors to manufacture the front-wheel-drive Ruxton. Roughly 400 cars were built before that venture folded and, with it, Kissel and Moon.

1924 KISSEL SPEEDSTER 6-55

Fitted with a Kissel-made speedster body, this rare Golden Bug is owned by Bill Trollope, of Turramurra, New South Wales. Obviously designed for fine weather, it has provision for carrying two golf bags.

The car is believed to have been imported new into Rockhampton, Queensland, where it changed hands several times. In recent years it was purchased by Ron Griffith, a well known Ipswich collector, who restored it. It was then purchased by Frank Illich, of Sydney, and in 1973 passed to Bill Trollope. With his father, Bill dismantled the car, checked it thoroughly and rebuilt the worn components.

At least 70 Kissels are known to survive around the world and roughly twenty are Speedsters. The car photographed here is believed to be the only true Model 55 Golden Bug in Australia; another is in New Zealand.

MECHANICAL FEATURES

Engine: Six-cylinder, side valve, capacity 4346 ccs, rated at 26.3 HP, developing 65 BHP at 2500 rpm. Water cooling with Stromberg carburettor and coil ignition. Design features a three bearing crankshaft.
Gearbox: Selective sliding straight cut crash-type gearbox with three forward gears, single plate Borg & Beck clutch and spiral bevel drive.
Suspension: Semi-elliptic springs front and rear.
Brakes: External contracting rear wheel brakes, with internal expanding transmission emergency brake.
Steering: Worm-and-wheel with 1½ turns lock-to-lock.
Wheels: Wire wheels, size 550 x 20.
Dimensions: Wheelbase 10 ft 4 ins (3150 mm). Track 4 ft 9 ins (1448 mm). Overall length 14 ft 10 ins (4521 mm). Height 5 ft 2 ins (1575 mm). Kerb weight 29 cwt (1470 kg).
Performance: Maximum speed when new — 75 mph (120 km/h). Normal cruising speed — 50 mph (80 km/h). Fuel consumption at highway speeds — 17 mpg (16.6 litres/100 km).

1924 Minerva Tourer

THE MARQUE

As previously mentioned under the entry for the 1904 Minerva (see page 25), the Belgian company, Minerva, commenced with cycles, then turned to motorcycles and a twin-cylinder, chain-driven prototype.

For the next few years they launched a succession of models, ranging from a 5 HP voiturette to a massive racer.

The turning point came in 1909 when Minerva decided to use a new kind of engine recently patented by Charles Knight and incorporating double sleeve valves. The design's main purpose was to keep the noise level to a minimum, but the engines were lively enough and Minerva chalked up some impressive competition victories. One drawback was the smokey exhaust.

Minerva persevered with the Knight engine design and became noted as a manufacturer of fine touring cars, robustly built and sporting in character.

When World War One put an end to car manufacturing, the firm concentrated on aero engines. After the War a series of luxury touring cars emerged — powered by four and six-cylinder sleeve valve engines. Most of the sixes were 20 HP, a smaller number had the larger 30 HP engine. The tourers all had Perrot leading shoe front brakes.

In 1929, Minerva went into the Rolls-Royce market with the magnificent and massive 'AL' model, powered by a straight eight engine of 6.6 litres. With an overall length of 17 ft (5180 mm), it weighed 34 cwt (chassis only). The new car sold badly and hastened the company's demise. Though the Belgian government came to the rescue, Minerva was effectively out of the car business by 1936, but continued as a manufacturer of agricultural and allied products. In 1957 a brief attempt was made to launch a four-wheel-drive utility on world markets (including Australia) but sales were poor.

MODEL AC MINERVA TOURER

This rare and powerful chassis came to Australia in 1924 and was fitted with a well proportioned local body, complete with cocktail cabinet, picnic trays and full all-weather equipment.

After being purchased by a well-to-do Adelaide family, it was chauffeur driven for four years, then sold, the chauffeur transferring his services to the new owner. Four years later the car changed hands again and was regularly used until World War Two.

In 1946 it went up for sale, appearing in an Adelaide car showroom for only £50 ($100), despite the shortage of cars at the time. It was bought by a Mr Weeks, who lived in Wudinna on the west coast of South Australia, and who subsequently used it for about eighteen years, mostly travelling over rough limestone roads. Towards the end of this working stint, the Minerva's bodywork was chopped to form a buckboard type of truck. The rear doors were stored in a shed and when the car was eventually restored the doors proved to be the only sound part of the body.

Around 1964 Mr Weeks parked the car under a pine tree and awaited a buyer. It was complete mechanically and had the original lights, windscreen and mudguards.

Adelaide-based civil engineering contractor, Brian Macmahon, bought the Minerva and completely restored it to its original condition, with help from Gordon Eames who remade the upholstery. Apart from the machining of some replacement components, the mechanical and body work was done by the owner. He discovered several interesting points — the bolts are hand made and individually fitted, which made re-assembly a tedious business. The crankshaft is offset, allowing the pistons to come out without removing the cylinder heads.

Brian Macmahon's handiwork was good enough for the car to win the 1974 award as 'The Most Meritorious Restoration of the Year' given by the Sporting Car Club of South Australia.

Though many Minervas were sold in Australia prior to 1930, they were mainly four-cylinder and 20 HP light six-cylinder models. This 30 HP model, which weighs a substantial 2.5 tonnes, is rare. Only four are known to survive in Australia, all in various stages of restoration.

MECHANICAL FEATURES

Engine: Six-cylinder, double sleeve valve unit of 5.5 litres, rated at 30 HP. Fitted with Sthenos-Minerva twin venturi updraught carburettor and a Scintilla magneto. There is a Kygas pump instead of a choke for cold starts; the starter motor has a clutch and stepgear.
Gearbox: Four-speed Minerva design with mainshaft and layshaft side by side. Double row ball bearings fitted throughout. The clutch consists of seven copper-lined driven discs.
Suspension: Semi-elliptic leaf springs at front, cantilevered semi-elliptics at rear. Shock absorbers, semi-rotary hydraulic at the front only.
Brakes: Four wheel with leading shoe drum brakes of 19 ins (482 mm) diameter.
Steering: Worm and segment, with only 1¾ turns lock-to-lock and a turning circle of 52 ft (15.8 metres).
Dimensions: Wheelsbase 12 ft 0½ ins (3670 mm). Overall length 16 ft 6 ins (5030 mm). Height 6 ft 8 ins (2032 mm). Kerb weight 50 cwt (2545 kg).
Performance: Maximum speed when new — 80 mph (128 km/h). Normal cruising speed — 50-60 mph (80-100 km/h). Fuel consumption at highway speeds — 14 mpg (20 litres/100 km).

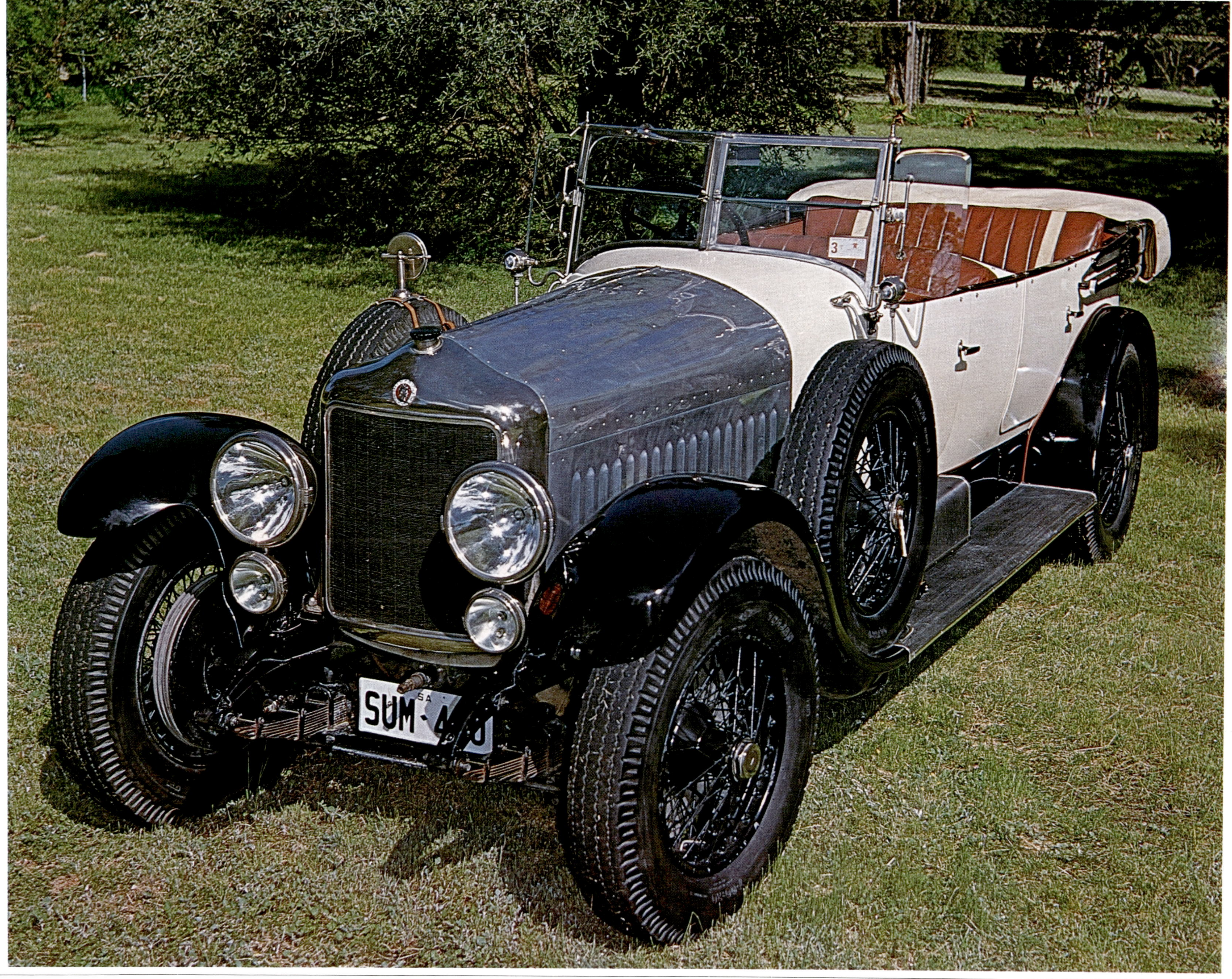
SUM

1924 Sunbeam Sports Tourer

THE MARQUE

The saga of Sunbeam is almost the story of a shadow. Looming over the success of Sunbeam as a sporting marque during the 1920s was the immense energy and individuality of a French engineering genius, Louis Coatalen. For thirty years the British-built Sunbeam reigned supreme. Then Coatalen left, and progressively the marque sank into mediocrity, then bankruptcy.

The company had been founded by John Marston, a mid-Victorian man of burly stature, elegant moustache and starched shirt. He had made a fortune from Sunbeam cycles but had no plans to enter the fledgling auto business until an apprentice, Tom Cureton, built an experimental car. The year was 1899. Marston liked the idea but not the design, and he helped Cureton build a second, then a third machine.

Finally the pair asked a local ironwork artist named Mabberley-Smith to design a car for them. He produced a curious design with one wheel on each side, one at the front and one at the rear. Hundreds were sold.

A separate car company was established and a prominent French designer and manufacturer, M. Berliet, asked to manufacture parts for a new car, which Sunbeam would assemble in England. The idea did not work well, so Sunbeam hired Angus Shaw to design a completely new model. Shaw then drove his 3½ litre 16/20 from the top of Britain to the bottom, and back again, without allowing the engine to stop.

Even this did not get the firm on its feet, so Louis Coatalen was invited to join the firm. He promptly produced a completely new range of models and thrust Sunbeam into the heart of motor sport. For twenty years Coatalen was chief designer, production executive and often racing driver or chief pit mechanic. He experimented with an amazing number of innovations, ranging from double-acting shock absorbers to hemi-spherical cylinder heads. His enterprise paid off and in 1923 Henry Segrave had become the first Englishman to win a Grand Prix in a British-built car. The year 1924 proved the zenith of Sunbeam's racing career, and Coatalen turned to record breaking. In 1927 his 1000 HP design, driven by Segrave, became the first to exceed 200 mph (320 km/h) on land.

The publicity did Sunbeam little good. Some years earlier the company's board of directors had made a disastrous merger with the shaky Talbot-Darracq organisations. Sunbeam made money but the profits were swallowed by Talbot and Darracq.

Coatalen pulled out, his health broken by overwork. The company went downhill so rapidly that, in 1935, the once famous organisation was bought cheaply by a major creditor, the Rootes Group.

1924 SUNBEAM 20/60 HP SPORTS TOURER

In January 1924 the English motor magazine *Autocar* published a road test of the new six-cylinder 20/60. After a technical description of the cantilever rear springing, the magazine said: "The car sits four square on the road and handles as if glued to the surface. Speed does not disturb its feeling of safeness, nor bad roads its poise. The springing is very comfortable and road shocks are barely noticeable".

These comments may have prompted the Adelaide Sunbeam agents to import the new model, though its selling price (around £1300) was similar to that of a 30/98 Vauxhall or a Rolls-Royce 20 HP chassis. It is possible that the agents used this car as their demonstrator, as its number plates are the same as the model designation.

One thing is certain. This most impressive sports tourer, now owned by John Ellis of Adelaide, is a very early example of a 20/60. Its small radiator, rounded rocker cover and other detail differences, place it apart from the later 20/60s.

The car's early history is unknown. John Ellis heard about it from the owner during a bar conversation. It had belonged to an Adelaide man who had dismantled the derelict car, then lost interest in the restoration. John Ellis acquired the parts around 1968 but did not start serious work until 1975. He spent two and a half years rebuilding the car. New body panels were made by Giovanni Pagnussat and the car painted by Stuart Sparke. Gordon Eames faithfully matched the original upholstery and all-weather equipment.

The Sunbeam-built body is unusual in having glazed side curtains instead of celluloid, and upholstery which matches the body colour rather than contrasts with it.

As a road-going machine, the Sunbeam is superb. The engine is smooth and tractable, the gearshift delightful and the handling outstanding. The 20/60 also features unusually powerful brakes for its era.

MECHANICAL FEATURES

Engine: Six-cylinder, 3.2 litres, OHV, rated at 20.9 HP, developing 60 BHP at 4000 rpm. Claudel Hobson carburettor and BTH polar inductor magneto. Unusually robust construction.
Gearbox: Non-synchromesh with four gears and right-hand gate change. Renowned for smoothness of change, this box operated in conjunction with a single dry plate clutch.
Suspension: Offset semi-elliptic springs at front, long cantilever springs at rear, torque tube, Hartford shock absorbers.
Brakes: Four wheel system with self-energising shoes at the front and Perrot actuation. Handbrake is separate with extra shoes in rear drums.
Steering: Worm-and-nut with 36 ft (11 m) turning circle and 2½ turns lock-to-lock.
Wheels: Rudge-Whitworth centre-lock type, 6.00-21 size, early example of wheel-base rims.
Dimensions: Wheelbase 10 ft 11 ins (3327 mm). Overall length 15 ft 1 in (4597 mm). Height 5 ft 8 ins (1727 mm). Kerb weight 35 cwt (1782 kg).
Performance: Maximum speed when new — 75 mph (120 km/h). Normal cruising speed — 60 mph (100 km/h). Fuel consumption at highway speeds — 18-20 mpg (14.1-15.6 litres/100 km).

QLD
VINTAGE
006

1924 Turcat-Mery T.T. Sportster

THE MARQUE

Though little known today, the French firm, Turcat-Mery, was one of the pioneers of the motor industry. Working in Marseilles with his brother-in-law, Simon Mery, Leon Turcat gained experience with some early Panhard cars. They were friends of the Peugeot family. They then designed the first Turcat-Mery. Completed in 1896, it featured several advanced ideas for the time including a four-cylinder engine, coil ignition and pneumatic tyres. Leon Turcat then forecast that the streets of Paris would soon be cluttered with cars.

The partnership continued to innovate with new ideas. By 1899 they had a car with a five-speed gearbox and in 1905 a unique racing model with six wheels and chain drive to the centre pair. A racing program was established and several notable victories won, though not with the six wheeler. In 1911, the firm won the first Monte Carlo Rally.

Hampered by tight finances, Turcat-Mery renewed vehicle production after World War One, though their designs were clearly dated. The 2.9 litre four-cylinder engine, for example, bore a strong resemblance to the Vauxhall 30/98 design. By 1923, Turcat-Mery was producing an advanced overhead cam engine as well as the ageing side valve design.

Turcat-Mery never entered the volume production business and had little interest in export. No examples of their work are known to exist in the United Kingdom, and it is doubtful if there are any in the United States. However a Frenchman, named Houssard, came to Australia and established a Turcat-Mery agency in Sydney. He exhibited cars at the Royal Agriculture Motor Show in 1923 and evidently sold quite a few before closing the agency in 1925.

During the mid 1920s things started to go badly for the small French manufacturer. The firm tried to market a small car, then a couple of six-cylinder models and finally a most interesting 2.3 litre straight eight. None achieved success. Production ceased in 1928.

Harry Cape, of Buderim, Queensland, has thoroughly researched the field and believes there are five complete Turcat-Mery's in Australia. Two are fully mobile and a third was nearing completion at the end of 1979. Two of the cars are SG models with Smith and Waddington (Sydney) roadster bodies, one is a shorter wheelbase version with an overhead cam engine. The third, with a glorious Smith and Waddington body based on the Californian hardtop design, is owned by Bill Millard, of Sydney.

Harry Cape has also contacted the owners of two veteran Turcat-Merys in France. Both owners, Oliver Turcat and Andre Turcat, are direct descendants of the original builder. Before his retirement, Andre Turcat was chief test pilot of the Concorde supersonic aircraft.

1924 TURCAT-MERY SG ROADSTER

Owned by Harry Cape, of Buderim, Queensland, this unusual car was imported by M. Houssard in 1924. However, it may have been an earlier model as its engineering features are closer to 1920-22 design.

The car came to Australia in chassis form and was fitted with a Smith and Waddington tourer body, and delivered to Mr Nesbitt, of Inverell, in New South Wales. The T-M apparently spent most of its life in Inverell, and was found by a Mr Burge in 1957. By then it was standing in a yard with a tree growing through the chassis and the remains of the body.

The Turcat-Mery was sold to Mr Ted Pollard, of Brisbane, who restored it and partially rebuilt the original body, turning it into a replica of the Tourist Trophy sports body, popular during the 1920s.

The present owner, Harry Cape, has done further restoration work.

MECHANICAL FEATURES

Engine: Four-cylinder cast enblock, side valve, capacity 2.9 litres, rated at 15.9 HP, developing approximately 40 BHP. Thermo-syphon cooling, Zenith carburettor, magneto ignition. Non-detachable head.
Gearbox: Four-speed crash type with central gear lever, reverse gear engaged through first gear position. Disc-type clutch.
Suspension: Semi-elliptic springs at front and rear.
Brakes: Four wheel Perrot type expanding brakes, mechanical operation.
Steering: Worm-and-sector with 1½ turns lock-to-lock.
Wheels: Beaded edge, wire spokes, 23 x 4.40.
Dimensions: Wheelbase 11 ft 0 ins (3353 mm). Overall length 15 ft 0 ins (4572 mm). Hood height 5 ft 6 ins (1676 mm). Kerb weight 27 cwt (1372 kg).
Performance: Maximum speed when new — 60 mph (100 km/h). Normal cruising speed — 40 mph (64 km/h). Fuel consumption at highway speeds — 20 mpg (14.1 litres/100 km).

1924 Vauxhall 30/98

THE MARQUE

Before being taken over by General Motors in 1925, Vauxhall Motors developed two sports/touring cars which soon became classics. The Prince Henry (introduced in 1910) and the 30/98 (introduced in 1914) were thoroughly conventional designs which transcended contemporary standards of performance and road-handling ability.

Though the 30/98 was catalogued for 13 years (until 1927), less than 600 were built. According to historian, G. N. Georgano, two-thirds of the total production came to Australia.

The 30/98 was in some ways a larger edition of the legendary Prince Henry. Because competition success was an essential ingredient for the success of this type of vehicle, Vauxhall increased the Prince Henry's engine capacity from 3 to 4.0 litres and, in 1913, built a very fast prototype with a 4½ litre engine.

They changed the wheelbase and modernised the chassis, giving birth to a new model which became the 30/98 HP. When launched, its price was almost 50 per cent higher than the lighter Prince Henry, and sales were slow.

Around twelve were built when production ceased for World War One. The 30/98 was relaunched for the post-war market at the exceptionally high British price of £1670. It was not until 1924, when production reached its peak, that the chassis price came down to a more reasonable £1000.

The early 30/98's were powered by an exceptionally robust side valve 4½ litre motor developing 90 BHP at 3000 rpm. The car was sold in chassis form for coach builders but the most popular body was the elegant Velox four-seater tourer, made in the Vauxhall factory. With its light guards, small doors and near perfect proportions, it was an exceptionally good looking design and very few closed versions were ordered.

In 1919, the 30/98 was probably the fastest production car made in Britain, with a guaranteed maximum speed of 100 mph (160 km/h) in racing trim or 85 mph (136 km/h) fully equipped.

Exciting and powerful, it offered an unusually high power-to-weight ratio, with safe handling and competition proven durability. The original model had rear wheel brakes only and even when the firm moved to four wheel brakes, the stopping power was little different. In all other respects it was a magnificent machine which can still be driven with considerable enterprise.

The initial 30/98, known as the E-type, ceased production in 1922 by which time some 270 had been sold. The designer, the famous Laurence Pomeroy, had left the company but one of his suggestions, an overhead valve engine, was adopted. Production of the new OE model commenced in 1923.

Based on the previous engine, the overhead valve OE unit was quieter and livelier than the side valve equivalent, though some owners consider the E-type the more enjoyable car to drive. Be that as it may, the OE was certainly the more advanced. The free revving engine developed 112 BHP at 3300 rpm with plenty of potential for special tuning. Other changes included a stiffer chassis frame, a less direct axle ratio and, after the car had been in production for some months, four wheel brakes.

By 1924 Sunbeam and Bentley were offering strong competition, not only in performance but also in price. Though Vauxhall again updated the design with hydraulic brakes and a more refined gearbox, sales continued to dwindle. The new owner of Vauxhall, General Motors, decided to concentrate on small family sedans. A total of 312 OE type 30/98s were built.

1924 30/98 OE VELOX TOURER

Owen Bourke, of St. Ives, New South Wales, spent several years trying to persuade a friend, Jeff Clampett, to part with his 30/98. Jeff had paid £240 ($480) for the car in 1950 but after dismantling it had left the parts stored in an outside 'loo', dubbed Vauxhall House.

After finally acquiring the car in 1975, Owen completely rebuilt it to factory-fresh condition, with Brian Hawke handling the bodywork and Bob King the trim.

The car has proved a reliable and delightful open road performer. According to Owen Bourke, it drives and handles as well as a Bentley. He should know, as he owns a couple.

MECHANICAL FEATURES

Engine: Four-cylinder, OHV, 4.22 litre developing 112 BHP at 3300 rpm. Five bearing crankshaft, detachable cylinder head, honeycomb radiator, Zenith carburettor, Watford magneto and monobloc cylinder casting. Twelve volt electrical system.
Gearbox: Conventional four-speed crash type, geared to give 28 mph (45 km/h) per 1000 rpm in top gear. Open propeller shaft, 3.3 axle ratio with multi-plate clutch.
Suspension: Conventional semi-elliptic springs front and rear with Hartford shock absorbers.
Brakes: Four wheel system. Handbrake operates internal expanding shoes on rear wheels, foot brake operates front wheel and transmission brakes.
Steering: Worm-and-wheel.
Wheels: Well-based Rudge-Whitworth, 6.00 x 20.
Dimensions: Wheelbase 10 ft 1 in (3073 mm). Track 4 ft 9½ ins (1460 mm). Overall length 14 ft 2 ins (4318 mm). Height 5 ft 2 ins (1575 mm). Kerb weight 29 cwt (1476 kg).
Performance: Maximum speed when new — 100 mph (160 km/h) in racing trim. Normal cruising speed — 55 mph (88 km/h). Fuel consumption at highway speeds — 12 mpg (23.5 litres/100 km).

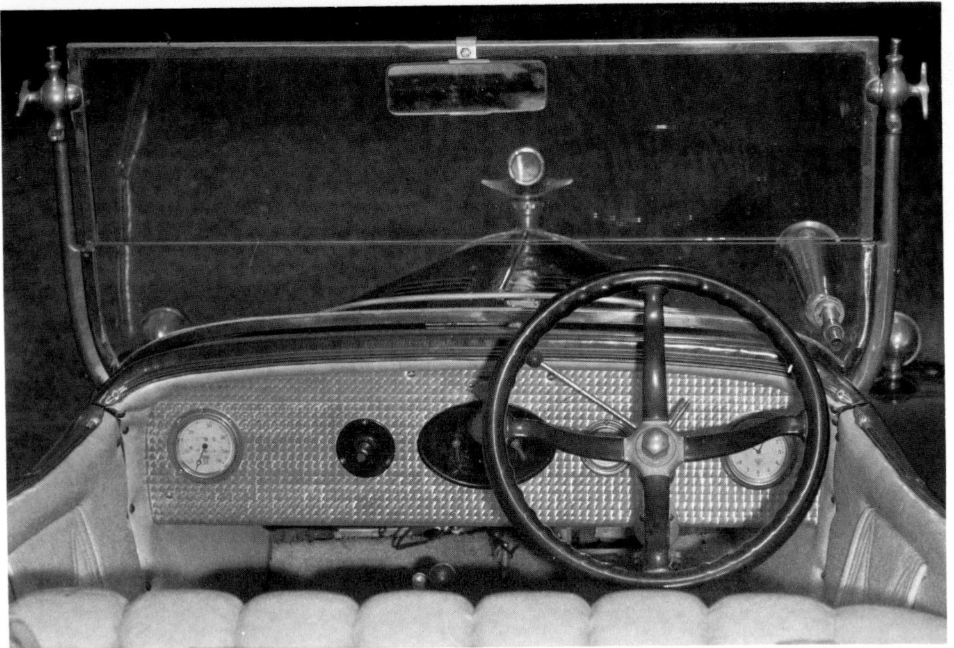

1925 'Bullnose' Morris

THE MARQUE

William Morris went into business on his own when his boss refused to raise his salary from four to four and a half shillings. Morris was employed as a cycle mechanic, so he started his own shop in his home town of Cowley, near Oxford, England.

After one initial setback, the cycle business thrived and Morris set his sights on becoming a car maker.

Just before World War One, he launched his first four-wheeler, the 10 HP Morris Oxford, which was quickly dubbed 'Bullnose' because of its distinctive rounded radiator. Morris announced this car at the 1912 London Motor Show, priced at £175 in the United Kingdom, and billed as "the car that does 50 MILES AN HOUR AND 50 MILES PER GALLON".

A major car distributor, Gordon Stewart, liked the prototype so much that he put in a large advance order. His substantial down payment helped establish the factory where the car was built. Stewart later became the main Morris distributor and, like William Morris, a self-made millionaire.

Thoroughly conventional in design, the Bullnose was a smash hit in Britain. Some 1300 were sold during 1913 and by 1925, the year the car pictured was built, Morris was making 54,000 cars a year, commanding half the British market.

The Bullnose was extremely popular with learner drivers as it stripped away the mystique of owning and controlling a car. Extremely easy to drive, it had a very sweet clutch (with wet cork inserts) and a gear change that was easier to master than almost any other of its era. The design was also reliable and durable, often outlasting cars costing three times as much to buy.

The Bullnose was also extremely lively. William Morris in person won the last hill climb held in Britain before World War One, driving an almost standard Oxford.

Morris started in business as an assembler rather than a builder, using proprietary parts where possible. The early 10 HP engines were made by White and Poppe. He did a deal to import the cheaper Continental four-cylinder engine from Detroit but World War One put an end to the scheme.

After the War, Morris had an engine designed to his own specifications, sub-contracting the manufacture to the Hotchkiss factory, located at Coventry. In May 1923, when Hotchkiss was building engines for him at the rate of 1000 a month, Morris bought the factory. He also bought S.U., the carburettor makers, and the firms making his radiators, bodies, chassis frames and other components. Wolseley and Riley were also acquired and M.G. started, using Morris Oxford components. Together they formed the Nuffield Group which later merged with Austin as the British Motor Corporation. Many of the companies still survive as part of British Leyland.

The Oxford (and the cheaper Cowley version) ran until 1926 when the distinctive radiator was replaced by a conventional straight-sided design. One hundred and sixty eight thousand Bullnoses were built. The basic design remained substantially the same, though the engine size increased in two stages to 1.8 litres and the wheelbase was stretched from 7 ft 6 ins (2.3 metres) to 8 ft 6 ins (2.6 metres).

The suspension was conventional. Though Gabriel snubbers were optional, they did not become standard until 1926. Front wheel brakes also became standard that year.

William Morris (later Lord Nuffield) was Britain's most successful car maker, but he had his failures. He lost a small fortune by buying the former Leon Bollée factory in France to make Morris cars. He also lost some costly legal battles. Many of his top executives left abruptly after a clash of wills. But Morris did more than anyone to successfully introduce motoring to the masses in Britain, and the "Bullnose" was the car that did it.

1925 BULLNOSE MORRIS

One of the larger engined 1.8 litre Oxfords, this pretty Bullnose roadster is now owned by Frank McMahon, of Ainslie, Australian Capital Territory.

The car's early history is not known but it was found and purchased by John Ham, of Canberra, on a farm in Victoria. Half of the body had been cut off to form a primitive 'ute'. John completely restored the car mechanically and made a new rear section for the body, faithfully duplicating the original roadster-and-dickey-seat design. The trim restoration was done by Harry Brown.

MECHANICAL FEATURES

Engine: Four-cylinder, 1.8 litres side valve rated at 13.9 HP, developing approximately 28 BHP at 2800 rpm. Thermo-syphon cooling, with Smith's 5-jet carburettor, Lucas magneto.
Gearbox: Three-speed sliding pinion unit incorporating dynamotor (starter-generator) with permanent chain drive. Gearbox in unit with motor. Double plate wet clutch with cork inserts. Propeller shaft in torque tube.
Suspension: Semi-elliptic springs at the front, three-quarter elliptics at rear.
Brakes: Foot brake operates the rear drum shoes, handbrake actuates separate shoes in the same drums.
Steering: Worm-and-spur wheel, with 40½ ft (12.3 metres) turning circle.
Wheels: Sankey spoked wheels 500 x 19.
Dimensions: Wheelbase 9 ft 0 ins (2743 mm). Overall length 12 ft 6 ins (3810 mm). Hood height 5 ft 5 ins (1650 mm). Kerb weight 17 cwt (865 kg).
Performance: Maximum speed when new — 55 mph (88 km/h). Normal cruising speed — 40 mph (64 km/h). Fuel consumption at highway speeds — 35 mpg (8.0 litres/100 km).

ACT
052

1925 Type 39 Bugatti Monza Grand Prix

THE MARQUE

The background to the Bugatti legend is given on pages 166 and 178 describing the Types 35C and 40.

Bugatti cars were outstanding on the road and track, but their racing history is phenomenal. During the 1925-26 racing season, Bugattis registered 1045 victories with a further 806 wins in the following season. Most of these successes were scored with the Type 35 and its variants, all with a 2 litre, eight-cylinder overhead cam engine, or the 1.5 litre derivative.

In 1926, a 1.5 litre displacement limit was adopted for Grand Prix racing in Europe, because speeds had become too rapid for the available tracks. This put Bugatti in an especially strong position, as the firm had already built some Type 35's with a modified engine, scaled down to 1.5 litres. It had also been tried with a Roots blower.

The Type 39 (unblown) and the later 39A (blown) were direct derivatives of the all conquering Type 35. Outwardly, they looked a little different, because of the larger radiator, but the chassis layout was the same.

The Type 39 is indeed a rare car. This writer looked in vain for one in the fabulous Schlumpf Museum, in France, where the 600 strong collection of cars includes 125 Bugattis. Most references to the Type 39 consist of just a few lines, even in books devoted exclusively to the marque. This writer has not been able to find out how many were built, though the official factory figures list a total of 290 for Type 35 and 39 combined, but the total number of Type 39, including prototypes, was probably only 50.

The few references available refer to the Type 39 as being produced in 1926, but the car photographed here was built in 1925 and had scored some competition success in Europe before arriving in Sydney in early 1926.

Produced originally as an eight-cylinder unsupercharged racing car, the Type 39 engine developed 90 BHP at 5000 rpm. The supercharged version developed 125 BHP, boosting maximum speed to 125 mph, or 200 km/h.

Ettore Bugatti produced seven Grand Prix models,the four-cylinder Types 37 and 37A with the cylinders en bloc, then a series of eight-cylinder cars with two sets of four cylinders. Apart from the Type 39 they comprised the 2 litre Types 35, 35A and 35C and the 2.3 litre Type 35B. All were bare of electrical components, except for the magneto ignition.

Though Type 39's are extremely rare, two are in Australia. The one pictured is owned by Ted Lobb of Grenfell, New South Wales, the other by Melbourne Bugatti enthusiast, Bob King. The latter car had a distinguished racing career in Europe before being imported by Dick Clarke and driven by him for several years at Maroubra speedway. Carl Junker drove it to first place in the 1931 Australian Grand Prix at Phillip Island, Victoria. The same car became the basis of the Ford-powered Day Special which raced with great success during the early post-war years. It was owned by Ted Lobb before being acquired by Bob King who is currently restoring the Type 39 to its original condition.

1926 TYPE 39 G.P.

This splendid example of a rare car has been owned by Ted Lobb since 1938, which is possibly some kind of ownership record for a Grand Prix Bugatti.

It had won the 1925 French Touring Car Grand Prix, fitted with a two-seater sports body with flared mudguards. According to its history related in the Australasian Bugatti Register, the car won its class in the Italian Grand Prix des Voiturettes a few weeks later and was third outright in the Italian Grand Prix run at the same time. In both races it was driven by Meo Constantini, later manager of Bugattis's racing team.

In 1926 the ex-Constantini car was imported to Australia by Frank Parle to race at Maroubra, where it had many lively outings with Frank Parle and Jack O'Rourke at the wheel.

Well known racing driver Bill Thompson (winner of three Australian Grand Prix) entered the car in the 1931 AGP but did not start. Two years later it was driven by Carl Junker in the Australian Grand Prix and was running well until the engine threw a rod.

The car was sold to Harold Edwards of Victoria and competed in trials and hill climbs organised by the Light Car Club. Ted Lobb bought it in 1938 and has since restored it to first class condition. The car is splendidly maintained and frequently driven around a short circuit on the owner's property.

MECHANICAL FEATURES

Engine: Straight eight of 1.49 litre capacity, single overhead camshaft, 3 valves per cylinder. Rated at 17.9 HP, developing 90 BHP at 5000 rpm. Water-cooled without fan, twin Solex carburettor, magneto ignition.
Gearbox: Four-speed crash box with wet multiplate clutch.
Suspension: Semi-elliptics at front, quarter elliptics (reversed) at rear.
Brakes: Mechanically operated four wheel internal expanding.
Steering: Worm-and-sector.
Wheels: Alloy wheels and optional wire spoked wheels; alloy size 710 x 90, wire 440 x 19.
Dimensions: Wheelbase 7 ft 10 ins (2387 mm). Overall length 12 ft 1 in (3683 mm). Height 3ft 6ins (1069 mm). Kerb weight 15 cwt (763 kg).
Performance: Maximum speed when new — 110 mph (176 km/h). Fuel consumption at highway speeds — 15 mpg (18.8 litres/100 km).

1925 F.I.A.T. 519A Limousine

THE MARQUE

There never was a Mr Fiat. The Italian company was founded by a former army officer, Giovanni Agnelli, in 1899 as Fabbrica Italiana Automobili Turino. The name was later shortened to F.I.A.T., and later still to Fiat.

Though Agnelli had designed and raced his own car before forming the company, his first production vehicle was really a Ceirano. Giovanni Ceirano and his brothers had come to Turin to make cycles, later cars, and in 1899 had a small factory and a staff of fifty workmen — but little capital. The newly formed F.I.A.T. bought out the Ceirano concern, renamed its small 3½ HP twin-cylinder car and put it into production as a F.I.A.T.

Progressive in his ideas and keen on motor racing, Agnelli soon had the factory humming. By 1908 it was building 1000 cars a year, so Agnelli installed equipment to boost production and reduce prices. By 1912 all was ready for a low priced car and the 1.8 litre Zero was introduced. The following model, the famous 501, introduced in 1919, brought motoring to the Italian masses.

Though mass production was the key to the future, Agnelli wanted to span the entire price field. This is why, in 1921, he produced the Superfiat, an enormous machine with a twelve-cylinder 6.8 litre engine, a wheelbase of 12 ft 6 ins (3860 mm), and such innovations as servo-assisted four-wheel hydraulic brakes. The car was monumentally expensive and few were made, but it made the point that Fiat could match Hispano in the luxury field. To consolidate the position, the 519 followed in 1922.

In many ways, it was a scaled down Superfiat, with the wheelbase reduced by 10 ins (260 mm). A six-cylinder engine of 4.76 litres was fitted and the vehicle's weight reduced to a more manageable 2035 kg.

Designed as a true luxury car, the 519 features an overhead valve engine, servo assisted brakes on all wheels, an adjustable steering column and optional power steering. Production ran for five years, with a variety of body styles and four basic chassis models — 519, 519A, 519B and 519C. The 519A has suspension changes, the 519B other mechanical refinements and the 519C was a 'colonial' model, with stiffened suspension, providing ground clearance of 259 mm (10 ins). When first produced, the standard 519 cost 78,000 lire in Italy.

FIAT 519A

Magnificently restored by Bob Robinson, of Gosford, this stately limousine has sumptuous seating for five, plus two occasional folding seats. Designed for chauffeur driving, it has a glass partition between the front and rear passenger compartments with a communication system to speak to the chauffeur.

It was one of a unique pair of matching 'his-and-hers' cars purchased by the Wormald family, of Pymble, New South Wales. The limousine was used by Mrs Wormald, and her husband, who had founded the fire extinguisher company. It had a sports body fitted to a similar chassis. The two cars were purchased together and arrived, fully equipped, in December 1925.

Charles Bowker acquired the 519A limousine in 1959 and sold it to Bob Robinson in 1977. Restoration commenced in May that year. It was completed eighteen months later, with Bob Robinson doing the mechanical and body work, Perc Cornish the trim.

About eleven similar cars are believed to exist around the world. This one gained the Best Vintage Award and the Best Continental Trophy at a Taree vintage meeting in 1978.

MECHANICAL FEATURES

Engine: Six-cylinder OHV of 4.76 litres rated at 28 HP, developing 80 BHP at 2600 rpm. Compression ratio 5 to 1, magneto ignition, thermostatically controlled water pump cooling system. Side draught carburettor.
Gearbox: Four-speed crash box, multiple disc clutch, torque tube to rear with 4.5 to 1 final drive ratio. Brake servo pump operated by gearbox.
Suspension: Semi-elliptic springs with friction type shock absorbers in front, cantilever rear springs.
Brakes: Servo-assisted hydraulic brakes on all wheels. Mechanical handbrake on rear wheels.
Steering: Helical pinions, turning circle 45 ft (13.8 m) 3½ turns lock-to-lock. Adjustable steering column and optional power steering system (not fitted).

Wheels: Sankey, beaded edge tyres 895 x 135.
Dimensions: Wheelbase 11 ft 9.7 ins (3600 mm). Track 4 ft 9.5 ins (1460 mm). Overall length 16 ft 4 ins (5000 mm). Height 6 ft 2.7 ins (1900 mm). Kerb weight 40 cwt (2035 kg).
Performance: Maximum speed when new — 70 mph (115 km/h). Normal cruising speed — 50 mph (80 km/h). Fuel consumption at highway speeds — 12.5 mpg (22.5 litres/100 km).

1925 Fiat 501

THE MARQUE

This car provides an interesting counterpoint for the Fiat 519A, a sumptuous limousine built in the same year and shown on page 155. The two cars show the scope of Fiat's activities in the vintage years.

At the turn of the century Fiat was one of several small firms struggling to build an Italian motor industry. However, the vigour of its management, its success in motor sport and the reliability of its products soon made it one of Europe's largest car makers.

Fiat has always diversified its models, producing cars for all tastes and purses. It has a distinguished racing history, dating back to 1900. The company won the Sicilian race in 1904 which pre-dated the Targa Florio and, in 1907, swept the board. Factory drivers Lancia, Nazzaro and Wagner won every European event which counted, including the French Grand Prix.

Fiat managed to combine brute force with elegant lines for their racing machines. As early as 1905 the company built overhead valve racing engines and, in 1911, a twin-overhead camshaft design. It pioneered four wheel brakes in 1914 and later led the field in superchargers and other innovations.

Not surprisingly, a competition version of their most famous vintage model, the 501, was built. Its 1.46 litre engine was tuned to give a maximum speed of 58 mph (93 km/h) and a 501SS won its class in the 1922 Parma-Poggio di Berceto hill climb at an average speed of 50 mph (80 km/h).

Relatively standard 501s, mostly in the hands of private owners, have won some 1000 races around the world.

Built between 1919 and 1926 the 501, 501S and the 501C were Fiat's first mass produced cars, with total sales of 40,000. The prototype, built in 1918, was dubbed the 'Lawyer's Masterpiece' being designed by legal man, Carlo Cavalli, who was also Fiat's works manager. The simple but robust mechanical design was a monument to reliability.

The relatively small engine was required to pull a fairly large and heavy body, and low overall gearing limited the maximum speed to 48 mph (77 km/h). Fuel economy was excellent. The standard engine developed 18 BHP at 2600 rpm, but the more sporting 501S was tuned to give 26.5 BHP at 3000 rpm. Lighter in weight, it had a top speed of 56 mph (92 km/h). The 501C was a colonial model with a widened track for use on rough roads.

Around 400 501's are believed to survive around the world. Australia has about 40 and New Zealand around 30, showing how popular the model was 'down under'.

1925 FIAT 501C

Fitted with a four door touring body built in Sydney by Garrets, this car is believed to have spent much of its working life in northern New South Wales. It was once owned by a jockey named Harris who is not a relative of the present owners, Peter and Marie Harris, of Southport, Qld.

Found some years ago in Lismore, the car was originally purchased to provide spare parts for a 1923 501 but was considered too good to scrap. Restoration commenced in 1973 with Peter Harris, Roger Pineri and Fraser Blackwell doing the mechanical and body work, Smith Brothers the trim.

The beautifully rebuilt car won the Vintage Section of the 1976 Speed Week Concours in Queensland and also the Vintage Section of the 1977 Vintage Car Club Concours.

MECHANICAL FEATURES

Engine: Four-cylinder, side valve 1.46 litres capacity, rated at 10.4 HP, developing 18 BHP at 2800 rpm. Water pump cooling. Fiat side draught carburettor. Magneto ignition.
Gearbox: Four-speed. Fiat made straight cut crash box with gate change. Multi-plate disc clutch.
Suspension: Semi-elliptic springs front and rear.
Brakes: Internal expanding drum brakes on rear wheels with four shoes per unit.
Steering: Worm-and-sector with 2¼ turns lock-to-lock.
Wheels: Sankey detachable wheels, 5.00 x 19 tyres.
Dimensions: Wheelbase 8 ft 8¼ ins (2650 mm). Track 4 ft 1 in (1250 mm). Overall length 13 ft 0 ins (3962 mm). Height 5 ft 11 ins (1803 mm). Kerb weight 19½ cwt (993 kg).
Performance: Maximum speed when new – 48 mph (77 km/h). Normal cruising speed – 45 mph (72 km/h). Fuel consumption at highway speeds — 30 mpg (9.4 litres/100 km).

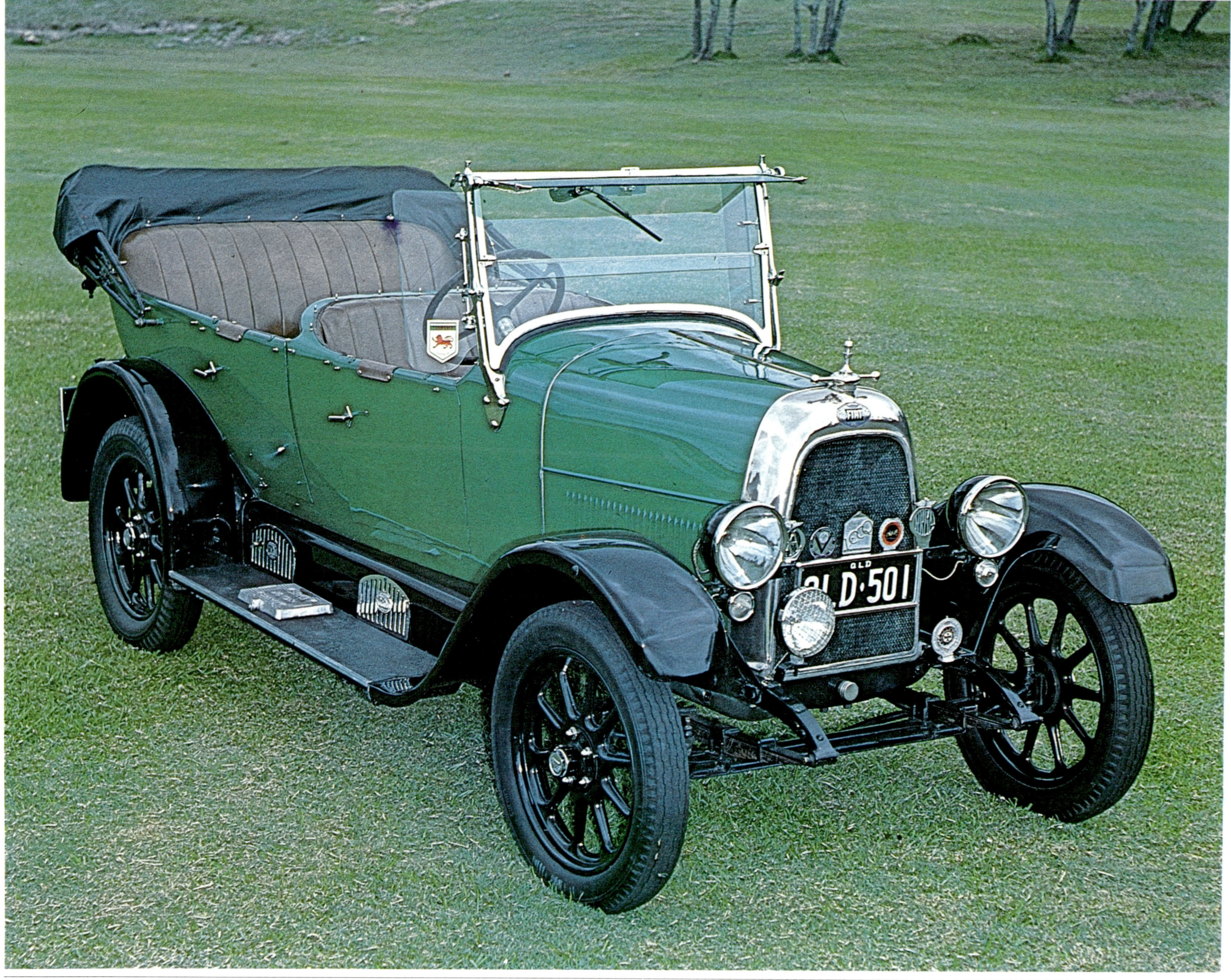

FIAT
QLD
D·501

1925 Rover Tourer

THE MARQUE

Rover's early history is told in a previous entry in this book, the 1906 Rover 6 HP shown on page 31. As soon as the company had the single-cylinder 6 HP successfully in production, it added two four-cylinder models to the range. The larger, the 16/20, earned its share of glory by winning its class in the 1907 Tourist Trophy Race at the Isle of Man.

Rover continued to produce the single cylinder car for some years, as well as twin and four-cylinder models. After World War One, the company decided to exploit the obvious market existing for a 'people's car'. The new design, known as the Eight, was cheap and basic, being powered by a twin-cylinder, air-cooled engine. An electric starter was never standard, but optional for the later cars. The Eight was noisy but economical — and popular. Some 17,000 were sold over a five year period.

In 1925 Rover introduced the larger and quieter 9/20 for its budget-conscious customers. For more affluent buyers, they offered the 14/45, later the 16/50, a new design with a remarkable cam in head engine incorporating hemispherical combustion chambers. A 14/45 won the R.A.C. Dewar Trophy for making 50 consecutive ascents of Bwlch-y-Groes, a steep hill in Wales, but despite this publicity, the car undoubtedly was under-powered. The engine developed 45 BHP, peaking at 3500 rpm. Despite a four-speed gearbox and a 5.0 to 1 axle ratio, the 14/45 was too sluggish for many motorists, especially the heavy sedan version.

In 1928 the company moved into the six-cylinder class with a more conventional OHV engine. Falling sales led to a major reorganisation in 1931. A new range comprised 10 HP, 12 HP and 14 HP models, as well as the celebrated Speed Twenty which gave the marque a new reputation as producers of conservative but fast and well engineered cars.

Rover commenced aircraft engine manufacturing during World War Two and, in 1950, made history by demonstrating the world's first gas turbine car. The large sums of money required for turbine development never led to a production design and the work was eventually dropped. The costly turbine project was probably the reason why Rover agreed in 1966 to the take-over offer made by Leyland trucks.

Today Rover is a leading division of British Leyland.

1925 ROVER 14/45 TOURER

Little is known about the car's early history. Though the aluminium body is original, it is not known whether it was made in Britain or Australia. The Torpedo-styled body seats five, with reasonable weather equipment in the form of hood and side screens.

Arthur Garthon of Hurstville, New South Wales, heard through the Rover Owners Club in 1976 that the 14/45 was in the hands of Adelaide's Rover agents, Champions Ltd., and had probably been traded in. It happens that Arthur was (and has since finished) restoring a 1927 six-cylinder Rover fitted with a similar body. He went to Adelaide to photograph the 14/45 and check some construction details, but returned to Sydney with it as a present for his wife, Val.

The body had already been restored by Dean Smoker of Champions Ltd. The mechanical components have since been rebuilt by Arthur Garthon. Three other 14/45's are known to exist in Australia and Alan Tester of Sydney owns and extensively drives the larger engined 16/50.

The 14/45's most unusual feature is the engine. The combustion chambers are fully machined to a hemispherical shape, the valves being operated by a camshaft in the cylinder head, through long rockers. Horizontal push rods run through the cylinder head to the exhaust valves.

MECHANICAL FEATURES

Engine: Four-cylinder, 2.283 litres capacity, valves inclined at 45 degrees, hemispherical combustion chambers. Rated at 14 HP, developing 45 BHP at 2500 rpm. Sloping S.U. carburettor, Lucas magneto.
Gearbox: Sliding pinion, crash-type with four forward speeds. Gear shift on driver's right hand side. Multi-disc clutch running in oil.
Suspension: Conventional semi-elliptics front and rear.
Brakes: Perrot system on four wheels with internal expanding design.
Steering: Worm-and-sector, lubricated by engine oil returning to the sump from the cylinder head. One turn lock-to-lock.
Wheels: Pressed steel artillery wheels, size 5.25 x 21.
Dimensions: Wheelbase 10 ft 2 ins (3099 mm). Overall length 14 ft 6 ins (4420 mm). Height 6 ft 0 ins (1829 mm). Kerb weight 28 cwt (1425 kg).
Performance: Maximum speed when new — 60 mph (100 km/h). Normal cruising speed — 40 mph (64 km/h). Fuel consumption at highway speeds — 20 mpg (14.1 litres/100 km).

1925 Straker-Squire 24/80

THE MARQUE

Sidney Straker and L. R. Squire were selling steam waggons and petrol buses in the British city of Bristol around the turn of the century. In 1906 they acquired the licence to build the Cornilleau-Ste Beuvre car and market it as a 25 HP Straker-Squire. Meanwhile, an engineering firm, Brazil and Holbarrow, joined forces with Straker-Squire and a brilliant young engineer, Roy Fedden, came to the company with the design for a new 2.0 litre four-cylinder car called the 12/14 HP Shamrock.

From the Shamrock (built in 1908 only) developed the 15 HP car on which the company established its "One Model Policy". It was advertised in 1913 as "The World's Best Fifteen". The Fifteen was raced at Brooklands both by the company and by private owners. The company's car broke many class records and its 98.74 mph (158 km/h) for the flying half mile and 92.02 mph (147 km/h) for fifty miles set in 1913, were still standing at the end of 1924.

The cars that raced at the Isle of Man in the 1914 Tourist Trophy were basically the standard Fifteen of the 1915 type (which did not go into production) and little different from the 1914 touring model.

Straker-Squire spent World War One building aero engines under licence and, in 1919, Roy Fedden designed the famous 24/80 model which earned the company a worthy niche in automotive history.

Its engine reflected the design of the aircraft units the firm had been building, the six-cylinders being separately cast, with a single overhead camshaft and exposed valve gear. It developed 80 HP and was sold as a sports 2/3 seater, torpedo four seater and as a limousine. The 24/80 was successfully raced at Brooklands, mainly in the hands of H. Kensington Moir, who once lapped Brooklands at 103.7 mph (166 km/h).

For some reason, the makers called the car a 24/90 from 1920 to 1922 and thereafter a 24/80, with no apparent reason for the change. Only 67 were made, four of which survive, including Moir's Brooklands car. The company's subsequent failure was due to poor management rather than the cars and commercial vehicles they built. There were frequent labour troubles and often long delays leading to cancellation of valuable orders. The 'One Model Policy' continued after World War One (apart from commercial vehicles) but a new board, elected in 1923, re-introduced the pre-war design, along with a 1½ litre light car.

Car production ceased in 1926, though a catalogue for that year was issued. The firm struggled on, mainly building commerical vehicles, eventually closing down in the late 1920s.

1925 STRAKER-SQUIRE 24/80

South Australia boasts the oldest veteran car movement in the country, dating back to 1934. The Sporting Car Club of South Australia is probably the second oldest club in the world which has consistently devoted attention to veteran car affairs. One early member, George Brooks, was instrumental in effecting firm ties with the Veteran Car Club of Great Britain and later became one of Australia's few recognised automotive historians.

George Brooks took his 1925 Straker-Squire on a 15,000 miles (24,000 km) tour of Britain and Europe in 1950-51, spending much of his spare time attending events conducted by the Veteran Car Club and the Vintage Sports Car Club. The car remains in excellent condition and is still driven regularly.

It was originally imported in 1925 by Mr S. R. Delmont of Adelaide and fitted with a locally made touring body. The present body is not the original, being taken from a 1923 four-cylinder 20 HP Straker-Squire and fitted after George Brooks had acquired the 24/80 in 1945. He worked on the car from 1947-49, then used it for nearly ten years as everyday transport. The 24/80 has never been restored in the true sense of word but has been maintained in sound serviceable condition.

It won several prizes in Concours events during the 1950s. It took part in the 1965 New Zealand International Veteran and Vintage Rally and the 1970 Australian International.

MECHANICAL FEATURES

Engine: Six-cylinder, 3.9 litre capacity, rated at 23.8 HP, developing 80 BHP at 3000 rpm. The engine features six separately cast cylinders, exposed valve gear and thermostatically controlled radiator shutters. An S.U carburettor and a Bosch magneto are fitted.
Gearbox: Four-speed sliding type with single plate clutch.
Suspension: Semi-elliptic springs at the front, cantilever springs at the rear.
Brakes: Four wheel brakes, internal expanding conventional design. Operated by rods with chain and sprocket equalisation.
Steering: Worm-and-wheel, with only 1¼ turns lock-to-lock.
Wheels: Rudge detachable wire, 5.25 x 21 tyres.
Dimensions: Wheelbase 10 ft 8 ins (3251 mm). Overall length 15 ft 0 ins (4572 mm). Height 5 ft 3 ins (1600 mm). Kerb weight 27 cwt (1374 kg).
Performance: Maximum speed when new — 75 mph (120 km/h). Normal cruising speed — 60 mph (100 km/h). Fuel consumption at highway speeds — 16 mpg (17.6 litres/100 km/h).

1925 Willys Knight Tourer

THE MARQUE

Willys is best known as the 'father of the Jeep', but the company has had two very successful past careers — as the makers of Overland and Willys-Knight. In fact, Willys built 140,111 cars in 1915, making it the world's second largest car maker, behind Ford.

The company which did so well fifty years ago was a composite of Standard Wheel Company (which made stage coach wheels), the Overland Company and eventually the Willys-Overland Company.

The first Overland (1902) was built because an engineering student named Claude Cox had written a thesis on gasoline engines. This made him a local expert and he was hired by Standard Wheel Company to design and build a small runabout, named after the famous stage coaches of the time.

Over one hundred Overland cars were made but by 1906 the company was desperately short of money and appeared likely to close. A New York car dealer, John North Willys, contracted to buy the entire year's output of cars in return for a controlling interest. He changed the name to Willys-Overland and, in three years, boosted output from 47 in 1907 to 4860 cars in 1909.

Production continued to rocket when Willys bought Pope-Toledo and moved the plant to Toledo and later introduced the industry's first time-payment plan for customers. In 1912 Willys drove a prototype car with a Knight double sleeve valve engine. By 1914 he had the first Willys-Knight ready for production. He went on a buying spree of supply companies.

Like so many company promoters, Willys over-reached himself. In 1919 he acquired Electric Auto-lite, New Process Gear and Duesenberg Motors, all for high prices. Within two years the company was floundering in a sea of red ink, with debts amounting to $46 million.

That extraordinary industry trouble-shooter, Walter P. Chrysler, was hired by the bankers (reputedly at a million dollars a year fee) to sort out the mess. It took him just one year to bring down the debts to $18 million and point the company in the right direction.

Chrysler ordered work to commence on the Overland Four, a highly successful design. He continued the 'silent' Knight series and originated the program which eventuated in the Overland 2.2 litre, four-cylinder Whippet of 1926. This series made a bid for the lion's share of the four-cylinder market.

The company's most successful model was, however, the Willys-Knight series of 'double sleeve valve' engines with 300,000 being built before production ceased in 1932.

But despite Chrysler's efforts, Willys went into receivership in 1921 and John Willys persuaded a syndicate of Toledo businessmen to put up $3 million and buy control of the company from the banks. In 1929 John Willys sold his shares and retired.

Unfortunately, like most car firms, Willys was severely hurt by the Depression of the 1930s. The production of the ugly model '77', known as the galloping pig, did not help. It went into receivership again in 1933 with production almost terminating.

The resurgence came when Willys, in conjunction with the United States Ordinance Corporation, developed the Jeep as a military all-purpose vehicle. Production commenced in 1937 and has continued ever since.

The company has since changed hands twice. The Kaiser-Frazer organisation acquired Willys soon after World War Two, mainly for its Aero design, the handiwork of former Ford engineer Clyde R. Paton. Production of all Kaiser vehicles, including the Aero, ceased in 1955 but Jeep lived on. In October 1969 American Motors Corporation signed an $86 million deal which bought Kaiser-Willys outright. Jeep manufacture was later to keep AMC afloat during some very lean years for its car making division.

1925 WILLYS KNIGHT 66

Willys built some exceptional four-cylinder designs until 1925 when the six-cylinder Model 66 was introduced, with a sleeve valve engine, front-wheel brakes and conventional chassis design.

Many thousands were built, but only seven are known to survive — two are in Australia. This model, owned by Anthony Switzer of Chatswood, New South Wales, is a superb example of a completely original Model 66. Its first owner, believed to be a Mr C. M. Whitmee, bought the car in Sydney and took it to Canowindra where it spent most of its life. It did little work and was eventually acquired by C. W. Sharpe, of Orange. In 1970 the car was still in first class mechanical order and complete in all respects.

Anthony Switzer acquired it in 1971. Over a three year period, he arranged for a complete paint job and new trim, but apart from that little attention was required to bring it to a first class condition.

Australia has an active register of Willys, Overland and Willys-Knight cars, with over 200 cars on its books, but this Model 66 is considered the pride of the fleet. As early as October 1903 a newspaper article said that A. Asher Smith, of Sydney, had ordered two Overland Runabouts "to be shipped at once".

MECHANICAL FEATURES

Engine: Six-cylinder, 3.9 litres, sleeve valves, rated at 25.35 HP, developing 60 BHP. Water-cooled with updraught carburettor and coil ignition.
Gearbox: Crash box with three forward gears and multi-plate clutch.
Suspension: Semi-elliptic leaf springs front and rear.
Brakes: Internal expanding brakes at front, external contracting at rear.
Steering: Ball-and-knuckle with two turns lock-to-lock.
Wheels: Timber spoked, 600 x 20.
Dimensions: Wheelbase 10 ft 6 ins (3200 mm). Overall length 14 ft 6 ins (4420 mm). Hood height 6 ft 5 ins (1956 mm). Kerb weight 30.5 cwt (1553 kg).
Performance: Maximum speed when new — 70 mph (112 km/h). Normal cruising speed — 50 mph (80 km/h). Fuel consumption at highway speeds — 12 mpg (23.5 litres/100 km).

1926 Salmson Ducktail

THE MARQUE

Between 1922 and 1930 Salmson cars were viewed by the racing world with a reverence approaching awe. The high cost of motor sport eventually proved too much for the small French firm, but not before its machines had given Bugatti and other designers a run for their money.

Salmson began as aircraft engine manufacturers with a factory close to the thriving Renault works at Billancourt, Paris. In 1922, Salmson started building the English G.N. cyclecar under licence, then followed with a 1.1 litre, four-cylinder car of its own. The engine was advanced for the day with overhead valves and a hemispherical combustion chamber. A single push rod operated the inlet and exhaust valves, using a clever system of springs and cams.

The first Salmson and most of the following models had a straight tooth-crown wheel and pinion, but no sun and planetary gears to give the usual differential action. The rear wheels were joined by a solid axle to reduce tyre scrub but the car took corners with a crab-like action.

This proved an asset rather than a drawback on the race circuit and before long Salmson was chalking up class wins in events as different as Le Mans 24 hour race and the Targa Florio.

Today Salmson is best remembered for its San Sebastian model, a two seater so named in 1926 after a racing version won the Spanish race. A year later, two San Sebastians finished 2nd and 3rd at Le Mans, being beaten only by the thunderous power of a big Bentley.

In a similar blown racing model, the French driver Goutte established a class record of 114.5 mph (183 km/h) at Brooklands. This led to two of Britain's top drivers, Major Goldie Gardner and Dr J. D. Benjafield, buying Salmsons.

The touring Salmson, the 10/15, was first produced in 1923, with a 1.2 litre engine. It had twin overhead camshafts but no differential. In 1925 the Series II arrived with front wheel brakes and other improvements, including a differential in the rear axle. A cozette supercharger was an optional extra.

By 1927 Salmson had an enviable track record but the arrival of the new M.G.s with their remarkably low prices and big sporting potential made inroads into Salmson sales. The firm responded by producing larger, more comfortable cars. During the 1930s they introduced a British model built in London. The two firms struggled into the post-war years with a succession of impressive looking coupés which never quite excited the buying public. In 1957 Renault acquired the company and Salmson, as such, disappeared.

1925 SALMSON D10CV Series II

This delightful looking roadster has an Australian made body with the then fashionable duck's tail rear end styling. There is only one door — on the left-hand side.

Its early history is not known but the car probably came here for competition purposes, being fitted with a low speed hill-climbing axle. Features include a fly-off handbrake and a starter/generator unit driven off the front of the crankshaft. Most unusual is the extremely direct steering — with only ¾ of a turn lock-to-lock.

The present owner, Des Hardman, of Armidale, New South Wales, purchased the Salmson in 1967. He re-sheeted the body and rebuilt the mechanical components.

There are only five known Salmsons in Australia.

MECHANICAL FEATURES

Engine: Four-cylinder, 1191 ccs, DOHC, rated at 10 HP, developing about 40 BHP at 4000 rpm. Thermo-syphon cooling with gear driven fan; side draught Zenith carburettor, high tension magneto. Crankshaft has only 2 main bearings yet the engine runs on a compression of 9 to 1.
Gearbox: Crash type with four forward gears. Shaft drive to rear axle.
Suspension: Semi-elliptics at front, quarter elliptics at rear.
Brakes: Rod-operated mechanical brakes with internal expanding design on all wheels.
Steering: Worm-and-wheel steering with ¾ turn lock-to-lock, 40 ft (12.2 m) turning circle.
Wheels: Beaded edge spoke wheels with centre lock, 730 x 130 size.
Dimensions: Wheelbase 9 ft 5 ins (2870 mm). Overall length 13 ft 0 ins (3962 mm). Height 5 ft 6 ins (1422 mm).
Performance: Maximum speed when new — 60 mph (97 km/h). Normal cruising speed — 50 mph (80 km/h). Fuel consumption at highway speeds — 30 mpg (9.4 litres/100 km).

1927 Bugatti Type 35C Competition Car

THE MARQUE

Ettore Bugatti was an Italian who spent most of his life in Molsheim in Alsace, which has been a part of Germany but is now attached to France. More than any other constructor, he produced cars of legendary character. A restless genius who died in 1946, Bugatti crowded more into his 66 years than half a dozen normal men, designing and building a total of 9500 cars, each one a consummate example of craftsmanship.

The very first Bugatti — a twin engined motorised tricycle — won eight of the ten races it entered. In future years Bugatti was to become the giant of European racing. His cars were also immensely successful around the world, including Australia, where W. B. (Bill) Thompson won three of the early Australian Grand Prix held on the Phillip Island circuit, Victoria. Arthur Terdich and Harry Drake-Richmond were also virtuosos, racing Bugattis in the early Australian Grand Prix events mainly driving Type 37 and 37A's. Hope Bartlett was another exponent and is best known for his winning exploits at Maroubra Speedway near Sydney.

Ettore Bugatti started making cars in 1909 and won his first grand prix in 1911. During the next 28 years his cars won more road races than any marque in history.

The epitome of a racing Bugatti, the Type 35, had a relatively small 2 litre engine but was light in weight, beautifully engineered and magnificently stable. For six years it showed a clean exhaust pipe to Europe's big budget racing teams. It was at its best on tight, torturous circuits such as the Grand Prix of Monaco. Once a pair of Type 35's, in the hands of amateur drivers, narrowly beat the immortal Rudolf Caracciola at the wheel of a Mercedes whose engine was three times larger than the Bugatti!

1927 BUGATTI TYPE 35C

Owned by Gavin Sandford-Morgan of Adelaide, this magnificently rebuilt 'Bug' started life as a Type 37 and was driven by Drake-Richmond in the early Australian Grand Prix's on Phillip Island.

Drake-Richmond was one of the colourful characters of the racing circuit. He boasted that he and his riding mechanic had combined ages totalling 120 years — yet they achieved memorable results under very difficult conditions. During the 1930 Australian Grand Prix, Drake-Richmond rammed his Type 37 into the rear of a Brooksland Riley, yet he stopped only long enough to change a wheel and carry on — coming second outright. The same car came third in 1931, second in 1933 and fifth in 1934.

It subsequently had a very patchy career and was later cut in half to make a speedway car. Subsequently, the chassis was welded back to its original condition and soon after World War Two, Arthur

Chick bought it from Arthur Wylie and installed a Type 43 engine, this being the supercharged eight-cylinder engine virtually identical to the Type 35B engine. For the next five years he engaged in a variety of competition events, after which the car lay unused for seven years. It was then bought and restored by Stuart Anderson. Since then it has been entirely rebuilt as a Type 35C with a supercharged 2 litre engine by Gavin Sandford-Morgan. He received help from G. Loveday (body) and Tom Butterfield (trim). The Type 35 and Type 37 had virtually identical chassis and bodies, apart from the engine and road wheels.

The Type 35 made its debut at the 1924 French Grand Prix and created a sensation. Its unsupercharged engine featured three overhead valves per cylinder and it ran on a combination of ball and crankshaft roller bearings. The supercharged versions, the Type 35C (2 litre) and the 35B (2.3 litre) were introduced for the 1927 racing season.

MECHANICAL FEATURES

Engine: Eight-cylinder, overhead valves, 1990 ccs capacity, developing 135 BHP at 5500 rpm in supercharged form. Zenith carburettor, Bosch magneto.
Gearbox: Sliding spur, with four forward speeds and a Bugatti built multi-plate clutch.
Suspension: Semi-elliptic leafs at front, reversed quarter elliptics at rear.
Brakes: Four wheel drum brakes, cable operated.
Steering: Worm-and-wheel with 19 ins wire wheels.
Dimensions: Wheelbase 7 ft 10 ins (2387 mm). Overall length 12 ft 1 ins (3683 mm). Height 3 ft 6 ins (1067 mm). Kerb weight 15 cwt (764 kg).
Performance: Maximum speed when new — 130 mph (208 km/h). Normal cruising speed — 80 mph (128 km/h). 0-50 mph (80 km/h) acceleration — 6 seconds. Fuel consumption at highway speeds — 18 mpg (15.7 litres/100 km).

1927 Citroen B14 Tourer

THE MARQUE

Louis Renault and Andre Citroen were intense business rivals who spurred each other to greater heights. Whilst Renault was a born engineer with a profound understanding of how to make and conserve money, Citroen was a super-salesman, with a gambler's instinct for borrowing and risking large sums.

During World War One Citroen had the controlling interest in a firm making gears and shells. The armistice left him with a large factory, ideally suited to car manufacture. Citroen studied Henry Ford's operation and set out to become the Ford of France.

His first car, released in May 1919, was the Type A 8 HP open tourer designed to be as near full proof as possible. Some 16,000 orders were taken immediately it was announced and production soon reached 10,000 units annually.

In 1921 the Type A was joined by the B2, one of the world's first sports cars directly derived from a production model. The same 9 HP four-cylinder engine later powered five Citroens which made the first ever crossing of the Sahara desert. The specially built machines with two-speed axles and caterpillar tracks publicised the Citroen name around the world.

By 1924 Citroen was building 250 cars a day on an advanced assembly line, including a lovely little 5 CV open tourer designed to be a true 'woman's car'. Driven by a missionary — Mr N. R. Westwood — a 5 CV (known here as a 7 HP) made the first officially recognised car trip around Australia. It left Perth in August 1925, completing the journey in five months.

The B12 Citroen, announced in 1925, set new standards for a European family car. The design featured a one piece spot-welded steel body, four-wheel brakes and an exceptionally good spray painted finish. The car proved popular and production was stepped up to 400 a day. Factories were also established in Britain, Italy and Belgium, with Citroen setting his sights on being an international car maker. He already commanded 36 per cent of the French market and borrowed huge sums to further modernise and enlarge his plants.

By 1930, Citroen was proving such a threat that Louis Renault launched a cut-throat offensive which gave and asked no quarter. The cost of the rivalry came close to breaking both firms.

Citroen responded by conceiving a revolutionary car which would make all Renaults look old-fashioned. He studied the work of several French men who were perfecting front-wheel-drive models, then committed his factory to build the world's first mass produced FWD. Simultaneously, he decided to finance work on a new fully automatic transmission and torque convertor, and use it as standard equipment in the new car.

Though his engineers told him the FWD model would not be ready before mid 1936, Citroen instructed them to have it ready by 1934. As a result, it went into production badly under-developed. The transmission proved so troublesome that Citroen was forced to design a conventional three-speed transmission almost overnight. Hundreds of automatic transmissions were scrapped and replaced by the new standard-shift box, but the cost was so high that Citroen's previously generous lines of credit closed up.

More trauma came when the first production front-wheel-drives gave endless trouble and the dealers' showrooms were soon overstocked with unsold cars.

The design itself was brilliant with front-wheel-drive, torsion bar suspension, hydraulic brakes, overhead valve engine and a completely modern unit-construction body. Its lack of development and the resulting sales resistance sent the company to the wall. At the request of the French Government, Michelin — a major creditor — took control in 1934. Citroen died a year later, a broken man.

His dream car — later famous as the 'Traction Avant' — was quickly modified. It became thoroughly reliable and stayed in production for twenty years. All Citroens have since had front-wheel-drive and engineering which put them years ahead of their time. The company is now part of the Peugeot group.

CITROEN B14 F

The most successful of the early Citroens, the B14 was noted for its simplicity and durability. Their reputation was endorsed in 1960 when a 1928 B14 taxi cab operating in Budapest was officially confirmed as having travelled 2.2 million miles, or 3.5 million km, driven by the same man since new.

The B14 was built with a range of body styles, including landaulet. In touring form, it boasted a maximum speed of 50 mph (80 km/h) with fuel economy around 33 mpg or 8.5 litres/100 km.

The car illustrated here was found in Ashfield, New South Wales by the Formby family of Bexley and restored by them to its present condition. It is currently exhibited at Green's Motorcade, near Liverpool, New South Wales.

MECHANICAL FEATURES

Engine: Four-cylinder, side valve, 1539 ccs. Rated at 9 HP, developing 22 BHP at 2300 rpm. Thermo-syphon water cooling, with Solex carburettor and magneto ignition. Two bearing crankshaft and gravity feed fuel tank.
Gearbox: Three-speed crash box with ball change in centre of floor. Single plate clutch, drive shaft with universal joint at each end.
Suspension: Semi-elliptic springs front and rear, with four friction-type shock absorbers.
Brakes: Four wheel drum brakes, Westinghouse system with servo assistance.
Steering: Worm-and-nut with 3 turns lock-to-lock.
Wheels: Michelin disc wheels, 5.50 x 19.
Dimensions: Wheelbase 9 ft 5 ins (2870 mm). Track 4 ft 0½ ins (1230 mm). Overall length 13 ft 6 ins (4115 mm). Height 4 ft 7 ins (1397 mm). Kerb weight 22.6 cwt (1150 kg).
Performance: Maximum speed when new — 50 mph (80 km/h). Normal cruising speed — 35 mph (56 km/h). Fuel consumption at highway speeds — 33 mpg (8.5 litres/100 km).

1927 Hudson Super Six

THE MARQUE

Hudson is possibly better known in Australia for the company's cheaper line (the Essex) than for the Hudson marque itself. The Essex did excellent business here during the 1920s, being widely publicised by a succession of interstate speed records.

Hudson was the superior car technically, but its price as much as anything else kept its Australian sales to a moderate number. The 1927 Super Six Brougham cost when new about $1300 in the United States, against $US600 for a Chevrolet with a comparable body. An Essex Phaeton with seating for five sold at $US695.

When this Super Six was built, the American industry was suffering its first taste of the Depression. Sales had plummeted down from 3.9 million in 1926 to 3.0 million in 1927. Hudson managed to build 53,000 cars that year, which was sound business if not spectacular.

Hudson had been formed in 1909 by Roy Chapin, father of the present Roy Chapin, the recent chief executive of American Motors. Roy Chapin, Snr., was an astute marketing man. His early cars were very keenly priced and promoted with considerable vigour. The first production car was described as 'the Model 20, having sliding gear transmission (selective type), its engine being a European-type with four cylinders, four cycle, water-cooled.' Some 4000 were sold during the first year of production.

A year later the company graduated to a new 'fluid cushion' clutch, a single plate affair with cork inserts running in oil. That same basic design was used for many years. When Brian Boardman, who owns the Super Six photographed on this page, was restoring the car he used the corks from 132 bottles to overhaul the clutch!

Hudson moved into the six-cylinder engine field in 1914, the new 4½ litre design establishing the company's considerable reputation for durability. In 1916 a Super Six made the first recorded two-way crossing between New York and San Francisco. In 1927 the engine capacity was enlarged to 4.7 litres, and an overhead inlet valve and side exhaust cylinder head fitted.

The Super Six represented the company's finest hour. The straight eight model produced in 1930 made little impact on the market and the company had a lean time.

In 1948 Hudson introduced a Step Down design, with a new high compression engine. The body and chassis were combined in a unitised structure (as on almost all modern cars), with independent front suspension system. The company built 145,000 cars in 1950 but

fierce competition from the larger companies forced them to seek a less crowded market. An attempt to create demand for a new compact car failed and in 1954 Hudson merged with Nash, forming American Motors Corporation. The last Hudson was built in 1958.

1927 HUDSON SUPER SIX

Typical of the cars produced by Hudson, this unusual Brougham has a five seater American body, made from timber and aluminium, with a fabric roof, built by Biddle and Smart.

The custom built body with its large rear luggage trunk sits on a standard 127 inch wheelbase Hudson chassis, the same wheelbase used for the company's seven passenger limousine.

The car was originally imported by Dalgety & Co. and sold to a family in Mittagong, New South Wales. It travelled extensively around the area, with frequent trips to Bathurst, staying with the original owner until the late 1950s when it passed to John Giddy. The present owner, Brian Boardman, of Lugarno, New South Wales, purchased the car in 1975. He found it almost complete, stored in a chicken shed in Kenthurst, New South Wales.

Brian Boardman spent three years restoring the Super Six. Every component was dismantled and rebuilt, the owner attending to the mechanical work and Bill Kay the body restoration. Bob Hutton Motor Trim restored the trim. They did the job so well that the Super Six won the Vintage Motor Club 1978 Annual Concours d'Elegance on its first major outing.

MECHANICAL FEATURES

Engine: Six-cylinder, 4.7 litre capacity, F-head with overhead inlet valve and side exhaust. Cast iron detachable block with aluminium crankcase, splash feed lubrication, Schebler carburettor (optional extra), rated at 29.4 HP, developing approximately 100 BHP at 3000 rpm. Cooling assisted by radiator shutters.
Gearbox: Hudson three-speed; single disc clutch with 132 cork inserts running in oil.
Suspension: 39 ins (990 mm) long semi-elliptics at front. The rear semi-elliptics are almost 58 ins long and splayed outwards at the rear to reduce body roll.
Brakes: Four wheel brakes with Bendix self energising 3-shoe in 14 ins (355 mm) drums.
Steering: Gemmer worm-and-peg type with 2½ turns lock-to-lock and approximately 40 ft (12.2 m) turning circle.
Wheels: Felloe brand wood and steel, 19 ins diameter, 650/600 x 19 tyres.
Dimensions: Wheelbase 10 ft 7 ins (3236 mm). Overall length 15 ft 8 ins (4775 mm). Kerb weight 32.6 cwt (1660 kg).
Performance: Maximum speed when new — 65 mph (104 km/h). Normal cruising speed — 45 mph (72 km/h). Fuel consumption at highway speeds — 14 mpg (20.1 litres/100 km).

1927 Jordan Sports Saloon

THE MARQUE

Jordan cars were built in Cleveland, Ohio, United States, between 1916 and 1931, but never in large numbers. It is doubtful if total production over the fifteen years reached 80,000 cars; of these, only a handful still exist.

But Jordan remains a memorable marque, thanks to its elegant styling and the policy of appealing to the emotional senses in its advertising. The company ran some of the finest newspaper and magazine advertisements of the day, stressing the cars' good looks and the pleasure of driving them.

From the start Edward Jordan fitted Continental engines, then considered one of the best proprietary units around. Only six-cylinder models were built until 1925 when the first Jordan straight eight arrived. It appears to have scored a minor hit, for in 1926 the company recorded its best sales ever — 11,000 cars for the year.

Having tapped the top end of the market, the company launched the relatively small but well equipped 'Little Custom' sedan. The wheelbase was reduced from 116 ins in the standard model to 107 ins, the engine capacity from 4.5 to 3.5 litres.

The 'Little Custom' was intended to produce luxury motoring at a reasonable price. Jordan advertised it as 'A veritable cameo of clean cut lines and compelling charm.' Standard equipment included a full set of instruments, air cleaner, oil filter, electric air horn, automatic windscreen wiper, shock absorbers, stop light, rear view mirror, sun visor, double cowl ventilator and dipping headlights. Some were also equipped with a ventilating windshield, smoking case, dome light and vanity case.

The 'Little Custom' was not a success, but the larger six and the eight-cylinder model continued to sell steadily. Jordan dropped the 'Little Custom' and, in 1930, introduced what contemporary observers said was its best car ever, the 5.3 litre Speedway Eight. It offered buyers a remarkable 114 HP, a four-speed transmission and styling closely resembling that used by Bentley and other British high performance cars.

Unfortunately, the Speedway Eight was priced at $5000. Its debut almost coincided with the Depression and the company closed in 1931.

1927 JORDAN MODEL R

Despite extensive enquiries, the owner of this rare car, Noel Williams, of Toogoolawah, Queensland, is unable to find out how and why it came here. It appears that at least three Jordans reached Australia in 1927 and two survive. There is also one Jordan mobile in Auckland, New Zealand, another in Canada, and a few in the United States.

Noel's car is a 'Little Custom' chassis fitted with a Jordan-made body, described by the company as a 'Sport Salon'. In today's terms it would be called a fixed hardtop with a fabric hood and the rear window suspended loosely in the fabric, as in a tourer.

The car was extensively used in its earlier days; some time in the 1950s it was acquired for restoration by the late Rex Reno, of Nambour, Queensland. The work never started and the car was eventually left at a wrecker's yard. Peter Harris, of Southport, Queensland, heard about the wreck and inspected it with Noel Williams, who decided to buy it for the princely sum of £12.50 ($25). He found another Jordan in Brisbane which he purchased for spares.

The mechanical restoration was done by R. I. Cannell, of Toogoolawah. The owner replaced the woodwork and completely rebuilt the body with help from local tradesmen. Wilcox Motor Body Works of Brisbane repainted the car. The trim was done by F. G. and N. J. Somerwill, of Southport.

In its day, the 'Little Custom' was quite a car. According to the Owner's Handbook, the car can cruise at 55 mph (88 km/h), but Noel considers 50 mph (80 km/h) to be a more comfortable speed.

MECHANICAL FEATURES

Engine: Six-cylinder Continental engine, side valve, 3.5 litres. Rated at 25 HP, it develops 60 BHP. Stromberg carburettor and coil ignition.
Gearbox: Warner three-speed crash box with single dry plate clutch and bevel drive.
Suspension: Semi-elliptic springs front and rear.
Brakes: Four wheel hydraulic brakes with external contracting bands on drums.
Steering: Worm-and-wheel.
Wheels: Wire spoked 18 ins.
Dimensions: Wheelbase 8 ft 11 ins (2718 mm). Overall length 13 ft 8 ins (4166 mm). Height 5 ft 8.5 ins (2232 mm).
Performance: Maximum speed when new — 65 mph (104 km/h). Normal cruising speed — 50 mph (80 km/h). Fuel consumption at highway speeds — 17 mpg (16.6 litres/100 km).

1927 Lancia Lambda

THE MARQUE

Former racing driver, Vincenzo Lancia, quit F.I.A.T. in 1906 to start his own company. For fourteen years he produced heavy, well engineered, conventional cars. Then, in 1922, he broke with tradition and designed his personal dream machine. It proved to be one of the world's great cars, and a major trend setter.

The lean, sleek and beautifully proportioned Lambda was one of the most advanced and sophisticated cars of its day. It was almost matchless as a family car as well as a high performance tourer.

The prophetic design came from the hand of Lancia himself. His lifelong interest in boats prompted him to design a car body with sufficient structural rigidity to carry all the mechanical components without a separate chassis frame. To this unitary structure he added independent front wheel suspension, an overhead camshaft V-4 engine and remarkably effective four wheel brakes.

Even more prophetic was the manner in which Lancia provided maximum passenger room. The small engine, combined with an unusually compact gearbox, was placed as far forward as possible, leaving room for a spacious passenger compartment. The design also featured a hide-away hood (more easily erected than most hoods of the day) plus one of the first luggage boots seen in a mass-produced car.

The Lambda was strictly a road machine. When it first reached Australia, the advanced specifications so intrigued a Melbourne group of enthusiasts that they wrote to the Italian factory asking for hints to modify the engine for competition. Lancia tersely replied: "This is a touring car. No details are available for anything to do with racing."

The V-4 engine had its cylinders offset by only 13 degrees. The cast-iron cylinder liners are in an alloy block, with a cast iron cylinder head. The original capacity was 2121 ccs, but this later became 2353 and 2360 ccs, the HP progressing from 49 to 59 to 69 BHP.

Nine different series of Lambdas were

built over a period of eight years. Some had the shortwheel base chassis of 122 ins (3100 mm), the others the long wheelbase of 135 ins (3430 mm). In 1927 the factory started building Lambdas with conventional chassis, so that custom-made bodies could be fitted. Mechanically, these cars were similar to the classic design.

The Lambda was known as the 'Legendary Lancia', and not just for its advanced specifications. It was considered an exceptionally fine road performer, with lively acceleration for the day, excellent steering, strong brakes and delightful handling qualities.

At one time the factory reconsidered its ban on racing and prepared the only Lancia entered Lambda competition car. Built for the second Mille Miglia, it was leading the race when only 180 miles (300 km) from the finish. A minor road accident put it out.

A total of 13,000 Lambdas were built.

LAMBDA TORPEDO TOURER

The exceptional example of the 7th series Lambda is one of the Hardman family collection in Armidale, New South Wales. An unusually original car, it has had only two owners since new.

The Lambda was originally purchased in Sydney in May 1927 by E. R. M. Shannan and extensively used from 'Balmoral', his property near Coonabarabran, New South Wales. In 1967 Lyndon Hardman swapped a used Land Rover for the Lancia. At the time, it had done 150,000 miles without a major overhaul. The Lambda was then meticulously rebuilt by the late E. R. Hardman and Lyndon Hardman, the trim being done by Blencowe & Son, of Armidale.

MECHANICAL FEATURES

Engine: Four-cylinder, overhead camshaft, capacity 2.37 litres, rated at 15.6 HP, developing 59.4 BHP at 2350 rpm. Zenith sidedraught carburettor, Bosch magneto. The cylinder block has a 13 degrees vee with cast iron sleeves in an alloy casting.
Gearbox: Crash type with four forward gears, short throw remote control change lever. Multiplate dry clutch. Spiral bevel rear axle.
Suspension: Independent front suspension with coil springs and hydraulic shock absorber. Semi-elliptics with Hartford shocks at rear.
Brakes: Four wheel internal expanding, cable operated. Finned alloy drums with steel liners.
Steering: Worm-and-wheel with 2¾ turns lock-to-lock.
Wheels: Rudge-Whitworth wire spokes, 22 ins x 5.00 tyres.
Dimensions: Wheelbase 10 ft 2 ins (3100 mm). Track 4 ft 7 ins (1400 mm). Overall length 15 ft 2 ins (4623 mm). Height 5 ft 4½ ins (1638 mm). Kerb weight 21 cwt (1070 kg).
Performance: Maximum speed when new — 71.5 mph (115 km/h). Normal cruising speed — 55 mph (90 km/h). Fuel consumption at highway speeds — 22 mpg (12.8 litres/100 km).

8
394
NSW
Y FI·014 O

1928 Bentley 4½ Litre Tourer

THE MARQUE

Walter Owen Bentley headed the company bearing his name for only twelve years. In that time he built 3030 cars, gained five Le Mans victories (four in successive years) and wrote an indelible page of motoring history.

The very fast lorry — 'le camion le plus vite' — as Ettore Bugatti once called it, was an enormous success in every sense, except commercially. Despite financial support from some wealthy friends and clients, Walter Owen Bentley had no option but to put the company into liquidation in 1931 and sell the assets for a paltry £130,000. The buyer — British Equitable Central Trust — virtually held an auction between Napier and Rolls-Royce — the latter winning.

W. O. Bentley designed the rotary engine for the World War One Nieuport Scout aircraft before launching his own company in 1919. His prototype 3 litre tourer was running by 1921 and, in May that year, it won his first race at Brooklands. The company was closely tied to motor sport for the next twelve years — but Bentley never built racing cars. His were all road-going high-performance machines. Some had magnificent saloon bodies, though the sporting tourers do most to evoke the marque's halycon days.

Bentley built six different models between 1919 and 1931, ranging from the 3 litre (1921-29) to the 8 litre (1930-31). All carried a five year guarantee.

As early as 1925 the English magazine, *The Motor*, was proclaiming that Bentleys had engines and brakes that were amongst the smoothest the magazine had ever tested.

The original 3 litre chassis was sold with a guarantee that it could do 80 mph (129 km/h) on the Brooklands circuit and also return 25 mpg (11.3 litres/100 km) at a steady speed of 29 mph (48 km/h).

The four-cylinder 4½ litre was introduced in 1927, rather to the dismay of the English press who had expected a six. The original engine developed 100 BHP, the figure rising to 110 BHP and eventually 130 BHP. An unblown 4½ won the 1928 Le Mans.

Some 4½ models carried an Amherst Villiers supercharger, jutting from the front dumb irons. The blower boosted power to 240 BHP at 4200 rpm and was largely developed for Le Mans competition work. Bentley himself was never enthusiastic about the superchargers.

When subject to the stresses of high speed racing, the blown engines blew up with monotonous regularity. Despite Bentley's overall success at Le Mans (with unblown engines), the failures were widely publicised and, in W. O. Bentley's view at least, the bad publicity led to the company's downfall.

The Bentley factory team — comprising such notables as Dr Dudley Benjafield (a Harley Street bacteriologist), Tim Birkin, Woolf Barnato, Sammy Davis and Bertie Moir — was unusual in that the drivers bought their cars, thus paying for the privilege of racing under the factory banner. W. O. Bentley, himself a former racing driver, acted as pit manager.

In 1926 the company announced its big 6½ litre six, followed by the 180 BHP 'Speed 6' of 1929, launched just as Britain entered the Depression.

The large Bentley with the mammoth 8 litre six-cylinder unit of 220 BHP arrived in 1930. Just over 100 were made, half of which survive.

After his company collapsed, W. O. Bentley joined Rolls-Royce. Three years later he moved to Lagonda where he was chief designer until 1946. In later life he maintained he could not afford to own a used Bentley himself and attended Bentley Driver Club meetings in a Morris 1000.

W. O. Bentley died in 1971.

1928 4½ LITRE SHORT CHASSIS

Bentley made a total of 713 4½ litre models before being taken over by Rolls-Royce, but only eight had the 'short' chassis, reduced from the standard 10 ft 10 ins (3302 mm) to 9 ft 9½ inches (2985 mm). Three were built in 1927, two in 1928 and three in 1929 — all 'short chassis' models being built to firm orders.

The rare short chassis 4½ in these photographs was owned for more than thirty years by an English car dealer who spent his spare time meticulously rebuilding it to new condition. He completed the work in 1974 and the restored car had barely covered 50 miles (80 km) when Sydney collector Frank Illich heard of it and made an unrefusable offer.

The magnificent sports tourer has an original Vanden Plas fabric-covered body.

The 4½ litre was well summed up in a road test published (February 1929) in the English *Autocar* magazine: "It must be remembered that though, in a sense, the 4½ litre is a sports model, it is not so truly a sports model as to be outside the consideration of the average driver who wants a quiet, flexible and comfortable car. As a matter of fact, the machine is two cars in one, according to the type of driver at the wheel."

MECHANICAL FEATURES

Engine: Four-cylinder overhead cam design with 4 valves per cylinder. Bore-and-stroke 100 mm x 140 mm, giving 4.39 litre capacity. Water pump and fan cooling, twin SU carburettors and twin magnetos. Engine develops 110 BHP at 3500 rpm.
Gearbox: Conventional crash box detached from engine; 7 pitch 'D' type design with four forward gears. Single plate clutch.
Suspension: Semi-elliptic springs front and rear.
Brakes: Mechanically operated four wheel drum brakes.
Steering: Worm-and-sector steering. Two turns lock-to-lock.
Wheels: Rudge-Whitworth knock off wire wheels, well base rims, 5.25 x 21 tyres.
Dimensions: Wheelbase 9 ft 9½ ins (2985 mm). Track 4 ft 8 ins (1422 mm). Overall length 13 ft 3 ins (4038 mm). Height 5 ft 2 ins (1575 mm). Kerb weight 26 cwt (1324 kg).
Performance: Maximum speed when new — 92 mph (147 km/h). Normal cruising speed — 75 mph (120 km/h). Fuel consumption at highway speeds — 16 mpg (17.6 litres/100 km).

1928 Bugatti Type 40 Touring Car

THE MARQUE

Though Ettore Bugatti made the finest racing machines of the day, he also produced superb touring cars. His extraordinary skill ranged from designing the world's first true mini — the 1912 Peugeot Bebe — to creating the largest, most powerful and most sumptuous limousine ever, the 1929 Royale.

In all, Bugatti produced 9500 cars comprising 53 different types. They had one thing in common — flawless road manners combined with matchless performance for their class. Some, such as the 130 mph (208 km/h) Type 57SC, were unbelievably fast; others were enormous fun for the lucky owners.

Many were noisy, temperamental, often incredibly complicated machines, but collectively they wrote a saga of immortality.

One of his racing engines had four cylinders and sixteen valves; another featured a truly unique approach to the problem of brake wear when racing. Its drums were cast integrally with the wheels — and spare wheels with smaller drums were kept ready in the pits.

Bugatti dominated the European racing scene for nearly a decade. He achieved an incredible five successive wins in the toughest event of all — the Targa Florio road race in Sicily. Here the mountain circuit tested the cars to the last rivet and the drivers to exhaustion, with 1200 hairpin bends to be taken at racing speeds.

Bugatti lived like a feudal lord. His self-contained estate in Alsace contained his car factory, horse stables, kennels, aviaries, private distillery, vineyard, cinema, police station, museum and boat yard. There was also an exhibition hall, not for his cars but to display the sculpture work of his brother, Rembrandt.

Bugatti's private world came to an end in 1938 when his son Jean — then being groomed to take over the factory — was killed testing a new Bugatti. Months later, World War Two broke out and the Bugatti factory was seized by the German army.

Ettore Bugatti died in 1947, at a time when he was working on new models for the post-war years. The family unsuccessfully tried to carry on, but the marque effectively ended with the passing of its creator.

1928 BUGATTI TYPE 40

Known as a 'Grand Sport' and owned by Col Wagener of Glen Osmond, South Australia, this sporting tourer is described by the factory brochure as a 'close coupled 4 seat torpedo touring car'. In reality, it has room for two adults with very limited leg room behind.

The Type 40 first appeared in 1926 and was capable of 75 mph (120 km/h) — quite a speed from a 1½ litre engine at that time. It sold at the comparatively modest price of £500 ($1000) in Australia, yet incorporated many of the design features of more expensive Bugattis, including an overhead camshaft engine with three valves per cylinder. A standard Type 40 once lapped Brooklands at 70 mph (112 km/h) in appalling weather conditions and was generally regarded as a very pleasant touring car, with

comfortable springing and exceptional handling by the standards of the 1920s. The engine was unusually flexible and pulled smoothly from low speeds in top gear. It also revved willingly and could reach 62 mph (100 km/h) in third gear. An average fuel consumption was 31 mpg on the open road, under normal touring conditions.

The car on this page was once owned by racing driver, Bill Thompson, but not for competition purposes. Its early history is not known but after World War Two it was bought by Peter Clarke, of New South Wales, then sold to Brian Coxon of Armadale, Victoria. After having some work done, he sold the car to Jim Bell. In late 1948 it was swapped for a 30/98 Vauxhall and the new owner, John Keys, crashed it.

Col Wagener acquired the car in 1966 in good order from Bill Barber. The mechanical restoration was done by the late Dave Roberts, the trim restoration by the owner. The car competed in the 1970 Sydney-Melbourne-Adelaide International Veteran and Vintage Rally.

MECHANICAL FEATURES

Engine: Four-cylinder, 1.5 litre overhead cam unit rated at 11.9 HP, developing 50 BHP at 4200 rpm. Conventional cooling; Zenith carburettor and coil ignition. The engine has three valves per cylinder which is normal for a Bugatti, unusual for any other engine.
Gearbox: Central gate change with four forward speeds and multiple disc clutch.
Suspension: Semi-elliptics at front, with reverse cantilever at rear.
Brakes: Cable operated drums on all wheels.
Steering: Worm design with 35 ft TC and 1¾ turns lock-to-lock. Rudge-Whitworth wire wheels 5.00 x 19 ins.
Dimensions: Wheelbase 8 ft 11 ins (2718 mm). Overall length 11 ft 10 ins (3327 mm). Height 3 ft 8 ins (1117 mm). Kerb weight 19 cwt (967 kg).
Performance: Maximum speed when new — 75 mph (120 km/h). Normal cruising speed — 60 mph (96 km/h). 0-50 mph acceleration — 30 seconds. Fuel consumption at highway speeds — 28 mpg (10 litres/100 km).

1928 Morgan Super Sports Aero

THE MARQUE

British built Morgans have always been most improbable designs. In concept and appearance, the original three-wheeler scarcely changed between 1909, when the first was built, and 1935 when Morgan decided to put the engine under a bonnet. Even when the three-wheeler was finally dropped in 1951, four-wheeler Morgans remained as anachronistic and individual as ever.

Each is an eccentric piece of engineering, not only in chassis design but in the manner in which it must be driven. The accelerator is hand operated from a lever on the steering wheel. The driver pushes it up to go faster, down to slow, unless, of course, the steering wheel is on full lock, in which case the accelerator lever is upside down. The driver also stays busy with the hand pump which feeds engine oil to the total loss lubrication system. The bevel box and chains give a choice of two speeds, high ratio being almost twice that of low; no reverse gear was fitted to models built before 1931. Front wheel brakes were equally slow arriving, being first fitted in 1926.

For all its foibles, the Morgan three-wheeler was one of the greatest machines ever built for low income enthusiasts. The purposeful looking Super Sports Aero seen on opposite page cost £145 — the equivalent of $200 new in England in 1928. Yet it offered a tremendous power-to-weight ratio (128 BHP per ton), a maximum speed of 87 mph (140 km/h) and quite delightful motoring.

H. F. S. Morgan built his first three-wheeler in 1909 and personally guided the firm's fortunes (and raced his products personally) for fifty years. His son, Peter, then took over the reins. A third generation of the Morgan family, Charles, now works in the privately owned concern.

Despite the three-wheeler's quaint appearance, it is more stable and far quicker than one might think. In 1930, one clocked 116 mph (185 km/h), then a world record for its class.

Various engines were used in the production of three-wheelers — Blackburn, J.A.P., Matchless, British Anzani and later Ford. All models had extremely direct steering, cable-operated brakes, a frame that resembled two pieces of tubing, and a unique system of sliding pillar suspension.

Over the years an estimated 40,000 Morgan three-wheelers have been sold.

The last was built in 1950, the design being reluctantly abandoned only because the car had little export potential.

About 20 Morgan three-wheelers are known to exist in Australia, a further 12 in New Zealand.

MORGAN SUPER SPORTS AERO

This superb Morgan was originally raced by Jim Thoms at Penrith, New South Wales, and in 1929 he won the 1100 cc class of the NSW Sports Car Championship.

Joe Wilson, of Kenmore, Queensland, who now owns the car with his wife, Bev, is also keen on racing. He has driven it in historic racing events at Amaroo Park (NSW), Oran Park (NSW) and Lakeside (Queensland).

Joe acquired the Morgan in March 1972. He restored it over a four year period, doing the mechanical and body work himself, with help from Graham Pedley (paint) and Ron Harding (trim). The car was restored twice, because Joe crashed and extensively damaged it whilst racing at Oran Park.

The Aero was originally imported with a water-cooled J.A.P. engine but Joe fitted a new British Anzani air-cooled engine. This had originally been imported to power a home made light aircraft, but the engine was never used. As the British Anzani engine was an option when the car was new, the Morgan does not lose its originality.

Despite the simple construction, Joe finds the Morgan a challenging handful to drive. All controls are on the steering wheel, the oil pump needs constant attention by hand and gear shifting is an art in itself. With less than one turn lock-to-lock, the steering is heavy and almost diabolically direct. However, Joe loves every minute at the wheel.

MECHANICAL FEATURES

Engine: Twin-cylinder British Anzani (8 valve), 1.1 litres capacity, rated at 8 HP, developing 42 BHP at 4500 rpm. Air-cooled. Lucas magneto. Exposed valve, gear total loss lubrication by pilgrim pump. AMAL carburation.
Gearbox: Two-speed transmission, using two separate chains and sprockets to rear wheel. Sprocket sizes easily changed for motor sport. In standard form, the Super Sports Aero is geared so that maximum engine speed in top gear is equivalent to 90 mph (114 km/h).
Suspension: Morgan sliding pillar front suspension, with quarter-elliptic rear springing. Hartford shockers at front.
Brakes: Three wheels, cable operated with internal expanding on the front wheels and rear hand brake.
Steering: Model T-Ford style of epicyclic steering with only ¾ turn lock-to-lock.
Wheels: Wire, non-detachable, size 350 x 19 ins.
Dimensions: Wheelbase 7 ft 0 ins (2134 mm). Overall length 9 ft 3 ins (2820 mm). Height 3 ft 1 ins (940 mm). Kerb weight 6¼ cwt (318 kg).
Performance: Maximum speed when new — 87 mph (140 km/h). Normal cruising speed — 55 mph (88 km/h). Fuel consumption at highway speeds — 50 mpg (5.6 litres/100 km).

1928 Riley Brooklands

THE MARQUE

The story of Riley's earlier days is told with the 1923 Riley Redwing. Here it is of interest to note that the company's first four-wheeler, built in 1905, was successful in hill climbs and sprints and gave the company its first taste for competition.

Riley's best known and probably its most enduring design was the Nine, launched in 1927. Conceived by Percy Riley, it was the most stylish light car of its time, with coachwork developed by his brothers, Stanley and Allen. A fourth brother, Victor, was the firm's managing director.

The little car featured a 9 HP four-cylinder engine which proved exceptionally robust and efficient. Camshafts located high on each side of the cylinder block permitted short, light push rods actuating valves seated in a hemispherical combustion chamber.

The 1089 cc engine initially developed 34 BHP at 4000 rpm, giving the standard car a road speed of 65 mph (104 km/h). As the engine proved an ideal racing unit, its power was rapidly boosted, peaking at 99 BHP at 6300 rpm, running on alcohol fuel.

The production car was such a success that it became one of the few vehicles of its time in such short supply that it commanded black market prices.

The obvious racing potential of the Nine attracted men like Parry Thomas and Reid Railton. Parry Thomas held the world's land speed record at the time and started to prepare a racing version of the Nine. When he was killed (in another vehicle) Reid Railton, then working for Thomson and Taylor, the famous racing engineers at Brooklands, took over. He cut the wheelbase of the standard chassis, lowered the body until the aluminium bucket seat was only 6 ins (152 mm) above the ground. The chassis frame members were bent sharply inwards to allow a pointed tail. The radiator was placed low and a special light weight body built from aluminium.

The result was a highly desirable sports car with a fantastic performance, known as the Brooklands or Speed Model. Only a limited number were built, many ending up on race tracks. When new the four-cylinder Brooklands cost £420 ($840) in the United Kingdom.

The Brooklands and the refined versions which followed earned an impressive competition record. During 1928 a Brooklands model took the 6 hour international record with an average speed of 85.2 mph (136 km/h). Similar cars also won their class in the Irish Grand Prix, the Tourist Trophy (1929 and 1931) and the 1931 German Grand Prix. The Brooklands model was eventually given a six-cylinder 1.5 litre engine and the car promptly won its class at Le Mans.

A Brooklands won the 1932 Tourist Trophy outright, another won the 1933 Australian Grand Prix outright.

1928 BROOKLANDS RILEY

Thomson and Taylor built only 91 racing versions of the Brooklands car, though other less potent models were made by

the factory. Eight Thomson and Taylor cars were equipped with a special engine developed for the Tourist Trophy race, with a heavier crankshaft and a high degree of tune.

One of them, the car shown on page 134, was bought in late 1928 by the father of Ron Head of the Melbourne firm of Head Brothers, after it had been imported by the Victorian Riley agent, Cohen.

The car was raced in a variety of events by Bill Williamson, then sales manager for the agents and a friend of Jack Day, one of the best known drivers of his day. It competed in the 1929, 1930 and 1932 Australian Grand Prix.

The present owner, Lance Dixon, of Melbourne, purchased it from Ian Garth in 1966. In immaculate condition, it is still used for occasional vintage hill climb and track events and carries road equipment including Bosch headlamps.

Lance Dixon has one of the finest collections of vintage racing machinery in the world and he rates the Brooklands as an exceptionally enjoyable car to drive. He sums it up in one word — 'brilliant'.

MECHANICAL FEATURES

Engine: Four-cylinder, 1089 ccs rated at 9 HP, developing about 83 BHP at 5000 rpm. Twin S.U. carburettors, magneto ignition, 2 bearing crankshaft. One of 8 factory engines built for the Tourist Trophy.
Gearbox: Four-speed close ratio with very fast remote control gear shift. Single plate dry clutch.
Suspension: Semi-elliptic springs front and rear with Hartford shock absorbers.
Brakes: Cable operated brakes on all wheels, 12 ins (305 mm) diameter drums.
Steering: Worm-and-wheel with 1¾ turns lock-to-lock.
Wheels: Rudge-Whitworth wire wheels, 5.00 x 19.
Dimensions: Wheelbase 8 ft 6 ins (2590 mm). Track 4 ft 0 ins (1219 mm). Overall length 13 ft 4 ins (4064 mm). Height 3 ft 0 ins (914 mm). Kerb weight 18¼ cwt (929 kg).
Performance: Maximum speed when new — 85 mph (136 km/h). Normal cruising speed — 70 mph (112 km/h). Fuel consumption at highway speeds — 29 mpg (9.7 litres/100 km).

1929 Alvis Front-Wheel-Drive Sports Car

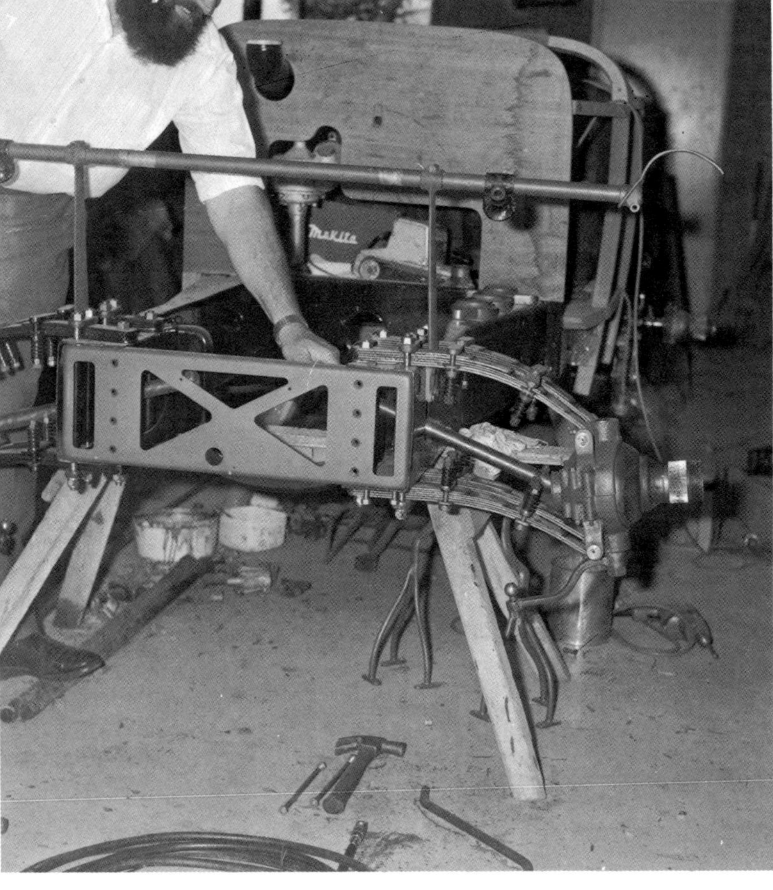

THE MARQUE

"The company thinks that purchasers should be experienced folk as the cars will be very fast and care will be taken in distribution to see that the cars reach only the right type of driver as they will require skilled handling."

Thus ended some brief notes on the F.W.D. Alvis, which appeared in *The Light Car* in February 1928.

The British company which expressed this unusual idea had an exciting history. Though it never really achieved complete success in the racing or the financial world, the company gained enormous respect amongst the sporting fraternity. Amongst other things, it produced the first production front-wheel-drive car, a full synchromesh four-speed gearbox and a competition history that comes close to being legendary.

The firm was founded in 1919 by T. G. John, a civil engineer and naval architect. He built a fairly advanced sports car, with a fabric body, four-speed gearbox and a lively character. Called the 10/30 (the engine was rated at 10 HP, developing 30 BHP), the car had a top speed of 60 mph (100 km/h).

No one is sure why he chose the name Alvis. One theory is that the word is a combination of aluminium (lightness) and vis (strength). All Alvis cars carried a simple insignia, in the form of a red triangle, the later ones all being inverted.

The original Alvis had a racey debut and its characteristic radiator became a prominent sight at motor sport venues through Britain. It chalked up 15 victories during the 1921 racing season, encouraging the firm to go public and launch a more powerful version called the 12/40.

A new chief designer, Captain G. T. Smith-Clark, developed an entirely new overhead valve engine which achieved considerable success in a new model, the 12/50. The car became a minor classic and the firm would have prospered had not they become over ambitious and tried to enter the mass market with the small Buckingham family car.

So much money was lost with this venture that by 1923 Alvis was ready to close. As a final fling the management entered three 12/50's 1.5 litre cars in the Brooklands 200 mile. A week before the race a fire swept through the workshop almost destroying the number one machine. The staff worked frantically to rebuild it, but even so, they were too late for the driver, Major Harvey, to take part in practice. Knowing that liquidation was close at hand, the staff lined up despondently to see Major Harvey compete in an untried car. He started relatively slowly but gradually made his way through the field and finally roared ahead of the lead cars, a pair of identical Fiats. He won at an average speed of 93.3 mph (149 km/h) and a remarkable fuel consumption figure just under 24 miles per gallon (11.7 litres/100 km).

The car all but expired on the lap of honour — but the publicity put Alvis back in business, with a big demand for the 12/50.

In 1924 a series of major improvements were announced and a prototype car shattered 39 class records at Brooklands. Seeking greater glory, the company turned a standard 12/50 engine around on the chassis and coupled it to a gearbox to drive the front wheel, using a front axle built along the lines of a De Dion rear axle. The prototype made fastest time of the day at Shelsley Walsh and clipped one second off the flying mile record at Brooklands.

In 1926 a 'production' version of the same car was announced, with a pair of ball joint drive shafts and independent front suspension using four-quarter elliptic springs. Only one was built, listed at £1000 ($2000). The engine and radiator were removed from this FWD car and placed in a rear drive chassis, No. 2929, and exported to Australia. It won fame at Maroubra Speedway in the hands of Phil Garlick. In 1928 a new overhead valve engine was introduced in a genuine production FWD series, and the company went to Le Mans, with a pair of unsupercharged front-wheel-drive models. They won the class and came sixth and ninth in the overall classification. By way of comparison, Tim Birkins 4½ litre Bentley came fifth.

Alvis built only 155 front-wheel-drive cars, including 39 of the special FD models. About twenty FWD Alvis are known to survive, eight being in Australia.

Noisy but not especially difficult to handle, the FWD model was replaced by a series of more conventional designs, the best known model being the Silver Eagle and the Speed Twenty. The latter was designed and built in a crash program to end all crash programs — rumour says just three weeks — thanks to yet another financial crisis.

During World War Two, the company

turned to aircraft engines and later produced a series of expensive luxury cars. They never recaptured the magic of early lightweights and today Alvis makes heavy armoured fighting vehicles.

1929 ALVIS FWD FD 12/50

Now owned by Evan Muir, with John Ham of Evatt, ACT, as custodian, this rare car has a boat tailed body built by Martin & King of Melbourne. Little is known of the car's history but it has been well maintained all its life and never required full restoration. It carries a Roots supercharger (a new car option) and is still capable of extremely high road speeds.

The driver is entirely surrounded by noise but the car offers a rare degree of exhilaration.

MECHANICAL FEATURES

Engine: Four-cylinder, overhead camshaft, 1.5 litres, developing 75 BHP; 68 x 103 bore and stroke, water-pump cooling, 40 mm Solex carburettor, magneto ignition. Roots type supercharger with 5 psi pressure fitted.
Gearbox: Alvis-built unit placed between motor and front-wheel-drive differential, the three components being bolted together. Axle ratio 4.77.
Suspension: Four wheel fully independent with four-quarter elliptic springs at each front wheel and quarter elliptics at each side of rear.
Brakes: Four wheel mechanical brakes, internal expanding.
Steering: Worm-and-wheel, with two turns lock-to-lock and 38 ft (11.6 m) turning circle.
Wheels: Rudge-Whitworth wire wheels, knock-off type, 500 x 20.
Dimensions: Wheelbase 8 ft 6 ins (2590 mm). Overall length 13 ft 0 ins (3962 mm). Kerb weight 22 cwt (1120 kg).
Performance: Maximum speed when new — 90 mph (144 km/h). Normal cruising speed — 70 mph (112 km/h). Fuel consumption at highway speeds — 26 mpg (10.8 litres/100 km).

1929 Austin Seven Chummy

THE MARQUE

An astonishing number of motorists seem to have started their careers in Austin Sevens, yet only 291,000 were made (between 1922 and 1937), compared with over 15 million Model T Fords. It is probably true that more Sevens survive than any other make of comparable production numbers.

An Englishman who learned his engineering trade in Melbourne, Herbert Austin worked for the Wolseley Sheep Shearing Company in Australia before being transferred to the English company. After designing a few cars for Wolseley's car division, Austin left in 1905 to put up his shingle outside a small rented factory at Longbridge, Birmingham. After a series of robust but undistinguished tourers, he produced a delightful little single-cylinder machine in 1909. It was almost a prototype of the future Austin 7.

In 1921 Austin Motor Company was on the rocks. As a last resort Herbert Austin decided to design a baby car to compete against the motorcycle-and-side car combinations then popular in Britain. The receivers refused to authorise the expense, so Austin, aided by a young draughtsman named Stanley Edge, designed the proposed new car on the billiard table at his home. Initially it was to have a twin-cylinder engine, then a three-cylinder radial unit, but eventually he decided to scale down the larger Austin 20 HP unit.

The prototype tourer, with a 700 ccs engine and an all-up weight of only 6 cwt (330 kg) created great amusement when it first appeared but went so well that the scorn changed to admiration. After a year, the engine was enlarged to 747 ccs and stayed that size until the Big Seven was introduced in 1938 with a 900 cc engine.

Because the Austin Seven was his personal design, Herbert Austin charged his firm two guineas ($4.20) royalty on each production car, making over a million dollars in royalties alone. The Seven was also produced under licence in France, Germany (by BMW), Japan and the United States.

When the first Austin 7 appeared, the English car trade dismissed it as a cheeky piece of entrepreneuring. Herbert Austin decided to prove his design with a 'baptism of fire' and immediately plunged into motor sport. The Seven made its competition debut in August 1922, winning the Shelsley Walsh hill climb. Then Arthur Waite, Austin's Australian born son-in-law, won the Small Handicap race at Brooklands, at an average speed of 59 mph (94 km/h). In the 1923 Whitsun Handicap, he came second after lapping at the sensational speed of almost 70 mph (112 km/h).

Specially tuned competition cars were soon clocking 80 mph (128 km/h) and, in 1925, a supercharged Seven won the 50 Mile Handicap at Brooklands with an amazing average of 89.9 mph (144 km/h).

The first Austin 7 to reach Australia landed in Sydney in 1924 and was an immediate hit. Arthur Waite created a sensation by winning the first Australian Grand Prix, held on Phillip Island in 1928. Two New Zealanders, Hector Macquarrie and Dick Matthews, drove from Sydney to Cape York over virgin terrain and through tropical forests — a combination which had already defeated two Model T Fords attempting to cross the same terrain.

In 1930, a supercharged racing Seven covered ten miles on the Montlhery (France) speed track at an average speed of 109.06 mph (174 km/h), a world record for the 750 cc class. By then Austin Seven was a household name around the world.

1929 AUSTIN 7 CHUMMY

Most Austin 7's in Australia have locally made bodies and it is rare to find two identical machines. This car, owned by Pedr and Anthony Davis, of Sydney, has a Holden body. The touring model was known as a 'Chummy', presumably because the four seats can only be occupied by four people on very friendly terms.

The car was purchased in 1971 as a collection of bits and pieces left over after another enthusiast, Paul Butler, had stripped two 1929 models to build a 'Chummy' for himself. Pedr Davis carried out the rebuilding of the second car, with generous help from Ron Muir, Peter Glover and John Lofthouse. Bob King, of Leichhardt, Sydney, made the trim and hood.

The Seven took part in the 1978 International Rally, proving a fascinating little car to drive.

MECHANICAL FEATURES

Engine: Four-cylinder, monobloc, capacity 747 ccs. Rated at 7.8 HP, developing 10.5 BHP at 2400 rpm. Side valve design with detachable cylinder head and two bearing crankshaft. Coil ignition, splash lubrication, Zenith carburettor and water cooling.
Gearbox: Three-speed crash type. Single plate dry clutch. Open shaft drive to rear axle, with fabric universal joint.

Suspension: Semi-elliptic transverse spring at front, quarter-elliptic springs at rear, friction-type shock absorbers front and rear.
Brakes: Cable-operated internal expanding drums. Handbrake operates the front brakes only, the foot pedal the rear brakes.
Steering: Worm-and-wheel, with 1¼ turns lock-to-lock.
Wheels: Wire spoked, 4.00 x 19 tyres.
Dimensions: Wheelbase 6 ft 3 ins (1905 mm). Track 3 ft 4 ins (1016 mm). Overall length 9 ft 3 ins (2820 mm). Height 5 ft 1 in (1550 mm). Kerb weight 8.5 cwt (425 kg).
Performance: Maximum speed when new — 45 mph (72 km/h). Normal cruising speed — 35 mph (56 km/h). Fuel consumption at highway speeds — 40 mpg (7.0 litres/100 km).

1929 Chevrolet With Holden Body

THE MARQUE

Louis Chevrolet was born in Switzerland and schooled in France. He came to America, working for De Dion-Bouton in New York. Following the arrival of his brothers, Gaston and Arthur in the USA, Louis established himself as a fast and fearless racing driver. In 1905, he achieved considerable notoriety by beating the great Barney Oldfield three times in six races. He raced his huge Fiat in the Vanderbuilt Cup, but crashed and wrecked it.

Chevrolet's next move was to join Walter Christie in launching the world's first large front-wheel drive car. The venture failed, so he had a crack at the world land speed record, in a giant Darracq V-8, clocking a new speed of 119 mph (190 km/h).

Whilst Chevrolet's reputation was soaring, the legendary Billy Durant had formed General Motors. Looking for publicity, he hired the Chevrolet brothers to build and race Buicks. When the bankers squeezed Durant out of General Motors Corporation, he had Chevrolet design him a brand new car which Durant launched. He called it Chevrolet because the big Swiss had become an idol in many households.

The first Chevrolet, released in 1912, named the Classic Six, was the largest and most expensive Chevrolet produced until the 1950s. Some 3000 were sold in the United States at the high price of $US2150 but Durant was not interested in the luxury market. Keen to compete with Ford, he turned out the H4, followed by the cantankerous and somewhat unreliable 490 four-cylinder model. It ran from 1916 to 1922 and sold reasonably well in Australia.

The 490 was a great success in the States, however, earning Durant $3 million, thus helping him to sweep back to control of General Motors, bringing Chevrolet as the bait. Louis Chevrolet and his brothers had, meanwhile, quit the company to concentrate on racing.

Four-cylinder Chevrolets were popular in Australia, especially when the Superior arrived in 1923, the Capitol in 1927 and finally the National in 1928. These cars were all assembled by General Motors Australia and, in the main, fitted with bodies built by the independent Holden organisation.

In 1929 the National was replaced by the six-cylinder International and soon Chevrolet was the best selling car in the country. By 1938 General Motors Holden (the two companies merged in 1931) held 38.4 per cent of the Australian market, against 19.5 per cent for Ford, the nearest competitor.

1929 INTERNATIONAL TOURER

Like most General Motors cars of the day, this five seater tourer was assembled by G.M. Australia and fitted with a locally made Holden body.

Owned by the Hardman family, of Armidale, New South Wales, it is almost unique, having had only two owners since new. The late Mr E. R. Hardman acquired the car from its first owner living near Walcha, New South Wales. The original invoice, still in the car's glovebox, showed that the big tourer had cost the equivalent of $370 when delivered in 1929.

When Mr Hardman acquired the car it had done only 40,000 miles, though it was in a well used condition. He restored the car himself, with help from Blencowe & Son, of Armidale, who re-trimmed the body.

MECHANICAL FEATURES

Engine: Six-cylinder overhead valve of 3.14 litres, rated at 26.3 HP developing 46 BHP at 2600 rpm. Conventional cooling system; updraught carburettor; coil ignition.
Gearbox: Crash type with three forward speeds and dry plate clutch.
Suspension: Conventional, with semi-elliptic springs front and rear.
Brakes: Internal expanding front brakes, external contracting rear drums. The handbrake works on the inside of the rear drums. Mechanical operation for all brakes.
Steering: Worm-and-wheel, with 2½ turns lock-to-lock.
Wheels: Steel disc with detachable rims, 5.00 x 20 ins.
Dimensions: Wheelbase 8 ft 11 ins (2718 mm). Overall length 13 ft 6 ins (4115 mm). Height 5 ft 6 ins (1676 mm). Kerb weight 22 cwt (1120 kg).
Performance: Maximum speed when new — 60 mph (100 km/h). Normal cruising speed — 50 mph (80 km/h). Fuel consumption at highway speeds — 20 mpg (14.1 litres/100 km).

NSW
BR·979

1929 Ford Model A

THE MARQUE

Henry Ford called the car he launched in 1907 a Model A, which was logical enough, as it was his first production vehicle. No one knows why he also used the same name for the 1928 model which succeeded the stunningly successful Model T.

The Model T had been in production for nineteen years and was such a hard act to follow that Ford delayed introducing a replacement until the last possible moment. It was only when Chevrolet sales were overtaking Ford at a catastrophic rate that Ford closed down his vast River Rouge plant and hurriedly switched to the Model A.

Work on its design had started in 1926, some years after Edsel Ford and other top executives had pleaded at board meetings for a new car. The Chevrolet Four was clearly superior in design, but Henry Ford was convinced that the public still

wanted the Model T. It was only after Ford dealers started going bankrupt that he agreed to a change.

Once the decision to build a new car had been made, Ford personally approved every detail. The first prototype was completed in October 1927, about four months after the huge plant had closed. Ford took it to the River Rouge test track, announced he was delighted and said production would start immediately.

The car went on sale in December that year — a record production feat. The speedy development and tooling was one of Henry Ford's most striking achievements, though his stubborn refusal to allow earlier development work was one of his greatest failures. Retooling cost $100 million.

That was not all. Whilst Ford was designing the four-cylinder Model A,

Chevrolet was tooling up for a new six-cylinder engine. As soon as the Model A was launched, Ford was forced to start work on a new V-8 engine which cost a further $50 million. The V-8 model was launched in 1932.

Meanwhile, Ford sold 5 million Model As in four years, with American prices between $385 and $570, depending on the body style.

Buyers could choose between a coupé, sports coupé, roadster, phaeton, Tudor sedan (two doors) and Fordor sedan (four doors). Four basic colours were offered.

Ford advertisements claimed a maximum speed of 65 mph (104 km/h) from the 40 BHP engine and said that it would deliver 30 miles per gallon. The car proved tough, robust and reliable, often working for years on end with little attention. The basic mechanical design was more conventional than the Model T, with a simple selective sliding gearbox replacing the planetary transmission. The Model A also boasted a good set of brakes, with self-centering, internal expanding shoes. The suspension was comparatively crude but at least it had double acting shock absorbers.

The Model A sold well around the world, especially in Australia and New Zealand. Today New Zealand is credited with having more working Model A Fords per head of population than any other country.

1929 FORD A TOURER

Owned by Bob Robinson, of Gosford, New South Wales, this touring model has a Ford Motor Company body with seating for five. Bob purchased it unrestored in 1973 from David Cummings, of Blakehurst, New South Wales, and restored it over twelve months. Harry Croft did the trim.

The car won the Best Vintage Trophies at vintage car meetings in Taree, New South Wales, in 1974 and again in 1976.

MECHANICAL FEATURES

Engine: Four-cylinder, side valve, 3.2 litre capacity rated at 24.3 HP, developing 40 BHP at 2200 rpm. Water pump cooling system. Tillotson or Ford-Zenith carburettor and coil ignition.
Gearbox: Selective sliding type with three forward speeds and single plate dry clutch.
Suspension: Transverse semi-elliptic springs front and rear. Adjustable hydraulic double acting shock absorbers on all wheels.
Brakes: Four wheel internal expanding brakes. Rear wheels have two-in-one drums, giving independent parking brakes.
Steering: Irreversible worm-and-sector system with 34 ft (10.4 m) turning circle and 2½ turns lock-to-lock.
Wheels: Wire spoked wheels 450 x 21.
Dimensions: Wheelbase 8 ft 7.5 ins (2629 mm). Track 4 ft 8 ins (1422 mm). Overall length 14 ft 1 in (4293 mm). Height 6 ft 0 ins (1828 mm). Kerb weight 22 cwt (1120 kg)
Performance: Maximum speed when new — 65 mph (104 km/h). Normal cruising speed — 40 mph (64 km/h). Fuel consumption at highway speeds — 22 mpg (12.8 litres/100 km).

1929 Gardner Closed Coupé

THE MARQUE

Russell E. Gardner joined the auto business in 1916 and between then and his final car in 1930, built distinctive four, six and eight-cylinder cars. He also produced bodies for Chevrolet and assembled complete cars for the St. Louis area of Missouri.

Despite their good looks, moderate prices and interesting specifications, the cars bearing his own name never reached the heights suggested by the gold-plated Griffin mascot. The first Gardner car, built in 1919, was powered by a four-cylinder Lycoming engine. Six-cylinder and a straight eight model, also Lycoming powered, quickly followed. After 1926 only the Straight Eight was produced, selling for $US1495 at a time when an eight-cylinder Pierce Arrow cost $US2775.

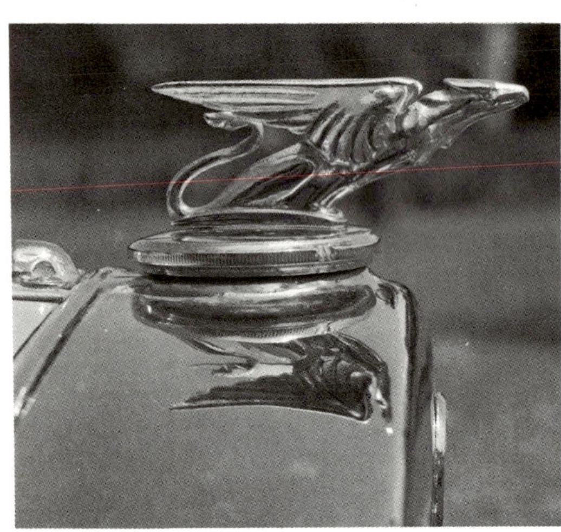

In 1930, the firm sold only 3000 cars out of a total United States production of 3 million. Despite competitive prices, good engineering and a choice of sixteen colours, the company's slogan 'The Great American Dream' dissolved into the nightmare of bankruptcy.

The Straight Eight Model 95, with its enlarged 4.8 litre Lycoming engine was to have resurrected the company's fortunes. Its interesting innovations included central oil lubrication, operated by a small pump which juggled up and down with the car's movement. The closed coupé also featured a three tone colour scheme as a factory option, along with wind-up windows for the doors and the main rear window. There were thermostatically controlled radiator louvres, twin inside rear mirrors (one for day, one for night), and an ornate dash panel finished in beautifully tooled brass.

When it became apparent that the 95 was not going to be a sales success, Gardner designed and built a prototype front-wheel-drive car, exhibited at the New York Motor Show of 1930. By the time it was ready for production, the bankers had moved in and closed the firm.

1929 GARDNER 95 COUPÉ

Dr Esma Anderson purchased this car in the United States when new and five years later brought it to Melbourne, where it was converted to right-hand drive.

After five years, she sold it to Preston Motors. It then went through a series of owners, no one keeping it for more than a few months, and had changed hands at least fifteen times by 1947 when it was acquired by John Wellard of Box Hill, Victoria. He moved to Queensland, taking the car with him and the elegant Gardner put in a working stint as a tractor on a pineapple farm. Eventually it fell into disuse and was taken apart, presumably for restoration, then stored in a shed in Woombye, on Queensland's Sunshine Coast.

Several enthusiasts heard about and inspected the Gardner, but the first to make an acceptable offer was Dick Vermeulen of Yandina, Queensland.

He bought it in November, 1977, and found the body timber had rotted, the body panels badly rusted, the engine in bits and lacking pistons. Despite the car's condition, Dick made up his mind to compete in the International Veteran and Vintage Rally, commencing in April 1978.

With the assistance of his wife, Fran, Dick spent 700 hours tediously rebuilding the car from the ground up. Dick did the mechanical, body and paint work himself, with Fran working on the trim. The car made its maiden run in restored condition just hours before the Rally commenced and proved a faultless performer.

MECHANICAL FEATURES

Engine: Eight-cylinder Lycoming, side valve, high compression head, rated at 33 HP, developing 115 BHP. Water-cooled with dual throat updraught carburettors, coil ignition.
Gearbox: Muncie with three forward gears and reverse with spiral bevel drive. Single plate dry clutch.
Suspension: Semi-elliptics front and rear.
Brakes: Four wheel hydraulic brakes, with internal expanding shoes and a contracting band handbrake working on transmission.
Steering: Worm drive with a 56 foot (17 metres) turning circle and 2½ turns lock-to-lock.
Wheels: 18 ins steel spoke wheels.
Dimensions: Wheelbase 10 ft 10 ins (3302 mm). Overall length 15 ft 10 ins (4826 mm). Height 5 ft 10 ins (1778 mm). Kerb weight 35 cwt (1782 kg).
Performance: Maximum speed when new — 100 mph (160 km/h). Normal cruising speed — 50 mph (80 km/h). Fuel consumption at highway speeds — 14 mpg (20.1 litres/100 km).

231·NEE
QUEENSLAND - SUNSHINE STATE

MG
1970 AUSTRALIAN INTERNATIONAL
VETERAN AND VINTAGE MOTOR RALLY
291
CX3
12
V.S.C.C.
022

1929 M.G. Midget

THE MARQUE

The M.G. was launched almost by accident. William Morris (later Lord Nuffield) had established a sales and service garage at Oxford before starting Morris Motors. The garage and the manufacturing company remained separate entities and, in 1921, motor sport enthusiast Cecil Kimber joined Morris Garages as sales manager. Believing a worthwhile market existed for lively lightweight cars, he arranged for a series of two-seater fabric bodies to be built on Morris Cowley chassis. Called 'Chummies', these hybrid models sold so well that a small production line was started.

In 1923 Morris Garages developed a stylish two-seater called the M.G. Super Sports Morris. It was followed by a similar four-seater on a 14 HP Morris Oxford chassis, but the name was shortened to M.G. Super Sports, despite the radiator displaying a Morris badge. In 1926 an improved version was introduced, but this time the Morris badge was replaced by the M.G. octagon. A new marque was born.

In 1929 Kimber decided that the smallest Morris production car, the Morris Minor, was the ideal base for a low priced sports car, especially as its Wolseley-designed overhead camshaft engine offered excellent opportunities for performance tuning. He designed and, in April 1929, launched a modified chassis fitted with a two-seater fabric body. Known as the M-type, it was an immediate success and became the first of the famous M.G. Midget series. The M-type stayed in production until 1932, and was replaced by the J-type.

The M-type was not designed for racing but a competition version made a successful debut at the Brooklands High Speed Trials in June 1929. Eleven months later three Midgets won the Team prize in the Double Twelve Hour race at Brooklands, the first of a long string of competition successes.

This victory inspired an era of intense competition with Austin. As M.G. began to assert their supremacy over the racing Austin Sevens, Austin developed a supercharged special with the aim of being the first 750 cc car to reach the magic 100 mph (160 km/h) mark. Cecil Kimber heard about the project and started work on a competition version of the M-type. Known as the EX120, it had a scaled-down engine which complied with the much publicised 750 cc capacity class. The new M.G. established a class speed record of 87.3 mph (139.7 km/h) unblown. When Sir Malcolm Campbell drove the supercharged Austin 7 to a new class record of 97 mph (155.2 km/h), a blower was quickly fitted to the little M.G. With George Eyston at the wheel, it became the first 750 cc car to exceed the magic 'ton', clocking a speed of 103.13 mph (165 km/h) at Montlhery in France. The same car went on to become the first car in the class to travel 100 miles (160 km) in one hour.

Racing M.G.'s were to score numerous racing, trial and record-breaking successes around the world. The marque was prominent in Australian racing circles, especially immediately before and after World War Two. The rear-engined M.G. built in Sydney by Gordon Stewart in the early 1950s pre-dated the more famous Cooper Climaxes by some years, bringing a new kind of racing car to these shores.

Australian assembly of the M.G.B. ceased in Australia in 1972, because the company could not meet the new exhaust emission and Australian design rule safety regulations. British Motor Corporation marked the end of the era by holding a formal 'wake' for the dead marque.

1929 M.G. M-TYPE

Ian Heather jnr, of Blaxland, New South Wales, heard that a rolling M.G. chassis was available at the Sydney suburb of Hurstville. He inspected it, realised it was almost identical to his father's M-type and purchased the machine in 1964. It turned out to be the oldest M.G. Midget in Australia.

The chassis had been used as a beach buggy on the south coast sands and was in near derelict condition. Over a four year period, Ian and his father, aided by various firms and individuals, rebuilt the chassis. Ian jnr., built a timber-and-fabric body of the type widely used in M-types. Standard bodies for this particular model are virtually unknown in Australia because M-types were imported as rolling chassis and fitted with a local body to suit the owner.

Since its restoration, Ian Heather's car has travelled more than 11,000 miles (17,600 km). It toured New Zealand for the 1972 International Rally and has travelled extensively throughout Queensland, Tasmania and South Australia on other major rallies.

A total of 3235 M-types were built but few survive. Their numbers have been supplemented by modified Morris Minors fitted with suitable bodies. Both cars owned by the Ian Heathers are genuine M-types. They are two of the few Midgets built in Oxford before M.G. moved to Abingdon in September, 1929.

MECHANICAL FEATURES

Engine: Four-cylinder, single overhead cam, capacity 847 ccs, rated at 8.5 HP, developing 20 BHP at 4000 rpm. Thermo-syphon water cooling, single S.U. carburettor, coil ignition.
Gearbox: Three-speed non-synchromesh, single plate dry clutch.
Suspension: Semi-elliptic springs all around with Hartford friction shock absorbers at rear.
Brakes: Four wheel drum brakes, rod actuated at rear; rod and cable actuation for front brake. Transmission brake controlled by handbrake.
Steering: Wormwheel with 1⅝ turns lock-to-lock and 39 ft (11.8 m) turning circle.
Wheels: Bolt on wire spoked 19 ins wheels.
Dimensions: Wheelbase 6 ft 6 ins (1981 mm). Track 3 ft 6 ins (1067 mm). Overall length 10 ft 0 ins (3048 mm). Scuttle height 3 ft 6 ins (1067 mm). Kerb weight 10 cwt (509 kg).
Performance: Maximum speed when new — 65 mph (104 km/h). Normal cruising speed — 52 mph (83 km/h). Fuel consumption at highway speeds — 36 mpg (7.8 litres/100 km).

SA
SMW·500
353
1929 PACKARD

1929 Packard Roadster

THE MARQUE

Packard once held 50 per cent of the American luxury car market and no stock broker, real estate magnate or industrialist considered his stable to be complete without a straight eight roadster.

During the 1920s, Packard was the undisputed American leader in style and appointments. Who cared if the engine was bolted rigidly to the chassis frame or that the radiators and hoods vibrated at speed? The magnificent straight eight engine could pull the heavy car from walking pace in top gear, accelerating like a sports car to a speed of 80 mph (128 km/h). Packard Eights reigned as America's top automobile for twenty years, and at one time were selling at the rate of 60,000 a year. Yet, surprisingly few pre-1930 models survive.

James and William Packard planned their first car in 1893. They did little about it for five years until a brand new Winton owned by the brothers broke down. An irate James confronted Alexander Winton who — according to Packard lore — replied: "If you are so damn smart, build your own car."

The brothers set up a workshop in the family electric lamp factory and the first Packard ran late in 1899. Powered by a single-cylinder engine developing 12 HP, it had tiller steering, wire wheels and a patented mechanism to advance the spark. The car still survives.

The brothers scored a major truimph a year later when they sold two cars to William Rockefeller. According to another legend, when someone wrote asking for literature, James Packard (who had none printed) replied, 'Ask the Man who Owns One'. Thus an advertising slogan, lasting almost as long as the marque, was born.

From an early stage the Packards hired a clever engineer named William Hatcher who developed several novel features, including the H-slot gearshift. In 1903 the company graduated to a four-cylinder car, selling more than 500 in the following year. Larger and more powerful models appeared, climaxing in the

twelve-cylinder Twin Six of 1915. During 1916 the company sold 10,000 cars — but the Packard brothers had earlier retired leaving a Detroit financier in control. During the early 1920s, Packard held more land, sea and air speed records than anyone else. Their magazine advertisements are still regarded as the most eloquent car promotions ever done. By 1937 the firm was selling 110,000 cars a year.

The man most responsible for the company's great engineering was Colonel Jesse Vincent, a self-taught engineer who had joined Packard in 1912, retiring in 1949. He was responsible for the development of the firm's first high speed six. When Cadillac answered with a V-8, Vincent designed a twelve-cylinder unit which, for eight years, was the ultimate in car engines.

In 1923 the Double Six was followed by the classic 5.9 litre straight eight and was the best balanced and smoothest engine available at the time. In 1927 Vincent introduced a hypoid rear axle to lower the drive shaft and floor boards.

The post-war years were unhappy times for the great marque. In 1952 a new president, James Nance, tried to create a youthful image and ordered that all historic records be destroyed. Fortunately some were secretly saved by company employees. The company merged with Studebaker and made its last car in 1958.

1929 PACKARD MODEL 633

Owned by Brian Macmahon of Adelaide and restored by him with help from Ben Long and V. Fischetti, this elegant roadster has a double bench seat at the front and a double dicky seat behind. Small side doors provide access to a golf club compartment. There are courtesy lights and reversing lights, with a folding luggage rack at the rear.

It was first imported to South Australia in 1929. After use as an ambulance, it was sold to Greenleaves Caravan Park in Alice Springs and converted to a buckboard-type truck. When a piston finally disintegrated, the car was abandoned. Brian Macmahon discovered it and, in 1971, purchased the buckboard for $100. The dismantled engine came too — in a large box.

It took seven years to rebuild the car to original factory specifications. The job has been so well done that the car won the 1978 Sporting Car Club of South Australia trophy, as the 'Most Meritorious Restoration of the Year'.

Mechanically conventional, the straight eight engine has a special device to feed extra oil to the cylinders when the choke is in use. The chassis is lubricated by a Bijur 'one shot' system, operated from a lever under the dash.

MECHANICAL FEATURES

Engine: Straight eight of 5.25 litres, side valve, rated 32 HP, developing 90 BHP. Packard updraught carburettor, twin make-and-break distributor points, 9 main bearings.

Gearbox: Three-speed Packard unit with air compressor on side for inflating tyres.
Suspension: Semi-elliptic springs, front and rear. Hydraulic shock absorbers front and rear.
Brakes: Four wheel brakes with Bendix three-shoe drums.
Steering: Worm-and-segment, with 3 turns lock-to-lock and 50 ft (15.2 m) turning circle.
Wheels: 20 ins disc.
Dimensions: Wheelbase 11 ft 1½ ins (3365 mm). Overall length 16 ft 5 ins (5003 mm). Height 5 ft 9 ins (1752 mm). Kerb weight 39 cwt (1985 kg).
Performance: Maximum speed when new — 80 mph (128 km/h). Normal cruising speed — 50-60 mph (80-100 km/h). Fuel consumption at highway speeds — 14 mpg (20.1 litres/100 km).

1929 Studebaker President 8

THE MARQUE

When mass production cars turned to six-cylinder engines, America's luxury trade moved into straight eight designs. By 1929 straight eight-cylinder models were produced by Auburn, Chandler, Duesenberg, Dupont, Elcar, Graham-Paige, Gardner, Hupp, Jordan, Kissel, Locomobile, Marmon, Packard, Roamer, Pierce-Arrow, Stearns, Studebaker and Stutz — to name but a few.

To gain strong competitive advantage, Studebaker offered a choice of ten body styles with its top-of-the-line President 8. They ranged from a 'convertible cabriolet' to a 'state limousine'.

All had a 5.5 litre engine which pulled the big car from 20 mph to an effortless 90 mph (144 km/h) in top gear. Inevitably, the sporting gentlemen of the day wanted this kind of performance in a more personal kind of car, and Studebaker obliged with a stylish sports-roadster, boasting a rumble seat and golf bag compartment.

The company also grabbed a competitive edge through record breaking. In 1929 four President 8's each covered 30,000 miles in 30,000 minutes or less, establishing eleven world records. Less spectacular was their victory at Pikes Peak, the famous American Hill Climb, where a President 8 established a new record against all comers.

These triumphs were enough to encourage Al Jolson and Johnny Weismuller (Hollywood's original Tarzan) to drive President 8s. So did thousands of others, and in 1929 the company declared a mammoth profit. Unfortunately, almost all of it was given to the shareholders as dividends and when Pierce-Arrow, the luxury car firm which Studebaker had purchased in 1928, began to flounder

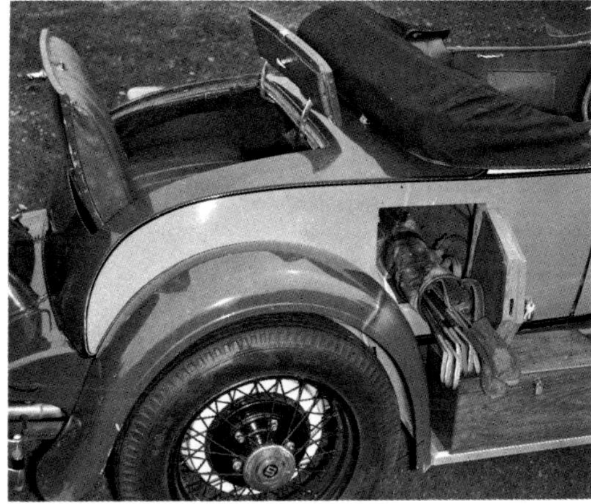
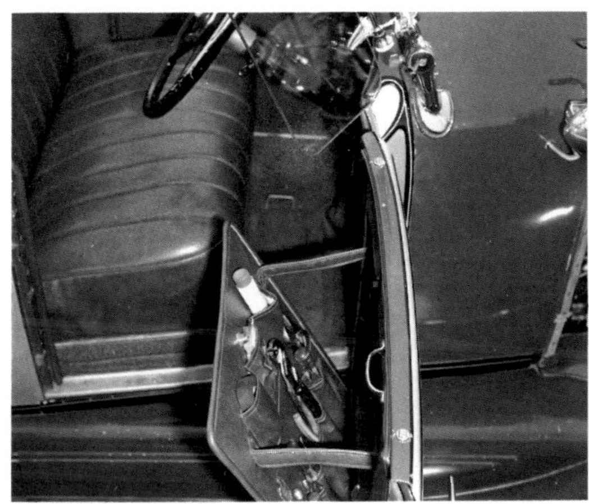

there was no money in the bank to support it. Eventually Pierce-Arrow was sold at a large loss and, in 1933, Studebaker was in receivership.

Studebaker had commenced in business building horse-drawn carriages and buggies and, in 1852, claimed to be the world's largest. In 1902 the firm built an electric carriage, quickly followed by a successful petrol buggy. By 1915 it was building four and six-cylinder models with a yearly output of 45,000 cars. It moved into the eight-cylinder field in 1928, and in 1932 was racing at Indianapolis, with some success, using a car based on the President 8.

Though sales were very depressed during the 1930s, Studebaker bounced back after World War Two with the revolutionary coming-and-going model created by stylist Raymond Loewy. In 1950 the factory sold a record 335,000 vehicles, giving it 4.2 per cent of the American car market. From then on it was all down hill. The merger in 1954 with Packard did nothing to help the ailing financial position. The move into Paxton superchargers and the sporty Avanti was little more than a final fling.

The American factory closed in 1963 and the Canadian factory three years later.

1929 STUDEBAKER PRESIDENT 8 ROADSTER

The early history of this elegant and powerful car is not known, but it is believed to have spent most of its time in New South Wales.

After World War Two, the car was owned by John Jones and later by Don Whitby, both from Sydney suburbs. Ben Bronk added it to his growing collection of cars and had intended to restore the Studebaker but fellow enthusiast John Cooper, persuaded him to sell it along with a 1929 Packard. The price paid in 1963 was £25 ($50).

A year later John Cooper sold the Studebaker to John Dowsett, of the lower Blue Mountains in New South Wales. He found it in fairly good shape mechanically and drove it almost daily. Progressively he cut out extensive body rust. After eleven years he sold the car to collector Frank Illich. Meanwhile, the late Toby Bent, a man well known in motor sport and veteran car circles, had first seen the President 8 in 1970. He set his heart on ownership and bought it from Frank Illich in 1975.

With Arthur Garthon, Laurie Fitzpatrick and Jock McGowen, he spent a year restoring the car to its present condition. In May 1976 with his wife, Betty, Toby attended the Sydney-Alice Springs Vintage Rally. The powerful Studebaker covered 7200 miles (11,500 km) towing a caravan.

MECHANICAL FEATURES

Engine: Straight eight-cylinder, side valve, of 5.5 litre capacity, rated at 39.2 HP, developing 115 BHP at 3200 rpm. Water-cooled with pump and fan, Stromberg dual throat updraught carburettor, twin coil ignition.
Gearbox: Conventional crash box with three forward gears, spiral drive to semi-floating rear axle. Twin-disc clutch.
Suspension: Semi-elliptic springs front and rear, hydraulic shock absorbers.
Brakes: Bendix internal expanding brakes on four wheels, with handbrake operating on four wheels.
Steering: Ross cam-and-lever system with 40 ft (12.2 m) turning circle and $2\frac{1}{3}$ turns lock-to-lock.
Wheels: Wire spoked well-based wheels with 6.00 x 20 tyres.
Dimensions: Wheelbase 10 ft 5 ins (3175 mm). Overall length 16 ft 0 ins (4877 mm). Height 5 ft 6 ins (1676 mm). Kerb weight 34 cwt (1731 kg).
Performance: Maximum speed when new — 90 mph (144 km/h). Normal cruising speed — 50 mph (80 km/h). Fuel consumption at highway speeds — 15 mpg (18.8 litres/100 km).

1930 Graham-Paige Sedan

THE MARQUE

It is not often that car makers seek to immortalise their profiles on the radiator, but brothers Joseph, Robert and Raymond Graham designed a bold radiator badge resembling a Roman shield. Their profiles are clearly displayed in helmets and mail armour.

The brothers gained control of the long established Paige factory in 1927 and displayed an off-beat but effective approach to marketing their products. They each signed all catalogues and invitations to the public to inspect their wares and involved themselves personally in all aspects of the business.

Paige Detroit Motor Car Company had built its first machine in 1908. A rather curious roadster, it was powered by a two-stroke, three-cylinder engine of 2.2 litre capacity. Two years later they switched to a conventional four-cylinder engine, at the same time dropping the word 'Detroit' from the car's name.

In 1914, following the automotive tide, Paige launched a six-cylinder car, with a Continental engine. It also announced the low priced Jewett (which sold between 1923 and 1926) to help boost total output. The idea apparently failed as the Graham brothers were soon in control.

Their energy and enterprise paid off. The first Graham-Paige was on the road within months of the take-over. Its four-wheel hydraulic brakes and optional four-speed 'twin top' gearbox were so much to the public's liking that they bought 78,000 in the first year. The brothers promptly expanded the range to cover three sixes and two straight eight models. A remarkable range of body styles included five and seven passenger sedans, two and four passenger coupés, a cabriolet roadster and a five passenger phaeton.

A determined effort was made to sell the cars in England through motor sport publicity. In February 1928, Captain D. M. Marendaz, driving in fog, established an impressive number of long distance records for a sedan. He also broke the existing Brooklands sedan lap speed, clocking 90.06 mph (144 km/h). Incidentally, the same open Graham-Paige won the very last race ever held at Brooklands, in August 1939.

Few Graham-Paiges were raced in Australia, but one feat has gone down in the history books. In March 1930, Sydney driver Don Robertson set out to beat the official Sydney-Melbourne road record, then barely above 10 hours. Driving a six-cylinder Graham-Paige 615, stripped of all unnecessary weight and fitted with a 3.3 axle ratio, Don roared from Sydney General Post Office with car club officials and newspaper representatives in attendance. The car performed faultlessly and he raced to Melbourne GPO in 9 hours 15 minutes driving time, or 10 hours 5 minutes elapsed time — a new record.

After this the police stepped in, declaring all interstate speed records to be illegal. Don Robertson's Graham-Paige, therefore, still holds the official Sydney-Melbourne speed record.

The Graham brothers made some major changes as they entered the 1930s. They dropped the name Paige and commenced production of the straight eight Blue Streak. An optional supercharged model, introduced in 1935, was capable of 95 mph (152 km/h). Sales were slow, so the firm reverted to less powerful, less costly machines. They designed a small 2.8 litre six and became one of the first firms to have an engine copied by a Japanese car firm.

Sales continued to drop. In desperation the company bought up the dies for the Cord 810/812, introducing a conventionally engineered version of the famous front-wheel-drive sports car. It, too, failed.

After World War Two, Graham-Paige's new president, Joseph A. Frazer, got talking to Henry Kaiser, the man who built the liberty ships. The talks led to a merger between Graham-Paige and Kaiser, producing two new cars — Kaiser and Frazer. Both were crushed by competition from Detroit's Big Three.

1930 GRAHAM-PAIGE 827 SEDAN

Fairly expensive for its day, this five seater sedan came with one-shot lubrication, tyre pump, tail light and back-up lamp, four 2-way hydraulic shock

absorbers, interior lamp, vanity mirror, curtains, clock and tasteful indirect lighting.

Its history is not known, but like many Graham Paiges it shows signs of having been extensively used. The marque was very popular for carrying passengers, mail and parcels over commercial routes, many having the chassis frames extended for extra room. When this car was discovered in a carport near Adelaide airport, it was complete but in a very poor state.

John Lasscocks, the present owner, gains great pleasure from driving the older American style cars, so he spared nothing in having the Graham-Paige restored to its former glory. Dudley Foster did the mechanical and body work, Harris Motors the trim.

The finished job is a remarkably lively, pleasant and smooth riding car, easy to drive and fairly light on fuel for a straight eight.

MECHANICAL FEATURES

Engine: Straight eight-cylinder side valve design, L-head, with 85.7 mm x 114.3 mm bore and stroke, giving total capacity of 5.3 litres. Engine rated at 36.45 HP, running on 5 bearing crankshaft, rubber mounted, dual Delco Remy distributor.
Gearbox: Selective sliding four-speed with first gear used for emergency starts. Double dry plate clutch, spiral bevel drive.
Suspension: Semi-elliptic springs front and rear.
Brakes: Four wheel internal expanding brakes, with 15 inch (381 mm) drums front and rear. Parking brake acts on transmission shaft.
Steering: Fully adjustable cam-and-lever type, 16 to 1 ratio; adjustable steering column; 47 ft (14.3 m) turning circle.
Wheels: Spoked wheels 19 ins, with 815 x 165 tyres.
Dimensions: Wheelbase 10 ft 7 ins (3226 mm). Overall length 16 ft 6 ins (5029 mm). Height 5 ft 8 ins (1727 mm). Kerb weight 40 cwt (2036 kg).
Performance: Maximum speed when new — 80 mph (128 km/h). Normal cruising speed — 60 mph (100 km/h). Fuel consumption at highway speeds — 15 mpg (18.8 litres/100 km).

211
1930 LA SALLE

1930 La Salle

THE MARQUE

La Salle is sometimes described as a poor man's Cadillac, because it was made by Cadillac to sell in a lower price range. This description is less than fair, for La Salle was a well engineered and expensive car by any standards. In 1930, the 5.6 litre V-8 four passenger sports phaeton sold for $2875 in the United States, against $US1225 for a similar Buick or $US3175 for a Packard. In comparison an Auburn Cabriolet cost $US1095, an Essex $US895.

Whilst certainly not inexpensive, La Salle was created by General Motors (and named after a well known explorer) to fill an obvious price gap between Buick and Cadillac.

The first La Salle appeared in 1927, introduced because Cadillac planned to announce a stunning new engine, a V-16, for 1930. The firm felt that a lower priced V-8 Cadillac would detract from the prestige of their tour-de-force. Hence the new marque.

La Salle's design and styling was done by Harley J. Earl, one of General Motor's legendary men. His concept was perfect for the day, for the new car had the same standard of engineering (and many components) from the Cadillac range. A very good looking car, it had overtones of European styling and was capable of a brisk road speed and pleasant travelling conditions.

Like Cadillac, La Salles were fitted with a range of bodies made by Fleetwood and Fisher, two companies owned by General Motors Corporation. Despite its close connection with Cadillac, the new model proved a quality car in its own right and, initially at least, sold well in the United States.

Cadillac introduced many innovations to the American scene, including synchromesh gearboxes and Hydra-matic transmission. Some innovations found their way into La Salle and the marque was chosen to pioneer the company's first all-steel sedan with a turret roof, though they had not originated this idea. The South Australian firm of T. J. Richards had been producing all-steel turret roof sedans for local Chryslers before General Motors had their American version off the ground.

Between 1927 and 1934, La Salle was virtually a small Cadillac, then the design changed to become an expensive version of the Oldsmobile (with an identical engine). It was priced to compete against the cheapest Packards and the Ford-built Lincoln Zephyr. Dwindling sales forced the company to borrow some of Cadillac's prestige and La Salle was given a Caddy V-8 engine. By this time, the whole project was becoming irrelevant, for Cadillac had a whole range of models starting with a V-8. La Salle was beginning to cut across the lower end of the Cadillac sales, and production ceased in 1940.

1930 LA SALLE CABRIOLET

Owned by Elizabeth Ryan of Fullarton, South Australia, this immaculate La Salle is one of those rare machines which have been meticulously maintained since new and has never required restoring.

It was originally imported by Mr Keith Angas (later Sir Keith), a prominent grazier from the Barossa Valley. He also owned Lindsay Park stud and, with his family, an extensive stable of cars.

The family's enthusiasm for motoring can be judged by the fact that the Angas homestead at Angaston was the site of the first privately owned petrol bowser in the State. Sir Keith designed the bodywork of several of his cars, and had local firms execute the work, but his La Salle was imported complete, with a Fisher cabriolet body. It has seating for four (two in the rear dickey seat), wind-up windows and other comforts.

Though fitted with synchromesh, the car is conventionally engineered throughout, with a pressed steel chassis frame, forged front beam axle and leaf spring suspension with lever action hydraulic shock absorbers.

MECHANICAL FEATURES

Engine: V-8 of 5.6 litres, rated at 35 HP, developing 95 BHP at 3500 rpm. The 90 degree V-8 is cast in iron in two blocks with detachable cylinder heads and an alloy crankcase with 3 main bearings. Cadillac updraught carburettor.
Gearbox: Three-speed synchromesh, with floor shift. The dry clutch has twin plates.
Suspension: Conventional semi-elliptic leaf springs frong and rear, with lever arm hydraulic dampers.
Brakes: Mechanically operated Duplex drum brakes on four wheels. Separate handbrake operating on rear wheels.
Steering: Worm-and-sector type. Wire wheels 700 x 18 ins.
Dimensions: Wheelbase 11 ft 2 ins (3403 mm). Overall length 15 ft 9 ins (4800 mm). Kerb weight 38 cwt (1935 kg).
Performance: Maximum speed when new — 85 mph (136 km/h). Normal cruising speed — 60 mph (100 km/h). Fuel consumption at highway speeds — 14 mpg (20.1 litres/100 km).

1930 Mercedes 38/250 SS

THE MARQUE

Mercedes' legendary sports cars, built between 1927 and 1932, are generally known as the S, SS, SSK and SSKL models.

Reflecting the thunder and glory of its era, the series was conceived during strikes at the Daimler-Benz factory and born at the height of the political unrest leading to World War Two. The brutally powerful performance epitomised the turbulent 1930s and these supercharged sportsters were noisier and faster than anything else on the road.

The series grew out of a design by Paul Daimler but displayed the unmistakeable hand of Dr Ferdinand Porsche. Though deservedly considered the finest series of sports cars of all time, it had a curious 'Achilles heel'. The gearing was so high (41 mph per 1000 rpm in top gear) that most driving was done in second and third gear. The gears themselves just could not take the immense loads imposed by the high torque and failed rapidly and noisily.

Introduced in 1927, the first of the line was the K model, with a 6245 cc single overhead camshaft engine with blower. It was known in Germany as 24/110/160 and everywhere else as the 33/180K.

In 1927 the factory produced a bigger and better model, first seen at Olympia. The engine was extended to 6789 cc blown. Longer, lower and much faster, the new car was called the 26/120/180 S in Germany. All others knew it as the 36/220.

Late in 1927 came the biggest and best Mercedes. The blown engine was 7020 cc (in all three models supercharging is optional; the blower can be cut in and out at will). The output of the basic sports touring version was 225 BHP blown. This car was designated the 27/170/225 SS but is always called a 38/250 SS.

Later, two modified versions appeared. The first was the SSK (K for 'kurz' meaning short). These were blown to higher pressures and produced about 250 BHP.

The last of the line was the immortal SSKL (L for 'licht' meaning light) with the chassis elaborately drilled out and blown very hard to produce about 300 BHP.

The German designation, such as 27/170/225, indicated the taxable HP, the unsupercharged power and the supercharged power. In England, the same car was known as the 38/250, indicating the British taxable HP and the theoretical maximum power.

In 1931, an SSKL clocked 156 mph (250 km/h) on the Avis speed circuit. Few people believed that a car of such power and weight could stay together on a long race. Yet, in the same year, Rudolf Garacciola won the 250 mile German Grand Prix at Nurburgring, with two Bugattis snapping at his heels all the way to the finish.

Fewer than 400 of the series were built. Of these probably half survive, including three or four in Australia.

1930 MERCEDES 38/250 SS

Correctly called the 27/170/225 SS, this rare and enthralling sports car is usually known as the 38/250 SS. Manufactured in 1930, it has a touring foursome body, built by Karosserie Mercedes, with steel panels over a hickory frame. Features include cycle type guards with tool boxes on the running boards, double locking doors, full weather equipment and twin spare wheels.

The car is completely original in every detail and has done only 11,000 miles (17,600 km) since new. It was delivered to Paris in October 1930 and is, therefore, a true vintage car.

It is believed that it was used for practice in the 1930 Le Mans, then returned to the factory and fitted with a new engine and paint work. After being exhibited at the Paris Salon, it was purchased by H.R.H. the Maharajah of Jumna and Kashmir. He returned the big car to the factory for various modifications, including a bright red light on the scuttle, below the windscreen. The many cars in the Maharajah's stable were similarly equipped, presumably for ready recognition by his subjects.

Early in 1931 the Maharajah had the car driven from Cannes, where he was holidaying, to his palace in India. Soon after it arrived, the big Mercedes was laid up on blocks, alongside a stable of Rolls-Royce's. The word was that the Maharajah had given himself an unholy fright in the powerful Mercedes.

The car was still sitting on blocks in 1969 when the Maharajah's heirs sold it to an American enthusiast who had it shipped to New York. The present owner, Geoffrey Davis, of Sydney, heard about the 38/250 SS and bought it. He had it shipped to England where it was completely stripped, inspected and reassembled by Antique Automobiles of Baston, Linconshire. The car was repainted, the bright work re-chromed and the wheels respoked as a precaution. The deteriorating leather and hood were replaced.

By coincidence, one of the late Lord Howe's racing mechanics was living in retirement close to Antique Automobiles. He had helped prepare the ex-Garacciola's 1930 Irish TT and Le Mans car for Lord Howe during the early 1930s. Without reference to notes of any kind, he sorted out all the problems of forced or atmospheric induction and tuned Geoffrey Davis's 38/250 SS to perfection.

MECHANICAL FEATURES

Engine: Six-cylinder, supercharged, 7.0 litres capacity, SOHC valve gear, rated at 37 HP, develops 225 BHP at 3200 rpm. Twin Pallas Mercedes carburettor; Roots blower running at three times engine speed; 12 psi. Engine can be driven supercharged or unsupercharged.
Gearbox: Four-speed straight cut non-synchromesh, centre mounted ball joint stick. Car geared to give 41 mph (65 km/h) per 1000 rpm in top gear. Multi-plate dry clutch.
Suspension: Long semi-elliptics overslung leaf springs in front; similar underslung springs at rear. Houdaille hydraulic shock absorbers front and rear.
Brakes: Large diameter drum brakes on four wheels, can be uniformly adjusted by a turn wheel on the cockpit floor.
Steering: High geared worm-and-nut, with about 1¼ turns lock-to-lock; 50 ft (15.2 m) turning circle.
Wheels: Rudge-type knock on wire spoked wheels, 20 x 700 tyres.
Dimensions: Wheelbase 11 ft 1.9 ins (3400 mm). Track 4 ft 8 ins (1422 mm). Overall length 16 ft 8 ins (5080 mm). Height 5 ft 7 ins (1702 mm). Kerb weight 37.3 cwt (1900 kg).
Performance: Maximum speed when new — 125 mph (200 km/h). Normal cruising speed — 80 mph (128 km/h). Fuel consumption at highway speeds — 8 mpg (35.3 litres/100 km).

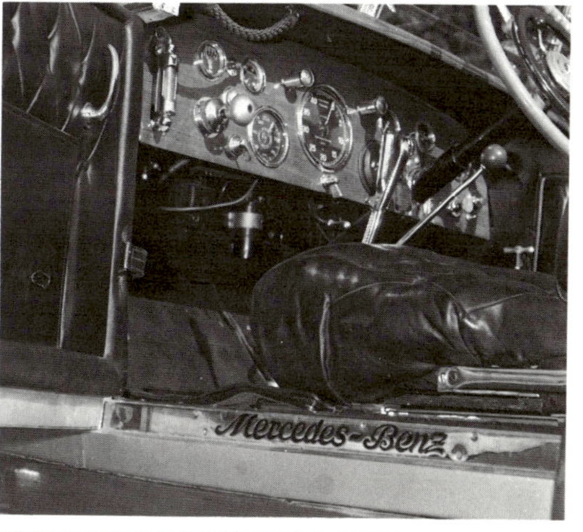
Mercedes-Benz

1930 Nash 8 Sedan

THE MARQUE

Nash began its automotive career as a Rambler, built by Thomas Jeffery in 1897. Rambler was very successful but when the founder died in 1910, the car's name was changed to Jeffery as a mark of respect. With the guiding hand gone, the firm floundered for a while. In 1916 Charles W. Nash resigned as president of General Motors and bought the Thomas B. Jeffery Company.

He organised a new 4.0 litre overhead valve six-cylinder model which he introduced as the Nash marque in 1918. Four years later the firm followed with an OHV Four and bought out Mitchell and Lafayette, two rather weak competitors. By 1926, Nash was selling 100,000 cars a year. Two years later it had become the world's largest producer of trucks.

Though Lafayette produced a luxury V-8 car, Nash decided to design a brand new straight eight for a top-of-the-line model. The new engine, of 4.9 litres, first appeared in the 1930 Model 490, featuring overhead valves, dual coil ignition and a willingness to rev to 3600 rpm, a high speed at the time.

The new four door sedan sold in the United States for $1295, against $695 for a 4-door Model A Ford, or $1845 for a Hudson Great Eight.

Though the Nash design was conventional, mechanical innovations set it apart from some competitors. Four small coil springs at the rear of the right hand front shackles act as steering dampers. The hand and foot brakes work off the same cables on all four wheels. A Bijur central lubrication system was fitted to feed oil to the spring shackle bolts, steering knuckle pins and clutch release bearings — and is operated by a small foot pedal located under the dash. Unusual, too, is the thermostatically controlled radiator shutters.

1930 NASH MODEL 490

Owned by Jennifer Tweedie of Carlingford, New South Wales, this superbly restored sedan has a body made by Seaman Body Corporation, with two bench seats. The original interior fittings include antique flower vases and vanity cases. There is also a pair of racks (made by Safety Auto Hat Rack Co. of New York) attached to the ceiling, for the convenience of passengers wishing to park their hats.

The original owners of the Nash probably lived in the Blue Mountains area of New South Wales. The second owner brought the car to Sydney in the early 1960s. It was purchased by the Tweedie family in 1968, by which time it had been repainted sky blue with black guards.

Spencer Tweedie, with his son Spencer, prepared the car to run in 'as is' condition for some years and it proved a consistent and successful competitor in Vintage Motor Club events. In preparation for the 1978 International Veteran and Vintage Rally, the car was fully restored by the Tweedies. The paintwork was done by Bruce Ross, in an original Packard Blue tone. The trim restoration was handled by Percy Cornish who carefully matched the colour, texture and pattern of the original fabric. After the 1978 Rally, the car was acquired by Jennifer Tweedie from her family.

Very few of the closed sedans are known to survive. There are three in Australia, one in New Zealand and a handful in the United States. Despite its size and considerable weight, the five seater sedan is capable of speeds to 85 mph (136 km/h).

MECHANICAL FEATURES

Engine: Straight eight overhead valve engine of 4.9 litres. Rated at 33.8 HP, developing 115 BHP at 3600 rpm. Conventional pump cooling with thermostatically controlled radiator shutters. Marvel carburettor with Autolite twin ignition system firing through 16 plugs.
Gearbox: Conventional with three forward gears. The gearbox can be key-locked in gear. Multiplate Borg and Beck clutch.
Suspension: Semi-elliptic springs front and rear.
Brakes: Cable-operated on four wheels, with handbrake linked to foot brake.
Steering: Worm-and-gear.
Wheels: Disc type, size 6.00 x 19.
Dimensions: Wheelbase 10 ft 4 ins (3150 mm). Overall length 15 ft 2 ins (4623 mm). Height 6 ft 0 ins (1823 mm). Kerb weight 37 cwt (1886 kg).
Performance: Maximum speed when new — 85 mph (136 km/h). Normal cruising speed — 50 mph (80 km/h). Fuel consumption at highway speeds — 13 mpg (21.7 litres/100 km).

ABOUT THE AUTHOR

Though widely known for his books and articles on modern cars, Pedr Davis has been an old car enthusiast since 1951 when he travelled as a passenger in a 1904 Mercedes driven by the late G. James Alldays in Britain's London-Brighton Veteran Car Run.

Pedr Davis served an engineering apprenticeship with the Austin Motor Company in England and, not surprisingly, now has a fully restored 1929 Austin Seven which he shares with son Anthony.

The author of twenty-four published books, mainly in the field of cars, motorcycles and aircraft, Pedr Davis contributes to major technical magazines around the world.

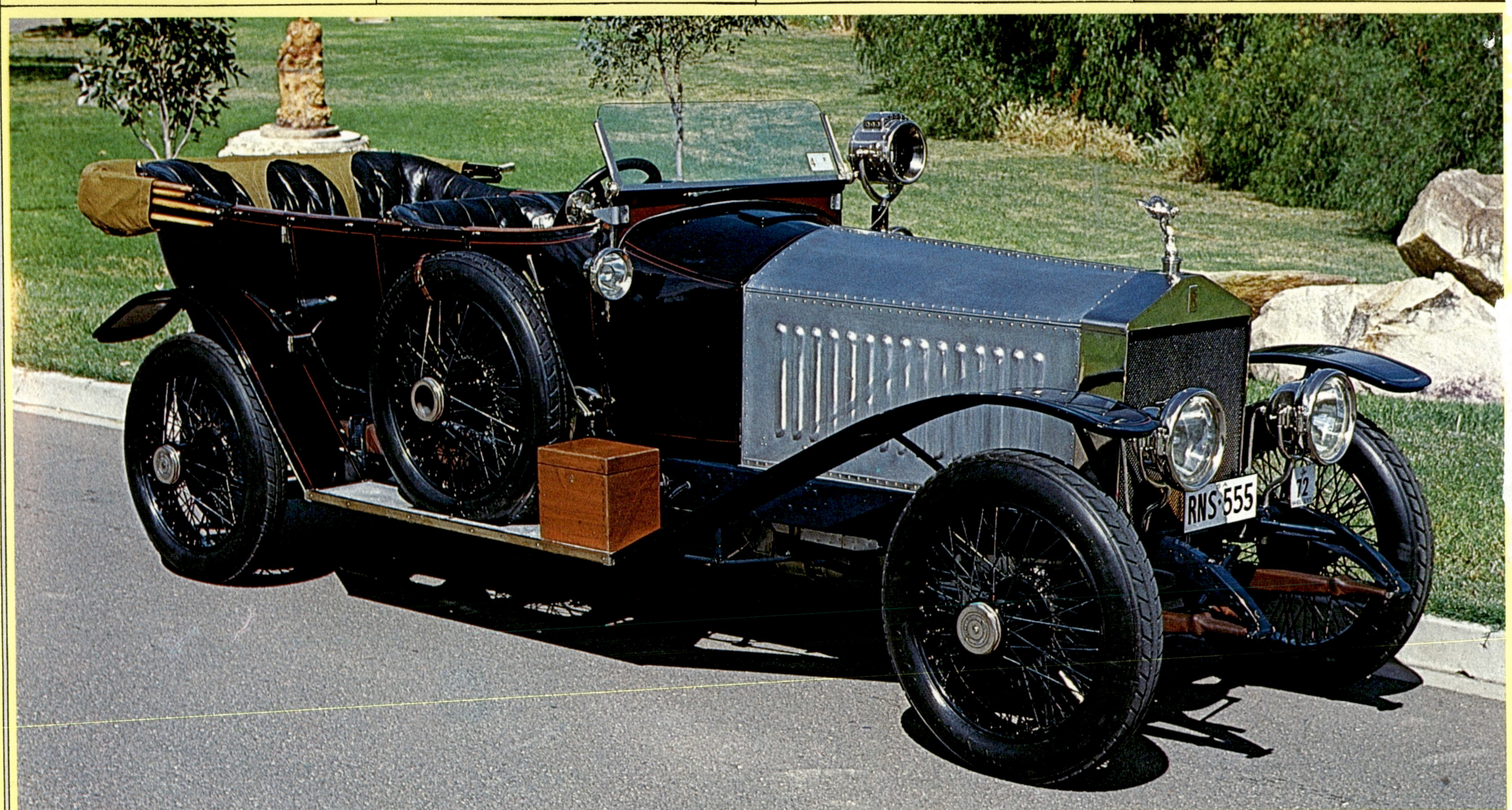

ACKNOWLEDGEMENTS

This book would not have been possible without the enthusiastic co-operation of veteran and vintage car clubs around the country and, of course, the owners of the vehicles selected for publication.

Only an enthusiast knows how much time and energy goes into restoring, maintaining, cleaning and polishing an old car. Many owners went to considerable trouble to ensure that their vehicles were at their gleaming best for photography. The weather was not always as helpful, but that's another story. If nothing else, my travels through four States inspecting and photographing these cars took me through some delightful territory and into the homes of many of Australia's keenest and most knowledgeable collectors. My thanks, indeed, for your hospitality.

Very special thanks go to the managers and staff of Australia's two most comprehensive car museums, Green's Motorcade, near Liverpool, New South Wales, and the National Motor Museum at Birdwood, South Australia. These people went to considerable trouble to make the vehicles in their exhibits available for photography. Valuable help with specifications and information was also willingly provided by Len Vigor of South Australia, George Roberts and George Green, both from New South Wale

The owners of the vehicles in this boc were invited to read and check the reports prior to publication, but if any errors have crept in, the writer accepts full responsibility.